# KELLEY'S JOURNEY:

## FACING A RARE DISEASE
## WITH COURAGE

By

**Denise Crompton**

ISBN: 1-4107-2184-1 (e-book)
ISBN: 1-4107-2185-X (Paperback)

Library of Congress Control Number: 2003091738

This book is printed on acid free paper.

Printed in the United States of America
Bloomington, IN

1stBooks – rev. 03/17/03

# DEDICATION

To my wonderful husband, Bob.

# ACKNOWLEDGEMENTS

I would like to express my sincere gratitude to my sister, Hilary Piccoli, for all of the hours that she devoted to editing this work. I appreciate the encouragement that she and my sister, Mary Lou Pursley, provided to me, while I completed this project.

I want to thank the many family members and friends who have offered support, understanding and prayers for Kelley through the years, as well as the priests who have offered Masses and counsel.

It would be impossible for me to completely express the gratitude I feel toward the people who have helped us during the years that Kelley has traveled on her journey through life. We have encountered many members of the medical field. Most of them have been humble, dedicated, and caring individuals. I would like to pay a personal tribute to some of them, however, they know who they are, and they all appear to be people who gain much satisfaction from the work that they do. I am under the impression that none of them are looking for accolades. To say that I am grateful for the help they have provided, is an understatement. They have kept Kelley alive, and as comfortable as possible, through some trying times. They have given her parents hope and encouragement.

We did have some negative experiences, also. Most of those incidents happened many years ago. It is very possible that some of the people we encountered have changed. Therefore, names of doctors, hospitals and cities have been omitted.

It is important for me to mention the National Organization of Rare Diseases (NORD); whose web site can be found at www.rarediseases.org.

It was through NORD that I learned of the National MPS Society; whose web site can be found at www.mpssociety.org.

Both of these organizations have supplied us with connections to others who are dealing with rare diseases, and the information we have gained has been invaluable.

# CHAPTER ONE

"What's wrong with Kelley's hands?" Mary Lou asked, trying to sound not too concerned. I knew my sister well enough, however, to realize that she was indeed concerned.

"What do you mean?" I asked, with a fluttering feeling in my stomach.

"Well," she explained, "I was playing some finger games with the girls, and I noticed she couldn't make a fist. Her fingers seem to be rather stiff."

"I never noticed," I responded before calling Kelley into the living room.

My three-year-old whirlwind ran into the living room (she rarely walked) and threw herself at me, laughing. I sank back into the chair, picking her up and laughing with her. What a fun kid!

"So, did Aunt Mary Lou teach you any new songs or games while we were away?" I asked.

"I dunno," she giggled while I looked at her fingers and glanced at Bob.

"Come here, Kelley," he said, taking her from me. He sat down with her on his lap and began to look at her hands.

Looking at them together, there was no mistaking her Crompton heritage. Except that her eyes were brown, and his blue, they looked a lot alike, with fair skin, fair hair and dimpled chins.

"Can you do this?" Bob asked, making a fist.

"Nope," she chirped, unconcerned.

"Let me see what you can do," he coaxed, wrapping his large hand around her little one. Her fingers simply would not bend all the way to make a complete fist. It was the same with both hands.

"You can go play now," her daddy said, putting her down from his lap. She trotted off to resume her activities with her two-year-old sister, Susan.

"I'm shocked!" I exclaimed, after she was out of the room, "I don't know how I missed that! I must be a terrible mother!"

"Well dear, you have had your hands full," my mother reassured, in her usual soothing manner. She was referring to the fact that, in addition to Kelley and Susan, we were proud parents of a nine-month-old son, David.

"Good thing you had that vacation in when you did," Mary Lou offered.

Bob and I had just returned, that Friday afternoon, from the first trip we had taken, since before Kelley was born, thanks to the generosity of Nana and Mary Lou. They had volunteered to stay with the children during Bob's vacation from work. We enjoyed five days of relaxation. I adored the children, but had to admit that it was refreshing to have a break from the constant demands of three little ones.

"Do you have any idea what could cause that?" Bob asked my mother.

"I wish I had an answer for you, but I've never seen anything like it," she honestly responded.

"It's too late for us to get in to see the doctor today," I said, "but I'll call and find out if he can see her on Monday."

We were fortunate to have a family doctor we trusted completely. His secretary knew me well, and found an opening on Monday, after I told her of my concern. It was going to be a long weekend!

We called Kelley our little firecracker, because she was born on July 4, 1963, and displayed a vivacious energy that indeed sparkled! She didn't simply like something; she *loved* it. She never sulked or whimpered. She *hollered*. At ten months of age, when she received an immunization shot from the doctor, she looked straight at him and told him off very loudly in her own language. We figured it translated to something like, "How dare you do that, when I thought we were friends!"

The band concert we went to on her first birthday entranced the little girl who, ignoring her parents, went right up to the bandstand and clapped her hands with joy throughout the entire performance. She also liked to play games. Before learning to walk, Kelley discovered the fun of rolling under my bed, in essence hiding from me. She would laugh heartily when I found her! However, I didn't think it to be particularly amusing that she had hidden her good shoes, when we were about to leave for Grandma's house for dinner.

Like most children, Kelley didn't like to take "no" for an answer. When she couldn't get what she wanted one way, I could count on her to try another. Somewhere around the age of two, the inevitable temper tantrum challenge appeared. I refused to acknowledge it. She never tried that again. Such lessons were quickly learned. It seemed that perception was inborn. By the time she was three, the little darling knew enough to put her younger sister up to doing things she figured would not meet with my approval. I got after Susan numerous times before realizing she had become a scapegoat.

Kelley possessed a sense of humor that was always one step ahead of what I expected for her age. The house we bought before David was born was out in the sticks, so we were always delighted to see company. This gave her an idea for a new game. She would go to the front door, and then run to find me, yelling, "Nana and Grandpa are here."

Since I was usually in the middle of some sort of housework when she pulled this, I would drop what I was doing and rush to the front door, only to find Kelley very amused at being able to play a practical joke on her mom! She played a few on herself that backfired, however. She didn't believe that those burners on the electric range were hot when they were red, until she touched one for herself. I was standing right there when she did it, having just taken the kettle off the burner. The burn marks were on her hand for quite some time. Then one day, while playing outdoors, she got a hold of a piece of board, not realizing that her hands were picking up splinters until it was too late. Getting all those little splinters out of her hands was a lengthy project. Bob and I took turns. Another time, she pulled a bowl of hot soup over on her from the counter while, once again, I was right there! She had enough clothes on, so she didn't get badly burned that time. Gave me a good scare!

In general, Kelley managed to get into, under, around and over more things than my imagination could. She always had another trick up her sleeve.

I child proofed our home before our first baby was born, by putting anything potentially dangerous out of the way. However, I needed to watch her all the time, because she was very active. I remember a sister-in-law observing Kelley and remarking, "She is perpetual motion!"

How true! When I was pregnant with her, I wondered why no one had ever told me how much babies kicked before they were born. It was not until I had other pregnancies with which to compare that one, that I realized that she was much more active than the average baby.

Just when the problem with Kelley's hands started, I have no way of knowing. It had happened so gradually that those of us who were with her daily simply didn't see it happening. I thought she was playing with the big toys out of choice. Susan was the one who always wound up the little radios, while Kelley lugged around the big dolls and stuffed animals.

When our family doctor saw her, he wouldn't even give us an educated guess on a diagnosis. He did reassure me that he didn't think we needed to be alarmed. His secretary was instructed to make an appointment for us at a big city hospital.

We had to wait weeks before they could see us. During that time, all sorts of ideas went through my head. There was a soap opera on television that I watched, while I ironed during the children's naptime. The story at that time included a child with a brain tumor. That was great food for my vivid imagination! I prayed. I have always prayed. I didn't wait for this to happen to start praying, but at this point, my prayers became very intense. I asked God to help me to accept His will, and I fought back tears when I allowed myself to dwell on it. I learned that trying not to think about a problem was easier said than done, but I didn't speculate aloud. Since he is a very private person, Bob keeps most of his feelings to himself. I knew he was wrestling with this problem as much as I was, and felt it would add to his burden if I revealed my apprehension. We waited in silence.

Being an engineer, Bob has a propensity for details. He writes lists, draws plans, and does whatever necessary to insure that any job is well done. I have always been somewhat methodical myself, so between the two of us, we came up with numerous solutions to the tasks involved in the undertaking of raising a family. They outnumbered us. We had to have a strategy!

Once a month, the baby-sitter came, so we could grocery shop without the children. When we arrived at the store, we each took a cart and went off with our lists. I never ran out of the necessities. When you are eleven miles from the nearest super market, and five miles from the nearest *anything*, you plan ahead!

To solve the problem of the constant 'I want the toy she's got' game, we bought just about everything in triplicate, as did the thoughtful grandparents. We even celebrated all three birthdays together until the children reached school age. Too many toys can be just as bad as not enough. We realized they needed different types of toys to develop both large and small muscles, and to develop their skills and knowledge. However, when they had all the toys at once, they became confused and most unwilling to pick up at the end of their playtime. We got a few boxes to keep in the attic, then let them choose which toys they wanted to keep downstairs. The rest went away temporarily. When I was aware that a change was in order, on a rainy day, or when I was deeply involved in a sewing project, I brought down a box from the attic. They were delighted to play with toys that they had not seen for a while, as they seemed like new. I then packed away some of the toys in which they had lost interest, and the constant clutter was eliminated. Picking up after play wasn't as much of a chore, with fewer toys.

When Bob and I were up late at night, and wanted an extra half hour to sleep in the morning, I put something new or different on the foot of each of their beds before we retired. That worked very well in the morning!

After an early supper each evening, we attacked our routine of lining the children up for washing, brushing, and snapping into pajamas. Our system had them all bedded down, after a story, by 6:30 PM. We needed the evening to catch our breaths before 6 AM arrived. Once a week, they ate without us, and Bob and I would enjoy a steak after tucking them in to bed. I have yet to meet a three year old who appreciates steak!

I was very busy in those days feeding, washing, changing not one, but three babies, and I loved doing so. Other than Susan's allergy to milk, they were all healthy. I knew I was blessed to have them. They were a constant source of wonder and joy!

The day of our appointment finally arrived. The first impression I received at the big hospital, in the big city, was that the kids with the long faces belonged to parents with long faces. I made a decision that day. No matter what we had to endure (and an inner voice told me we were in for a long haul), we would not become morose.

It's difficult to remember all the events of those first few years. Some of it was forgotten as quickly as possible, to retain sanity. Some I wanted to forget, but I couldn't. Fighting discouragement was a battle.

It took an hour to drive from home to the big city. We were a one-car family in those days. I was fortunate to have healthy, helpful parents. They lived about twenty miles away, so for every appointment, Grandpa brought Nana to the house to mind the two younger children, and he drove Kelley and me to the hospital. It was not possible for Bob to get away from work for these visits. There were many visits, and they were tiring. Some of the doctors cared only about her joints and drew bleak pictures about the future of a child who had a diagnosis of Juvenile Rheumatoid Arthritis.

The remarks we endured were, "She will get worse," "She may never be well enough to go to school," "Don't allow her to become upset," "We just don't know what to tell you or what to expect."

Even the most cockeyed optimist can find it difficult to remain positive under such circumstances, but Kelley had a darling smile (like her Dad's), and a spirit that loved a good time. Grandpa did, too. We put all of our efforts into making each trip as much fun as possible. We planned outings, discussing where we would stop to eat on the way home, and what we would have to eat. Kelley always wore a special dress for the occasion, and we took along her favorite books and toys. The way Grandpa and I acted, one would think we were taking the child to a circus rather than a clinic. In some respects, that clinic did resemble a circus!

I never used baby talk with my children. The best way for them to become articulate is for adults to speak properly to them. However, it appeared that some of the nurses and doctors never progressed beyond baby talk themselves. Kelley was a child with whom you could level, but if you talked down to her, she became insulted and wouldn't cooperate at all. There is one picture that I still recall clearly. Two doctors were talking to me *about* her *in front of* her, as though she couldn't comprehend the language. They then turned to her with baby talk. Apparently she reasoned if they wanted to play games, she would play games with them. It always brings a smile to my lips when I picture four-year-old Kelley, in her pretty white dress with the red trim, and her fair hair in bouncy ponytails. She was squatting under a table looking at two doctors, with a big grin on her face, as they were bending over trying to coax her out, using this strange language of baby talk!

5

The clinic trips were wearing at best. We usually had to leave home very early in the morning. Knowing that Nana would be as firm, loving and understanding with Susan and David as she had always been with the five she raised, I was not concerned about them. I knew she wouldn't spoil them. Dad never complained about the hours of waiting, but it was difficult to keep Kelley amused and in good spirits during those long hours. We met many different doctors, most of whom were very impersonal. Occasionally we saw the same one twice, but mostly we experienced rounds of the same questions over and over again. My questions were usually brushed off, giving me the impression that they didn't think I should be asking any. Never once were we seen at the appointed time. We endured long waits at the clinic, long waits at the lab, and long waits in x-ray.

Often someone wanted to take Kelley away from me for some lab work or examination. It caused me a great deal of inner turmoil when someone said, "No, mother, you can't come."

I wanted to respect their positions, but I knew my little girl needed me. How could I submit her to having strange people examine her, or stick needles in her arm, and not be there to at hold her hand? At first I submitted, but maternal instinct was strong, and I learned to assert myself by saying, "If I don't go, she doesn't go, either."

They didn't like it, but they did consent to my wishes. What else could they do?

Grandpa, Kelley and I were all people who moved fast. When there was something to do, we *did* it. We didn't sit around thinking about it, mope around, or drag our feet. It's probably a family trait. Grandpa and I spent much of the time laughing about the 'busy' personnel at that clinic. We sat in the various waiting rooms, waiting our turn, and watched them perform their tasks S...L...O...W...L...Y! Rarely did we see anyone even walk fast, yet we often heard them complain about how far behind they were, and how overworked they were. I recall listening to three of them talk for five minutes about how they were not going to be done on time.

"If they'd stop talking about it, and *do* it, they might surprise themselves," I remarked to Dad, prompting us both to laugh, although I also felt annoyed about the amount of time we had to sit around. We did decide that the excessive heat throughout the place probably contributed to the general languor, and tried to be understanding.

Kelley's hands seemed to be the most important problem in the beginning, although it rapidly became apparent she was experiencing limited range of motion in all of her joints. The immediate treatment included physical therapy for all of her joints, and braces for her hands.

The man who made the braces was a very slow and patient man, who had a very thick accent. We had trouble understanding him at times. In fact, there were a few times when Dad and I simply looked at each other and shrugged after a third attempt. These braces were very elaborate and very difficult to adjust. It was also very difficult for Kelley to become adjusted to them. Although the brace maker was the kindest, most patient person we met there, Kelley did have some difficulty warming up to him. After all, he was the man who put those cumbersome things on her hands, and that interfered with her fun and games!

In the beginning, Kelley wore the braces for a few hours at a time. Once she adjusted to them, she was expected to wear them during all her waking hours. The braces were constructed with wire, and little elastics were used for tension and flexibility. These elastics were tightened as her fingers started to bend more. We broke many elastics during that time! We also had to soak her hands in warm water a few times a day, and follow it up with a dull Physical Therapy routine. If I had ever entertained the idea of becoming a physical therapist, this experience served to convince me that I had absolutely no capacity to answer such a call.

Kelley did not like PT! I tried all sorts of ways to do it, in an attempt to make it more pleasant. By doing it right before lunch and right before supper, we had something pleasant to look forward to after finishing. We did it to music. We made up games. We made up songs. We invited other children to join the games. I prayed a lot, and she still never liked PT. Consequently, neither did I! She liked the braces even less. They limited her ability to do many of the things she wanted to do. I wondered how effective they really were.

When the experts at the hospital decided that Kelley's elbow joints were bending too much, they made splints for her to wear to bed at night, which kept her arms straight out while she slept. The first night I put her to bed like this, she looked at me in panic and protested, "I can't reach my thumb!"

I felt like a very mean mother. I didn't think it was fair to take away a child's thumb! For years she hadn't sucked her thumb during the day, but, when going to sleep, she found it to be a comfort, along with hugging her favorite cottontail. The reaction of Kelley's arms, when the splints came off, in the morning, resembled springs being set free. She then grabbed for her beloved cottontail and put her thumb in her mouth to make up for lost time.

All three of the children had cottontails. One of the first toys Kelley had was a pink and white stuffed bunny. Of any of her many toys, this was the one with which she chose to sleep. Susan followed suit, so when David came along, we bought one for him, also. My first attempt to get rid of the old dirty worn out cottontail Kelley had, and replace it with a lovely new one failed. Oh, how children love to hang on to the old and familiar! Inspiration hit me one day just before Easter, when I was reading the tale of the Velveteen Rabbit to them. I followed it up with a story of how the Easter Bunny was going to come in the middle of the night to take their well-loved bunnies to turn them into *Real* and leave new ones for them to love. This started a family tradition that was carried on for years, and it made us all happy.

As soon as breakfast was done each morning, Kelley had to put on the braces until lunchtime. She soon learned to stretch out breakfast, lunch and dinner. Who could blame her? I did not rush her. I never once liked putting those things on her hands. It never felt right, and it tore at me emotionally. I knew it was necessary to help her joints, but I wondered about her spirit— could we keep it intact?

The clinic visits were exhausting. Thankfully, Grandpa was a great stabilizer. On the way home, we always stopped to eat somewhere; his treat. That's when he would tell his stories. He was not one to lecture, or to give unsolicited advice, but he could get a point across just fine. He helped me enormously in coming to grips with the situation. After letting me vent my feelings, he would say, "That reminds me of the time that..."

We always ended up laughing. Fred Kelley never ceased seeing the humorous side of life. What a blessing to have such a father! In the Kelley family, we were never allowed to feel sorry for ourselves. Now, I was not allowed to feel sorry for myself, and I could not allow myself to feel sorry for my daughter, or to let her feel sorry for herself. Self-pity can breed self-destruction. I prayed for strength and courage.

In searching for answers about JRA, I frequently learned more by comparing notes with other mothers in the waiting room than from the doctors. I also learned that the juvenile form of the disease differed from the adult. We saw some children at the clinic with very severe cases. I wondered if that was what we should expect for Kelley. No one could answer that question. There seemed to be no true course for the disease to run. There appeared to be no reason for the onset, or little hope for a lasting remission.

In addition to the splints, braces and physical therapy, we were directed to give Kelley twenty-seven baby aspirins daily. We tried all the different brands and flavors before settling on the right one for her taste buds. If she had to chew nine of them with each meal, they might as well taste good.

While Kelley was somewhat belligerent at times about wearing the braces (she was known to hide them), and she wriggled out of those arm splints at night (I'll never figure out how), she had spunk one had to admire! She decided not to let this problem stop her from having fun, period! Her idea of a good time in those days was taking every toy out of the toy box and telling Susan to put them away.

Sweet Sue was about three years old when she one day announced, "I'm tired of her making all the DEZIZZIONS," and she started to assert herself.

Kelley had gotten into so much and tried so many things, that Susan and David seemed like easy children to me. I think they were probably average. Susan could sit in the rocking chair by the hour singing to her dolls, while David played with his little cars and Kelley took a notion to pull all the books off the shelves or try to rearrange the furniture. I had read that children with JRA were frequently shy and retiring. I guessed that had Kelley never read that book!

We didn't allow this crippling disease to keep us from doing many of the things we wanted to do. Our humble little home site included a little beach. Bob and I both loved the water. When we bought the house, it was more for the location than for the house itself. We were able to go swimming every day in the summer. We were also surrounded by dirt roads and woods in which to go walking. The children and I enjoyed long walks almost daily. Some of my most cherished memories of their early years are those walks. The children loved to go exploring.

I discovered that lunchtime was less hectic if I read to the children while they ate. Then I put them in for naps. The three shared a room. It really was a humble home! It was fun to listen to them settle down for a nap or for the night. I used to stand outside the door listening to them, wishing I could see them without them seeing me. It was especially fun when the girls had their whisper dolls. These dolls whispered various phrases when one pulled a string. The children often giggled about them.

I had wanted a family very much, and I was most thankful to have them. When the girls were about three and four years old, Susan caught up to Kelley in height, and I had a wonderful time dressing my 'twins.' Their blond hair was just about the same shade. David's hair was blond, also.

When people said to me, "My, you have your hands full!"

I replied, "Yes, and I love them."

When they said, "But it costs so much to raise a family."

I quipped, "Can't think of a better way to spend my money."

Bob had experienced the joy of family camping when he was a child, and I had done some tenting as a girl scout, so we chose to give it a try the summer that Susan and Kelley were three and four years old. Using a little bit of wisdom, we left David with my folks. He was about to become a two-year-old boy—a very normal two-year boy—into everything! We felt the next year would be soon enough for him.

With a borrowed tent, we set off for the mountains. It was a beautiful experience. There were no clocks to obey, no telephones, radios or televisions to interrupt the wind whistling through the trees, the stream tripping over rocks or the birds waking us in the morning. It was very relaxing for me. I think that Bob was afraid that I might not like the adventure, so he knocked himself out to the point of cooking all the meals. How could I not enjoy it? We had the chance to spend some time together, hiking, reading, talking and sitting around the campfire at night.

There was one particular incident we remember from that week. We were driving back to the campsite one day from a sightseeing trip to a gorge, when a bird flew into the grill in the front of the car. Bob and I both noticed it, and heard the thud. We assumed it fell to the road. Once we were back to the campsite, Kelley was the first to notice the mangled body of the poor creature. She screamed, cried and carried on for quite a while. I hadn't seen her like that before. She said she was upset for the bird's family. It was very difficult to console her. She took it very hard, and talked about that poor bird's family for sometime afterward. We thought she had a remarkable capacity for compassion for such a young child.

At the end of that summer, when tents were on sale, we bought the largest one they had. We declared ourselves CAMPERS!

Our first trip to the big city hospital was in October 1966. In the fifteen months that followed, I learned a good deal about JRA, including the fact that there was a good deal the medical profession didn't know about the disease. It seemed that the doctors had as many questions as I did. We did become used to the trips to the city, and they did become less of a big deal.

I have been blessed with a very strong and abiding faith in God, and although I couldn't see the sense in the things He allowed, I knew He had more wisdom than I did. I had always heard that He doesn't give us more than we can handle, so I reasoned that He must have some faith in Bob and me to have given us this child. With His help, I knew we would be able to take care of her and get her the right help, no matter how painful it was for us.

When the Arthritis Foundation helper called to ask me to collect in our neighborhood, I said that I would even bring my own little poster girl around with me. I did. Everyone gave. After a while, every January the neighbors looked forward to our visit as well as a progress report of the bright and smiling little pixie. They had their donations waiting for us.

# CHAPTER TWO

One bitter cold January 1968 morning, we went to the city for what we expected to be a routine day of waiting and lab work, waiting and PT, waiting and doctors. When the doctors examined Kelley this time, they asked if she had been experiencing pain in her legs, knees and hip joints. Her answer being, "No," they seemed to be perplexed. I told them she had been taking dancing lessons and doing as well as anyone else in the class. She also kept up with her playmates with no trouble.

Frowning, the chief clinic doctor said, "I don't like it. Her joints are not right. We'll admit her today and put her in traction."

I grimaced. I had been in traction a few times myself, and I was an adult at the time. What would it be like for this little four year old?

"Oh, it will only be for a few days," the doctor assured me.

Stunned, I went to my father in the waiting room and said, "There is no need for you to hang around here all day. They are going to admit her."

He frowned, and I shrugged my shoulders responding, "This is a renowned hospital. They must know what they are doing!" I quickly made a list of the things that she would need, and asked him to have Nana round them up so Bob could bring them in after work.

For the following two weeks, we encountered a most negative hospital experience. There was only one nurse who showed any real concern for Kelley. It appeared that all anyone cared about was her joints. They seemed to be oblivious to the fact that she was a living, breathing human being with very human emotions and needs. They gave us the impression that they saw *parents* as *the enemy*. The last thing they wanted to do was to let parents in on their trade secrets. They wouldn't even tell me her temperature!

Kelley was put in a six-bed room, where all of the other children were babies. There was no one with whom to talk, and she was tied down in traction. A two-year-old boy in the room was in a full body cast and traction. The staff would just leave his tray by him, expecting him to eat. They picked it up after saying, "Oh, I guess you weren't hungry." I decided to take it upon myself to feed him his meals.

I had a pounding headache by the end of that first day. I hadn't left Kelley to get myself anything to eat, or even a cup of coffee, as they kept telling me that the doctor would be in to see me momentarily. I don't know what type of dictionaries they used for reference, but their "momentarily" lasted from noon until 9 PM. No one, in that period of time, was even able to find me two aspirins for my headache.

By 8 PM, Bob arrived with his questions, and I had no answers for him. While he didn't actually ask the questions, his concern about this unexpected turn of events showed on his face. Hospitals tended to make him very uncomfortable. Walking in to see his little girl in traction was a painful event.

A nurse appeared and told us that visiting hours were over, and we would have to leave. I was tired, hungry, headachy, concerned, irritated, agitated and out of patience. I emphatically informed the staff that I was not going anywhere until I saw the doctor who was assigned to Kelley, if I had to stay all night! The elusive doctor appeared in her room five minutes later.

It was clear that this man was very impressed with the title "doctor" and very unimpressed with the title "mother." I never did get a straight answer out of him until my brother arrived one day to impress the "doctor" with the title "reverend." My brother was not out to impress, but when the doctor saw his Roman Collar, he became communicative and cooperative.

Dad took me into the hospital each morning. I brought my thermos of coffee as well as some of Kelley's favorite foods. Bob met me there in the evening. My days on duty were usually twelve hours long. In the beginning, I went to supper at suppertime. Then I found out that the doctors made their rounds at that time, so I brought a sandwich and stayed in her room for supper. The group of them came in one night, on their rounds, and asked me to leave. I told them I intended to stay with my daughter while they examined her. Besides being one of those nuisance mothers, they now found that I was impertinent, too. They examined, conferred, and reported, "We don't know."

I asked repeatedly to have her room changed. They always said that they would do it tomorrow. They never did. The first few nights, it took the nurses until 10 PM to get her readied for sleep. I took over that job myself and had her all set for the night when I left around 9 PM. A few times, as I walked down the hall to the elevator, I could hear her crying and my heart would break. I felt terrible leaving her there, tied down in traction, and with splints on her arms. She couldn't even suck her thumb for comfort. I was very concerned about how the experience was going to affect her emotionally.

One of the nurses said to me, "Don't worry, she won't remember it."

That didn't make the immediate situation any easier. I tried to tell her that even though we don't remember some events, they still affect us. This was the same nurse who walked around eating the Popsicles that were supposed to be there for the children!

We did what we could to make the best of a bad situation. Family and friends sent in cards, and we decorated the room. We made paper dolls. I read to Kelley, sang to her, and made up games. Somehow, I even found time at home to make her a few new nightgowns. There are only so many things one can do while flat on one's back with weights hanging from one's legs. Passing the time of day in this situation called for all the resourcefulness I could muster.

Emerging from the elevator upon my arrival one day, I heard my little darling hollering. I rushed to the room and asked, "What's wrong?" While traction is uncomfortable, it is not really painful.

"My foot!" Kelley yelled, "My foot!"

I pulled the covers off to discover that the ace bandage holding the traction straps in place was on so tight; Kelley's foot was blue! Yet there was a nurse in the room who had been telling Kelley to quiet down! She had not bothered to see if there was anything wrong with the foot. The traction had to be left off for the remainder of the afternoon.

One Sunday, during Kelley's hospitalization, my sister Mary Lou said she would like to go with us to the hospital, while Nana and Grandpa took care of the little ones. We had a snowstorm that had the two of us on the edge of our seats all the way. Bob drove on, undaunted by off-ramps that looked impassable, and quietly delivered us to our destination. Mary Lou always remembered that day. A few years later, when she awoke the morning of her wedding day to find us in the middle of a snowstorm, she said to herself, "Bob Crompton will get me there!" She was right.

I have had some nursing experience. First I was a ward clerk, then a nurse's aide, next an EKG technician, and finally a student nurse. An accident causing a back injury was the reason I gave up that career. It all came in handy now, however. I knew what to do, and how to do it, when caring for a patient. I knew where to look for things and how to get the job done without getting in the way of the staff. They were glad to see this, and I in essence was Kelley's special nurse during the hours I was there. I was extremely concerned about her care when I was not there. I knew how things should be done, and on that floor, in that hospital, at that particular time, they really were not done correctly.

I didn't eat right. I didn't think it was all that necessary. I didn't sleep well, mostly because my mind was spinning with questions for which I was unable to obtain answers. When they admitted her, they had told us it would be only for a few days. After three days, Kelley started asking when she could go home.

The answer was, "We'll see tomorrow."

When the next day arrived, the answer was again, "We'll see tomorrow."

That scene replayed day after day.

When Kelley came down with a terrible cold, no one seemed to care. It was only her joints that were of interest. We became disheartened and disappointed, yet I thought that these people were supposed to know what they were doing, so I went along with their treatment. I didn't know what else to do. It *was* a very renowned hospital.

As the couple of days turned into a couple of weeks, I learned a new, more extensive physical therapy routine. We were instructed to create a traction set-up, on her bed, at home. Who else but Bob could have done such a thorough job of preparing her bed to take the traction? It was necessary to put the bottom of her bed up on shock blocks, as had been done in the hospital. Bob also had to make her a special platform to lie on to hold her at enough of an angle to counteract the weights. Otherwise, she would have slipped right out of the bottom of the bed. There were pulleys, ropes and clamps. I made bags to hold the sand, which we were able to get from our beach.

When we finally were able to take her home, we were told that it was very important that we not allow her to stand or sit. I was instructed to take her out of traction two times daily, carry her to the tub to soak in hot water for twenty minutes, and then go through the PT routine. That routine took us an hour to accomplish when we first learned it. Once we became familiar with what we were doing, and could remember what came next, without having to read it, we cut it down to half that time. I found as many ways as I could to make the process fun and varied. I made up games, rhymes and songs. I would be lying if I didn't admit it was a chore. I decided that physical therapists are a special breed. I can't identify with them at all. Kelley did not like PT, and I did not like playing the heavy in making her do it, but of course, I knew it was for her benefit.

There were sores on Kelley's ankles when she returned home from the hospital. They had been caused by the constant rubbing of the traction straps. I was able to successfully treat and eliminate them, using applications of tender, loving care and attention.

We borrowed a television from my brother for Kelley's room. I never imagined that a four year old of mine would have a television for her personal use, but there were some programs on that were good for children. They provided a distraction for her, when I was busy doing housework. Because the traction set-up took up so much room, the bedroom had to be completely rearranged. Consequently, navigating was a problem. It was good that I wasn't a very large person.

Kelley still had to wear the braces on her hands in the day, and splints on her arms at night. We were directed to return to the clinic in a month. At that time they would most likely take her out of the traction, put her in casts, and teach her to walk with crutches. A month is a long time to be tied down, so I started looking for help by reading up on caring for disabled children. I asked everyone I knew to visit. I did not want to make David and Susan spend all their time in that room playing with Kelley, so I was thankful when they did so often, on their own.

Now, besides being a busy mother of three little children, one of them was bedridden. I had become so busy, that I made the mistake of neglecting to take care of myself. I came down with the worse case of flu that I had ever had, and I needed for Bob to stay home from work for a few days to take care of me. I learned then how important it was to take care of myself when Kelley was in the hospital. She needed me to be well when she returned home. I never forgot that lesson.

We had to use a restrainer around Kelley's chest at times to keep her from sitting. I hated to do that, but she had developed very strong stomach muscles. She could sit up quite easily, and too often. She also became able to curl up in her sleep, pulling all that weight up with her legs, without even knowing it! Those weights occasionally awakened us in the night. Sometimes the wrap that held the traction straps in place loosened. When seven pounds of sand suddenly hit the floor in the still of the night, we knew it!

The month passed, and we anxiously went to see the doctors, carrying Kelley. Before we saw the doctors, a nurse, who told us she was involved in a study concerning clinic patients, interviewed us. I had plenty to say, and she suggested that I put it all in writing.

When the doctors did examine her, they said, "Go home and add a pound of weight to the traction. Bring her back next month to get casts and crutches."

We were so disappointed to realize that we had to face another whole month with her in traction!

When we returned the following month, I handed a letter to the nurse who had interviewed me. It best illustrates my thinking at that time, so I have included it here:

Dear_____,

For the past three months, our family has been going through the trying experience of caring for a bedridden four-year-old child. I am sure you can see what a difficult time this can be, not only for the child herself, but for her younger siblings, and indeed for father and mother, too. A child in traction is more care than she was as an infant. Mother is very much tied to the house, unable even to take the younger ones for a walk, unable, in fact, to give them the time and attention she once did. For many parents in such a situation, the financial burden caused by medical bills leaves little in the budget to provide for hiring help or buying the many toys that would help to keep the active mind of the confined youngster occupied and interested in things other than her affliction.

Unfortunately, we had very little to go on when our daughter came home from the hospital. We were led to believe it would be a short time that she would be in traction, so we tried to "make do" with what was at hand. When we realized (after going back to the clinic) that she would be bedridden longer than we had anticipated, we had to call upon all of our resources: friends, relatives, neighbors and books.

We have discovered during this time a number of inexpensive, as well as expensive ideas for occupying the time and mind of the bedridden child. It is for this reason I have felt it necessary to write this letter to you. Through our experiences we would like to help lessen the burden other parents will face. We feel the hospital personnel have been somewhat remiss in treating the *whole child*. When our daughter was discharged from the hospital, we were given pages of instructions concerning the traction set-up, the physical care of the child in traction and the necessary diet, but absolutely no help concerning the emotional needs of the child. I have taken some courses in child psychology, and have read numerous books on the subject. I have also had a few years experience at being the mother of three small children. However, I have not had the experience with the ill or handicapped child that the personnel of this hospital have had. It would indeed be a great help to parents if along with the pages of physical instructions, there would be a few pages of general ideas that the parents could adapt to the age and dexterity of their child. I have taken the liberty to present to you the enclosed list of suggestions that could and should be passed on to other parents. I feel this list could be greatly enlarged by the hospital staff. I am sure other parents who have shared this type of problem would be most helpful in adding their ideas, if only someone asked them. I must tell you quite frankly that until my conversation with you on March 8, I had the feeling that no one at the hospital (except perhaps the physical therapists) really cared about anything but my daughter's joints. I was encouraged by your interest on that day, and by the fact that a study was taking place concerning clinic patients. We have been visiting that clinic for over a year now, and have had mixed feelings about the way we have been received. One feels like a number, being told to report to a certain floor, then being told to sit and wait, and wait, and wait (while trying to keep the child in an affable mood right through her usual lunch time). After a few visits, we began to find our way around, and learned to bring snacks with us. We found out more from other parents in the waiting room than we did from the endless round of doctors to whom we had had to report the same story over and over again in front of the child.

Is it really good for the child to call more attention than necessary to her problem?

Is it good for the child to have the various aspects of her problem discussed in her presence?

Is it good for her if her parents are not told completely all of the implications, limitations and possibilities connected with this particular disease?

Is it possible for the parents to work more closely with the hospital staff concerning the child's emotional health?

The parent of the handicapped child needs assistance in helping the child to adjust to the limitations placed upon her by the disease. I personally believe in teaching the child to deal positively with what she has; to accept her limitations, but to find there are many things she *can* accomplish; to be interested in others and in helping others. I believe in obtaining all the help available to let the child realize she can have a useful and worthwhile life no matter what the handicap. The parent needs answers to questions such as: How does the weary mother find the energy twice daily, day after day to 'play games' in order to encourage the child to perform exercises which may be painful, or unpleasant at best?

Two weeks ago, I finally obtained a book that has helped us a great deal with our problem. How I wish someone at the hospital had recommended it months ago! Now I wonder why books of guidance are not given to parents, or at least made available by the hospital for parents to purchase. If the hospital could not make this or a comparable book available, could you at least provide a bibliography for parents?

In closing, I would like to assure you that I have written this letter only because I felt there was a need for it. I do not wish to unduly criticize the hospital, but I do feel there could be a greater rapport between parents and the hospital personnel. I do know my feelings are not unlike many parents I have talked to at the hospital, and my desire is to help them and their children. I know first hand of the emotional, physical and financial drain made upon the whole family (especially the conscientious mother) in these circumstances.

Thank you for your time and attention.
Sincerely, Denise Crompton

I enclosed four pages of ideas with my letter. I never did receive the courtesy of a reply, but I suspect that others like me made some suggestions, also. Things have changed dramatically in all hospitals since then, praise God!

Month after month we returned to the clinic with high hopes that this time they had meant what they had said. Month after month, we were met with the same shaking of heads. More and more I wondered if this was the right thing to do. More and more I questioned them, and more and more the answers were vague. I prayed, and so did everyone else who knew Kelley. If I had thought that having three babies in three years had been a challenge, I was to discover that to be just a prelude to this experience. While we waited for prayers to be answered, we kept following the orders of the doctors.

One of the answers to our prayers was that my parents bought the house next door to us. Now I had some good reliable help close at hand, plus a generous supply of moral support.

We were not without some humorous incidents during this time, like the woman in the business office at the hospital who said to Kelley, "Shame on you for sucking your thumb."

I had to hold my tongue. The lady was very much overweight. I wanted to say, "Shame on you for eating too much!" Nowhere in the Bible have I ever seen it say it is a sin for a child to suck her thumb, but I do remember seeing that gluttony was frowned upon. Judging others is frowned upon, too. That's why I decided to hold my tongue.

We had some neighbors that were not too neighborly. This was only one isolated family. The rest of the neighbors were the best you could find anywhere. This isolated family was just that. They spoke words that we did not use, nor want our children to use, and they always spoke them very loudly! One of them heard about the "poor kid who was tied to the bed" and came to the door asking to see her. That started a parade. They all came, from grandparents on down, to look at the poor kid. That was the only time, in the eight years that we lived there, that they had anything to do with us.

That spring, when Bob was away on a business trip, there was a heavy rain that caused an excess of water in the cellar. It made me very uncomfortable to think of all that dampness in the house, and what it might do to Kelley's joints. Just about everyone else in the area had water in their cellar, too, so we were on a list to be pumped out by the fire department. When I called them back at 10 PM to ask if they had forgotten us, they said the list was long. I explained the situation with Kelley, and the woman to whom I spoke said, "Why didn't you tell us that the first time you called? You are now next on the list."

The people who installed the furnace in that house had the foresight to put it up high, since we were so close to the water. They did not have the same foresight with the pump for the well. The strange thing was, that the whole time the pump was submerged it worked. Once they pumped us out, it quit!

A lightning storm hit that year, the likes of which I had never seen before, and hope to never see again. Kelley was close to a window, and the traction had quite a bit of metal attached to it. I whipped that equipment off in record time! The storm stayed around for a while, went away and came back again. Consequently, Kelley spent the whole afternoon out of traction, and thought it was a perfectly delightful storm!

That spring, Bob was offered a position with another company nearby; which meant a substantial raise in pay. He accepted. His colleagues threw a wonderful farewell party for him. I was proud and pleased to see them show such appreciation for him. I knew he was a very conscientious worker who asked for no praise. He deserved the honor!

The doctors gave us an allowance to keep Kelley out of traction for two hours a day just before Easter. On Easter Sunday, we decided to put that allowance to good use. We all dressed up in our best clothes to go out with friends to have an ice cream Sundae. It was a fun afternoon for all of us. Even though Bob was carrying Kelley, we felt like a normal family again!

We were not able to go camping that summer, but Bob did set up the tent in the yard so he, David and Susan could sleep outside. One of our clinic visits was during his vacation, so he had the joy and pleasure of taking us. He learned first hand why we always returned home exhausted. An engineer finds it difficult to witness waste of time and energy, as was apparent there. He felt the same frustrations as I did while trying to communicate with the doctors.

I said many prayers of thanks that summer for the house on the beach. The situation would have been much more difficult if we were still in that second floor apartment that was so hot in the summer!

Kelley was able to exercise in the water every day, and I considered that to be one of her PT sessions. Grandpa helped me whenever possible with the job of carrying her. Nevertheless, the constant lifting for so many months was taking a toll on me, and my old back injury kicked up again. I called the visiting nurses to see if there was some way to get some help, and a nice nurse came to visit to see if it was necessary. In general, I have always liked nurses. I had intended to be one myself, and I always felt that I had something in common with nurses. The situation at this point was that Kelley was now five years old, Susan four, and David going on three. He was big for his age, but because it was more convenient for me at the time, he still wore nap and night diapers. Kelley had been in traction six or seven months. I was on pain medication for my back, but still doing PT twice a day and keeping house as well as caring for the rest of the family. Yet, this nice nurse said to me, "Shame on you for not having that boy trained by now."

David was the best baby in the world. He was a darling toddler. He was well behaved, very respectful, quite bright, well dressed, clean, well fed and healthy. That nurse was just what I needed to have a good laugh! So quick to judge!

Even though I had a black mark on my motherhood by her, because of this neglect, we did get the help of a homemaker. She was assigned to do the lifting and heavy housework while I did the fun stuff like PT. This homemaker was another prayer answered. She was a beautiful little lady, but strong, as well as warm, kind and understanding. She was with us for two hours a day, which gave me some relief, and provided a break for my folks, too.

In September we went for yet *another* check-up, hoping for some good news. The doctors stood around shaking their heads and talking about attaching wires to Kelley's bones and putting her back in the hospital. With all she had been through already, and with the care (or lack thereof) I had already seen in that hospital, this idea spelled DANGER to me! It would be too easy for her to get an infection. Enough is enough!

I sat slumped on my mother's living room sofa late that afternoon thoroughly discouraged. I was drained. Kelley was at home back in traction, with Grandpa minding her. I said to my mother, "I don't know what to do now, but I just can't allow them to do that to her."

In her calm reassuring way, Mother asked, "Isn't there somewhere else you could take her, dear?"

"I don't know," I answered, "I thought this place was supposed to be the best. Where else can I go?"

God supplied the answer. I prayed that night for guidance, and I sent the prayer express to God. I didn't stop to chat with any of the saints in between.

The next day, as I sat at my desk to work on a grocery list, I saw it! It had been there all along, but this day, I really "saw it" for the first time. The pamphlet from the Arthritis Foundation made me realize where I could get some help!

That day I wrote a long letter to them, explaining what had happened, and what the doctors proposed to do now. I then asked if they knew of any alternative methods of treatment. It must have been a pretty desperate sounding letter. I was feeling pretty desperate, but I knew somehow that this plea for help would be heard, and I slept much more peacefully that night.

# CHAPTER THREE

I received an answer to my cry for help within two days. I must have sounded pretty desperate, indeed! The letter from the medical director of the Arthritis Foundation suggested we look into having Kelley admitted to a specialized hospital, only twenty miles from our home. In that way, he would be able to see her when he visited there weekly. I ran next door, filled with expectancy, to share my newfound hope with my parents. Dad offered to baby-sit while Mom and I went to investigate the hospital.

The building was new and modern in design. We were immediately impressed by the large, sunny and attractive waiting room. After explaining the reason for our visit to the receptionist, she cordially invited us to take a seat while she called the hospital's director.

In a matter of minutes, a very refined gentleman approached us, extended his hand, and introduced himself. We followed him to his office. Without rushing or interrupting me, he listened to my entire story. I knew that my prayers had been answered! It was wonderful to be so graciously treated by a doctor! He explained to us that there were many children in residence who would probably spend their entire lives there. Because he didn't want Kelley to get the idea that she wouldn't get better and go home, he planned to place her with another child who would also be leaving someday.

Mom and I chatted happily all the way home about our renewed hope. I don't think Kelley really understood it all, but she became caught up in my excitement when I told her about the hospital. When Bob arrived home from work, he could hardly understand us. Kelley and I were both talking to him at the same time about the events of the day. I had already filled out the application and dropped it off with our family doctor, so he could forward it to the hospital after signing it.

"Oh honey," I exclaimed, throwing my arms around Bob, "finally we have found someone to treat the whole child!"

"That's great! That's really great!" he said beaming happily with us.

Within days, we received a letter from the hospital as to the day Kelley would be admitted. They invited her to visit the following Sunday, so she could have a tour of the hospital and grounds before her admission.

We were welcomed that Sunday by a lovely young nurse who took us around and introduced Kelley to the other children. We saw a variety of braces, crutches, contraptions and wheelchairs. The nurse explained that some of the children were off for the weekend at home, or out visiting with friends, but to many of the children, this *was home*, and they operated like a family. Everyone had a routine, starting with getting fully dressed each morning. Then they went to physical therapy, occupational therapy, or the hospital school. The grounds were beautiful, with a large playground in the back. Local high school students came in the afternoon to take the children confined to wheelchairs out for walks on the grounds. Sunday afternoons were sometimes spent 'at the movies' in the hospital. At other times, live entertainment was provided. It all sounded too good to be true!

A few days before Kelley was admitted, I took some snapshots of the children in order to have them put on a Christmas card. Her little legs looked so thin in those pictures after nine months in traction! Her smile was as broad as ever, though! My favorite photo of Kelley from that day was not the posed one I chose for the Christmas card, but rather the one I snapped when she was clowning around. Any occasion was a good occasion to have fun!

We let her sleep without the traction her last night at home. We had come to doubt that the traction was beneficial by that time, anyway. We knew when we left her at that hospital that she was in capable hands. The building was well designed for the specific purpose of dealing with long-term illnesses.

Kelley's roommate was a little girl who wore a large brace to correct a problem with her spine. While she and Kelley didn't make life long friends of each other, neither did they have any real problems with being roommates. They just didn't have much in common.

"Miss Personality" came to "interview" us. She was about ten years old, and had spent most of her life hospitalized. This girl took it upon herself to greet all visitors to the children's floor. She knew where everyone was at all times, and made it her business to see that everyone had what they needed. Sporting a perpetual infections grin, she moved around better, in that wheelchair, than most of us do walking. I am sure this was no small task, since she shared a room with five other children, most of them victims of Cerebral Palsy. They were in various stages of growth and development, and unable to walk unaided. A few of them were able to get around somewhat with the aid of crutches and braces. The total picture represented hours and hours of PT, OT and surgery, not to mention good old-fashioned sweat!

The children had their problems getting along together at times, and Miss Personality would somehow always solve the problem better than any adult could. I was always grateful that I came to know this child during Kelley's stay. She was a genuine inspiration! She told me that her parents visited her, from the city, when they could afford to take the bus, but there were many other children in her family. It was a hot day when she came back from surgery that September. As she lay on the bed with a minimal amount of covers, I saw all the scars from the various operations she had undergone. They had all been done as part of a plan to help her to walk. It may sound like a sad note to report that she died about five years later, but I believe she was here on a mission, which she fulfilled. She was a powerful example to the rest of us who tend to complain about trivia! How the saints must have welcomed her into heaven. What a comforting thought to know her kind are there waiting for the rest of us!

The type of nursing in this facility was very different from that in the big city hospital. Nurses did get personally involved in caring for long-term patients. There was very little sickness, a small amount of surgery, and a great demand for cheerfulness and encouragement. Out of necessity, the hospital staff became surrogate parents, and as such disciplined their charges as parents would.

Kelley's room was a comfortable size, and very cheerful. It had very large windows on the ground floor, giving a panoramic view of visitors arriving and leaving. We had friends who lived near the hospital. Their young children were not allowed on the children's floor, but they could visit right outside her window. That was fun. She was also close enough to home, so that all the grandparents as well as many aunts and uncles, were able to visit. That gave me more of a chance to spend time with David and Susan. We had a constant exchange taking place. David and Susan made things and drew pictures for me to take to Kelley, and she did the same for them. It helped to keep their feeling of unity.

I wrote to the previous hospital when I knew that Kelley was being admitted, saying we were making the change so traveling would be easier. I requested them to transfer her records. It was seven months later when the new hospital received the report. They, of course, had done their own evaluation long before then. There was one doctor on staff who was in charge of Kelley's case. He shook his head upon initial examination.

"What a shame to have kept her in traction for so long," he said, "Look how those muscles have atrophied! It will take a lot of work to get her walking again."

"Do you mean she *will* be able to walk again?" I excitedly asked, "Will it be okay for her to do so?"

"Oh, yes, she should, after enough physical therapy."

"I have been doing PT with her at home all along, but I was told not to let her walk. I did catch her at it a couple of times during the summer," I admitted, "When she was out in the yard with the other children at the picnic table during her hour's release, I looked out and saw her holding onto the table and making her way around by walking. I didn't have the heart to stop her and take away a moment of joy."

23

The doctor's eyes sparkled as he smiled and said, "We will have the specialist see her when he comes in on Tuesday. I am sure he will agree with me."

The specialist was the one who had answered my letter. He could not have been any kinder or more understanding, and to top that all off, he did know something about this strange disease. Every time the other doctors said they didn't know, I was under the impression they were talking for the whole medical profession. It turned out that there were some people in the medical field who did know a great deal. What a relief!

They eliminated the traction, splints and braces. Kelley thought this hospital was an okay place, even though they made her do physical therapy. It was many weeks before the muscles in her little legs were ready to try a few steps at a time. I will never forget my feeling of gratitude and relief the day she actually walked again. As the tears ran down my cheeks, I noticed a few of the nurses had tears in their eyes, too.

During Kelley's two month stay there, the same wonderful woman, who had helped me out at home when my back was a problem, came in each day to care for the other two children. That allowed me to go to the hospital at a regular time daily. I borrowed a friend's car and arrived each day at lunchtime. Kelley and I always joined the crowd in the six-bed room for lunch. I enjoyed helping the children who needed assistance.

There was never a problem communicating with any of the nurses, doctors or therapists in that facility. It was good to know that I wasn't such a crazy lady, after all, in wanting to take care of the whole child. I started to have confidence again in the medical profession. The day Kelley put her arms around the doctor to give him a kiss when she was going home for a weekend; I knew her faith had been restored, too.

One evening during her stay, Mary Lou and I stopped in to see Kelley. I looked at her and looked for the thermometer. She always had a certain look, which I will never be able to explain, that let me know that she had a fever. I read the thermometer and called the nurse. She read the thermometer and called the doctor. The staff went into action! The lab was called to draw blood, and collect urine for study. The nurses commenced to bring her fever down with alcohol rubs and forcing fluids. At the last hospital, no one cared that she had a cold, which is what this turned out to be. At this hospital, they not only took care of Kelley, but also did all they could to protect the other children from contracting the cold. She did have to stay in her room, and away from the others for a few days, but the staff absolutely doted on her.

We had been saving to buy a new car. The one that we had purchased, when we were first married, was now seven years old. While it had been a good car, it had seen better days. Bob felt it would start costing too much money to keep up, so we went looking for a station wagon to accommodate a family with plans to go camping again. We fully intended to trade in the old one, but when the salesman told us what it would be worth as a trade in, I said, "It's worth a lot more than that to me."

Bob understood. I was thrilled to have my own car! I didn't need to borrow one anymore, and I could come and go, with the children when I pleased. I suppose it would have been nothing but frustrating, if I had obtained it much sooner, and had to see it sitting in the driveway, while we were all tied down by Kelley's traction. Instead, it was now an added liberation. That old run-down car that we were going to trade-in lasted five more years. Usually, Bob used it to go back and forth to work, and left the wagon for the kids and me. He is a dear! I don't think I ever took that car for granted.

Nine months of being tied down and being disappointed repeatedly had taken its toll on our little girl emotionally. Her cooperation and behavior were, at times, less than desirable, especially in PT. It was a relief for me that someone else was playing the heavy in that department. However, the therapists complained to the doctor about a very uncooperative patient. The consensus of all who worked with her was that she was a delightful girl who was also hyperactive.

Heck, I knew that all along! That was no news to Kelley's family. What was news, was that something could be done about it. I had assumed that she would calm down to her usual roar in time, and that, most likely, she was reacting to her new found freedom, trying to go in twenty directions at once. However, the new doctor gave me a paper to read on a new type of drug, which was being used successfully, to treat hyperactive children. He suggested we consider letting Kelley try it, under supervision, with the theory that she could accomplish more in PT if she would stay in one place long enough. It made sense to me. I certainly knew the frustrations of trying to get her to do PT. I also knew that these people were very experienced, and if they were having problems, perhaps we should try it. I also felt very confident that they would watch for side effects, so I gave them my okay.

My sister had volunteered to pick Kelley up on a Friday to bring her home for the weekend. Since she would be home in the late afternoon, I skipped a visit that day. It was the end of October, and she was walking quite well by that time. This sweet little thing came into the house, gave me a big hug and kiss as usual, and then offered to set the table for supper, which was not usual. She displayed a behavior that was so helpful and cooperative, I said to myself, "Wow! They have taught her in a matter of weeks what I have been trying to teach her for years!" I was pleased with her performance, but it did not do much for my ego!

Then Mary Lou produced a little bottle and said, "They started her on this today. You are supposed to give her one tablet three times a day."

My ego was okay again. It wasn't *me*. It was the *pills!*

"Boy, they sure do work!" I exclaimed.

I have always believed that medicine should be used only when necessary. In this case, I quickly decided that it was indeed necessary. The article had said that perhaps these children outgrow their need for this medication, but during this particular period of growth, it made life much better for patient, parents, and teachers. It was a very effective little magic pill!

The anticipation of Halloween at the hospital mirrored that of children everywhere. I bought Kelley a new costume for the occasion and put it in the locker in her room. The next day it was gone, and Kelley was crestfallen. I talked to one of the nurses who said, "Bet I know where it is! We have a resident pack rat."

There was one little girl there who never seemed to understand that she could not simply take anything she wanted. The costume was returned, and Kelley was able to go trick-or-treating, with the other kids, throughout the rest of the hospital.

PT became easier when Kelley's overall behavior changed to fairly normal. We were on the right track. The therapists instructed me as to their way of doing PT. It was more preferable than the method previously employed. A few months after her admission to the "answer to a prayer" hospital, Kelley was sent home. She was to return on an outpatient basis twice a week for PT, and every few months to see the doctors. They still had many questions concerning Kelley's condition. She did not have the typical type of flare-ups known to happen with JRA, and the curve of her fingers was different from what they usually saw. They asked me to please bring her in any time she experienced a flare-up, so they could witness, for themselves, just what was happening. I did rush her in one day when she had a flare-up, which produced hot inflamed joints, that lasted for a few hours. The doctor told me that she was not having a typical JRA episode. He did not theorize why, but he also said that her blood work was also not typical.

Thanksgiving 1968 was a very thankful one for our family. Our girl was home, and, except for doing PT twice a day, we were a normal family with three preschool children.

We shared a joyous traditional Christmas. Believing that children should know the spirit of giving, as well as receiving, at Christmas time we instituted a family tradition, as soon as they were able to comprehend. Every year on Christmas Eve, they each chose one of their own toys (preferably a treasured one) to put under the tree. It was a gift for Santa Claus to take back to the baby Jesus. The girls usually picked one of their favorite dolls. David chose from a variety of toys. When he put his little purple goat under the tree for the baby Jesus with no prompting from us, we knew that he understood the spirit of giving. That little goat had been his constant companion for a long time.

We also made a cake each year, and sang Happy Birthday to Jesus. Two pieces of cake were left out on Christmas Eve—one for Santa, and one for Santa to take back to Jesus.

The children were at delightful ages by this time. They were quite capable of doing many things for themselves, and they played together rather well. Their personalities were developing. Kelley was the ringleader. She usually set the scene and directed the play. Susan was, for the most part, content to go along with whatever was happening. As long as she was fed regularly, Susan made few complaints. Oh, how she loved to eat! Kelley was rather fussy at times about what she wanted to eat, but then, she didn't require as much food as the others, as she was growing slowly. At one time, Kelley's clothes were passed down to Susan, then Susan caught up and they were the same size. By this time, Susan was passing clothes down to Kelley. While Kelley was spontaneous in action, Susan came up with some good innovations, and David was the thinker and planner. When my sister Hilary gave him a large set of those little bricks that stick together, as a Christmas gift, I thought it was going to turn out to be one more mess to keep picked up. Hilary had a son first. She had chosen the right gift! David spent hours and hours creating buildings, boats and what-have-you with those bricks. Tumbling around with Susan on the floor was another of his favorite activities.

We went camping on vacation—off to the mountains again. It was even more fun than the last time. Kelley was six years old that summer, Susan five, and David almost four. We went hiking, swimming, on nature walks, and generally wore them out to the point where they would ask after supper, "Can we go to bed now?"

We slept in sleeping bags, on air mattresses that frequently deflated before sunrise. There was no electricity, and the living was easy. One night, for a treat, we got all cleaned up and went to a Chinese restaurant in town for dinner. Susan loved it. Kelley and David didn't care to try any of those strange things, and didn't think it was such a great idea. We did our share of sightseeing, and hit the usual tourist attractions, where they let the kids in dirt-cheap, and charge exorbitant prices to the adults. We toyed with the idea of letting them go in alone, in an attempt to beat the system, but decided we did want to see them again.

27

They all traveled well. We had a supply of games and toys in the car to keep them amused, not to mention food and drinks. Yes, there was a great deal of work involved in raising these children, but the delights of watching them grow and develop was well worth the effort.

After returning from vacation, Kelley was able to go to school. The town we lived in did not have a regular Kindergarten at that time, so they had a six-week summer session for those entering first grade in the fall. She went for a half day, in the morning. It was a good way to introduce the children to the routine. The first day of school, when I put her on that bus, I was glad I was wearing sunglasses, so she would not see the tears in my eyes. It was such a joy and blessed relief to see those little legs make that big climb up those bus stairs. I thought of the doctors who, a few years before, told us she might never be well enough to go to school. I said a deep prayer of gratitude.

In September 1969, I wrote the following letter to that wonderful man who had answered our plea for help a year before:

Dear Doctor_____,

It was a year ago this month when I first wrote to you seeking assistance in dealing with my daughter Kelley's problem.

I can't begin to thank you for the difference your answer to that letter, and your care, have made in Kelley's life, and the emotional health of our whole family.

Only rarely have we met a hospital staff to compare with that where you sent us. It is such a relief to know we are now receiving care for the whole child! Before meeting you and the resident we are working with, we had so many unanswered questions. Now I find I am frequently meeting people with scores of questions regarding arthritis. I have given away the pamphlets I have already read, but I don't feel qualified to answer questions about cases other than Kelley's. I would like to learn more about the disease and also would like to know if there is anything I can do to help the Arthritis Foundation. I do collect in our neighborhood every January, and I do have limited time to devote, but when I meet parents as bewildered as we were a year ago, I feel I'd like to do something to help.

A grateful thanks to you from the whole family! Kelley had grown distrustful of doctors in general. You have renewed her confidence—mine, too! She loves you and the hospital staff. God bless you all!

Sincerely,
Denise Crompton

# CHAPTER FOUR

Kelley entered the first grade that fall. It seemed that the only difference between her and the typical first grader was that she was taking pills for arthritis, the pill for hyperactivity, and had to do physical therapy, because of the limited range of motion of her joints. In the photo I took of her on the first day of school, she looked no different from any other six year old. We were aware, from previous testing, that her IQ was only slightly lower than average, so that was not going to bother us at all. Her radiance was more than slightly above average! IQ really has nothing to do with achieving success and happiness in life. I have known countless people who score high on an IQ test, yet are miserable. It is attitude that counts, and the only grades about which we were really concerned, on any of the children's report cards, have been attitude and effort. We knew Kelley might need help to keep up with the class. However, we felt so happy that she was well enough to go to school, we weren't going to be concerned about how soon she learned her times tables. We did not expect, however, that she was going to be unable to keep up physically with the rest of the class. She gave it a valiant try, but I began receiving calls from the nurse, almost daily, to go to school to pick her up and take her home. She was simply too tired to make it through the day. After a conference with her teacher, the nurse and the principal, we decided to have her come home daily, at noontime. She needed to take a nap when she got home. This was the first indication to us that she was not able to keep up with her peers. Socially, she loved school. Academically, she had no great desire to learn to read or add. I devised all sorts of games to play at home to aid her academically. Susan and David reaped the benefit of playing the games with us.

Kelley's first grade teacher was the best one she ever had. I have to say that. My sister Mary Lou was Kelley's first grade teacher. Kelley had no trouble separating her teacher from her aunt. In fact, she separated the two so well, that when Mary Lou stopped in for a visit one afternoon, Kelley took out her school papers to show to her aunt. We enjoyed that! It was also a treat for me to be able to be a "fly on the wall," receiving reports from Mary Lou, about how things were going at school. Whenever there was free time, Kelley organized the action just as she did at home, and directed the play. She had a number of followers who were very happy with this. Socially, school went well. She certainly wasn't going to be shy or self-conscious because she had a disease. We thanked God for that!

I started teaching that year, myself. When I took Kelley for her first Confraternity of Christian Doctrine class, Father asked me if I would teach the class. It was a small parish in a small town, and there were not enough teachers.

"Oh, Father," I said, motioning to Susan and David, "I have to take care of the little ones."

"Bring them to class with you," he said, "it won't hurt them any."

I was about to protest again, because I had never taught before, but I could see that he was in a tough situation. I supposed that if I wanted my children to have a Catholic education, I should be willing to do my part. I saw it as an opportunity to put to use the courses I had taken at the State teacher's college a few years before.

On the first day of teaching the first grade class, I told Kelley that in class, I was "Mrs. Crompton." She never forgot. I gave all the children papers to take home to be filled out and signed by their parents. Kelley held onto hers until we got home, and then handed it to me and said, "My teacher said to give this to my mother." She separated us very well!

I came from a family of teachers, including my father. We had been taught that having one's father a teacher in the school one attended did not automatically grant one any special privileges. Quite the contrary! We had better behave ourselves, or else! I enjoyed my little CCD class so much, that I spent a total of fourteen years teaching. I tried all different grades, and loved them all.

We were able to celebrate Halloween as a family that year. Our neighborhood was a delightful mix of a few families and many retired folks, who loved having the children visit. With all of the children in their costumes, we made the rounds in a large group. We went visiting at the neighborhood houses, rather than just standing at the door saying, "Trick or treat."

We were all invited into each of the homes, and offered all sorts of goodies, including cider and donuts at the last stop. It was a friendly fun evening, with the hosts guessing who was behind each mask, and the children being delighted when they guessed incorrectly!

Our neighbors directly across the street were often a Godsend to me. Grandparents themselves, they were most willing to add our children to their list of loved ones. Lucy and Ray became like family to us. Sometimes Lucy called me to say, "I'm not doing anything but sewing. Send the children over."

She was a very talented lady with her sewing machine. I used to wait until the children were at her house to attempt much sewing, myself. She would sew, and teach them too, at the same time. One day she sent them home with matching outfits that she made for them, without patterns!

We knew we could count on Lucy and Ray for anything, and it was fun being with them. We were indeed fortunate to be in such a neighborhood. When people used to ask us why we lived in such a remote place, we explained that it was worth driving four miles down that long road, where the only traffic one ran into was little animals crossing the road. It was a quiet, peaceful and friendly neighborhood where we could count on each other, yet everyone managed to mind their own business.

We did PT at home before school in the morning and again before supper. Twice a week, we went to the hospital for PT. They gave Kelley's hands a twenty-minute whirlpool bath before the exercises, which they kept updating. I found it reassuring that they educated me as to the reasons for each change. There were days when Kelley really gave me a hard time about doing PT. She gave them a hard time at the hospital, too. Sometimes I left her with them, and went to have a cup of coffee with a friend. It was difficult to impress upon such a young child the importance of keeping her joints moving, so they would not become any stiffer, and to impress upon her that she would be able to do more if she could loosen up those joints. Her resistance was to structured exercises. She was not lazy, she simply wanted to be able to go off and play like the other kids did, and there were times we had a battle of wills. I cringed at playing the heavy in this department, thinking it was enough of a job just getting her to behave herself in general, without this added to it. I prayed for patience.

Since I dislike medication, we experimented with her little pill for the hyperactivity. We decided we could handle her without it on weekends, thus making it more effective when she was in school on weekdays. On one occasion, I tried her without it for school. There was a noticeable difference. My sister said that she hoped I wouldn't do that again. Kelley really disrupted the class when she couldn't sit still.

Once a month, we had to visit the lab at the hospital to have Kelley's blood drawn. One day, when we got off the elevator, she realized where we were headed, and took off down the hall as if running in a marathon. I didn't blame her. I felt terrible having to make her do that, even though I knew it was necessary.

During one of our visits to PT, the head therapist told me that there was a social worker, at the hospital, who wanted to see me while Kelley was having her therapy. A new addition to the hospital, she was meeting with the parents of all the children. Her demeanor was pleasant as she asked me many questions about our family, and how we were handling all of the problems that Kelley's condition presented. I answered each of her questions matter-of-factly. We had already done all of our dealing with our initial emotions, and we had a good support system in our families of origin.

31

We knew how to ask for help when we needed it, and were able to get our needs met. At the end of the interview, the social worker sighed and said, "Mrs. Crompton, isn't there anything I can do to help you?"

"I don't think so," I said, realizing that she was disappointed, "but I wish you had been around when we were going through a terrible time with that other hospital a few years ago."

My sister Hilary visited us at Thanksgiving time. When she saw that I was suffering again with my old back injury, she asked, "Why don't you see a chiropractor?"

"I've thought about that for years, but the medical doctors keep telling me not to," I responded.

"What have they done for you?" she asked, "You're still having trouble."

She was right. In the past, I had been hospitalized numerous times for the problem, and it never seemed to get better for very long. I was reluctant to see a doctor who would put me back in the hospital again. I asked Bob his opinion. He was rather tired of my back problem, himself.

"What have you got to lose?" he asked.

Since he put it that way, my decision was easy. The medical doctors had talked about surgery. I chose to try the chiropractic way first. I had heard good reports about a man in the next town, so I made an appointment to see him. It was not without trepidation that I walked into the office. The man appeared to be as big as a bear! I promptly announced, "I must tell you that I am scared."

This kind gentleman assured me that he had never lost a patient on the table. That brought a good laugh from me, which helped me to relax. He was very gentle when he examined me.

"How long have you been having this trouble?" he asked.

"It started eleven years ago," I told him, "I had an accident which caused the pain in the lower back, and all the way down my leg, but now the pain is also in my neck and right down the arm to my finger tips."

"I can see why," he said, as his expert and talented fingers picked out the problem spots, "You give me eleven weeks, then."

"You mean I won't have to keep coming back every month for the rest of my life?" I asked, bearing in mind that I knew people who did just that.

"I have enough patients that I can fix most of them and send them on their way. Yours is not a chronic problem. At least it shouldn't be. If you let me, I should be able to correct this, and send you on your way. It will take some time, and you will back-slide until we have that spine in alignment, but if you will persevere, I believe you will find it worthwhile."

This was the most optimistic any doctor had ever been about my back problem. It was something I had thought I was going to have to put up with for the rest of my life. Eleven weeks did not seem very long under these circumstances.

It didn't even take that long. It was more like six weeks until I was pain free. Really pain free. What liberation! No pain and no medication!

In talking with the chiropractor about my family, I told him about Kelley's problems. He suggested I bring her in sometime when I had an appointment. He said that he just wanted to look at her. One Saturday morning he worked on my back, and that night, I sneezed myself into a very uncomfortable position. I called him to ask what to do. He advised me to use a heating pad for then, and to call him in the morning if it was still painful.

"Tomorrow is Sunday," I said. I never knew a doctor who went to his office on Sunday, and I had experienced back pain for so long, that I thought I could wait until Monday.

"Call me, anyway," he responded.

We had a snowstorm that night. On Sunday morning, the chiropractor called me.

"I'm going in to the office to shovel. Have your husband bring you in," he said.

I did, and took Kelley along. He put me back into alignment. This was the sliding-back he had warned me about, but he assured me we were still going in the right direction. Then he asked to see Kelley's feet. I told him that it was her hands about which we were most concerned. He said, "I know, but I can tell a lot from looking at feet."

I took off her shoes, and Bob and I exchanged glances while the doctor examined first Kelley's feet and then her hands.

"She doesn't have Rheumatoid Arthritis," he said after a while, "I don't know what to call what she does have, but I know it is not JRA!"

I told him that the doctors we were currently seeing had been questioning the diagnosis, also. He said that he wouldn't be able to cure her, but he would be able to help her somewhat, if I brought her along with me, whenever I went there, and he wouldn't charge me for her.

Thus began a very beautiful patient-doctor relationship. Kelley grew to love the man. She enjoyed going to see him. He never stuck needles in her, he never gave her medicine, and he never talked down to her. She made cards and drew pictures for him, and he picked her up in his big bear arms to let her kiss him goodbye, each time she left. He saw her regularly, long after my back was better, at no charge—he insisted. He said she brightened his day, and that was all he needed to collect. I sent him quite a few patients, on the testimony of what he had done for me, after all those years in pain. He was a gem!

When I was in nurse's training, I was fed a lot of propaganda about the greatness of the medical profession. Most people in the profession are under the assumption that their way is the only way, or at least the only right way. I could have saved myself years of aggravation, pain and inconvenience if I had seen a chiropractor the first time I injured my back. However, the doctors, in the hospital where I was in training, persuaded me not to. It was difficult defying all that I had learned and believed. This experience, coupled with Kelley's experience of nine needless months in traction, caused me to start re-examining many of my previous beliefs. It appeared to me that we had a sort of hero worship in this country regarding the medical profession. Perhaps that was why, in my youth, I wanted to be a part of it. We all like to be respected. At this point, I started to see the narrowness of some of the members of that profession, and began to grow surer of my own impressions and instincts. I came to realize that their opinions are just that— opinions based on education and their own personal experiences. I wondered how many people, including doctors and nurses, had gone through surgery for back problems, when a chiropractor could have treated them successfully without a knife.

It *was* a chiropractor that fixed my back. It was wonderful to walk out of his office without a prescription to be filled. All the medication did was mask the real problem. Experience is a great teacher!

I did not want to give up on the medical profession. That was not an option. I did learn to question, examine, weight the evidence, pray for guidance, and go with my gut instincts.

In January 1970, we sat in the conference room at the hospital with the doctors and nurses working on Kelley's case. Our specialist said, "I've shown Kelley's x-rays to a colleague at a large city hospital. I have been under the impression for some time that Kelley doesn't have JRA. This other doctor is in agreement with me. He would like to have you take her there, to let him see her. He specializes in diagnosing questionable diseases. If she were my daughter, I would take her."

I had confidence in this doctor. He had shown himself to be thoughtful, kind, thorough, and not given to drastic or dramatic treatment. The idea of going back to the city hospital was not all that appealing, however. True, it was a different hospital than the previous one, our new specialist was connected with it, and we really no longer had a diagnosis. I must have hesitated while all this was going through my mind, so he continued, "And we will be able to have all her studies and tests covered by a grant from the March of Dimes."

Throughout the years, when we donated to the March of Dimes and various other foundations, we never imagined we would become recipients. This would surely be a financial relief! Bob did have some insurance coverage at work, but there were limitations to it. This help would make a big difference to us.

I said yes, we would go to the city, and although I shook this doctor's hand when we left, I really wanted to give him a big hug. I let Kelley do that. At her age, she could get away with it, without embarrassing him.

Now, after all this time of learning about JRA, and coming to grips with it, we found ourselves in a whole new ball game, and a whole new ball park, yet!

I have always found it easier to deal with the known rather than the unknown, and here we were up at bat, and the pitcher was an unknown—someone from the big city. Would he throw fastballs or curves? Would we be able to keep up the team spirit? We certainly would try!

Very often in life, I have heard people ask, "Why me?"

I believe I am fortunate that I have never felt that way. I have always figured, "Why not me?"

I have yet to find a person who has not had problems.

Why Kelley? Well, why not Kelley? Because my trust is in God, I believed that no matter what we were to discover next, the ability to handle it would be given to us. I was thankful that we were not too far from the big city, and that we had a family willing to help us.

# CHAPTER FIVE

Little did we realize that winter, when we entered the waiting room of this new hospital, just how many more times we would cross that threshold — enough to write a book about!

It was with anticipation that we first met the specialist who was going to have the fun of coming up with a diagnosis. I really doubt that I saw him as a person that day. I guess I wanted him to be a magician who could say, "Oh she has XYZ disease. A little lemonade twice a day will take care of that!"

I do believe in miracles, as well as simple solutions to complex problems.

We went through the usual clinic hello, weight, height, insurance, and all. Then we were escorted into one of the little examining rooms, where a young doctor, working with the specialist, saw us first. Once again, there was a battery of questions to be answered. When did this show up? When did that happen? When did you first notice? What is happening now? I wished that I had made a tape of this recital to avoid having to repeat it ad infinitum. As time went by and more was added, the dates of different occurrences became more difficult to remember.

When this doctor was finished with the history and physical work-up, his chief, who was friendly, interested and interesting, came to see us. He ran over the whole case to date, and added a few questions and comments of his own. He was under the impression, he told us, that Kelley had some type of birth defect. With the help of tests, x-rays, computers and other doctors, he would try to find out what the problem was. He ordered only x-rays and blood work that day. He was careful to explain that he did not subject a child to tests just for the sake of compiling data, and that he would proceed slowly, testing only when indicated. Meanwhile, the facilities of this hospital complex were ours. He assured us that he would see to it that Kelley received whatever help she needed in that facility.

This doctor was very straightforward. He didn't talk down to either Kelley or me. He appeared to be a person who was truly interested in what he was doing, as well as interested in his patient. He was quick to assure us that the diagnosis of JRA was a natural one for the previous doctors to have made, as the symptoms so closely paralleled the symptoms she had. It really did not matter to me, at that point, that Kelley had been misdiagnosed. What mattered was that we were going forward looking for a new diagnosis.

Next we had the fun of finding our way around the place. We were taken care of quickly and efficiently that day. There was some waiting involved at the lab and x-ray, but nothing at all like it had been in the other hospital, a few years before.

Hospitals don't really get built; they just sort of evolve. One lays down a cornerstone somewhere, and buildings are constructed, after which someone thinks to connect them with bridges and tunnels. The elevators are placed in such a way, that no matter where you want to go, you cannot simply arrive there without going somewhere else first. In some cases, someone with a paintbrush has thought to paint arrows. However, one is never too sure where the arrows lead, and if there is any place on earth, where you do not want to end up in the wrong department, it is in a hospital! The most important places to find are rest rooms and cafeterias or coffee shops. After we had taken care of that, we started searching for things like labs. It always looked like everyone else knows just where they are going, and no matter how hard I tried to look the same way, I had to end up asking some questions. Sometimes, the people who looked like they knew where they were going couldn't give me the answer, anyway. It all seems so simple now because I know that place so well, but it was a challenge then.

Kelley always hated to have her blood taken. I managed to impress upon her that if she held her arm still, they would get the blood on the first try, and it would be done and over with quickly. She felt that she had to protest, so I told her to go right ahead and protest vocally, as long as she held her arm still.

Protest vocally, she did! Loudly, too! I was always quick to assure the lab technicians that she would make a lot of noise, but she would indeed hold her arm still. They didn't mind the noise too much, as long as she cooperated. Her favorite cry was, "Don't you do that to me! I don't want you to do that to me! I don't like to have you do that! It hurts, it hurts!"

By the time she expressed all of that, the blood would be drawn, and she would receive her Band-Aid. Then she would smile at the technician and say, "Thank you."

Kelley never held a grudge. She always seemed to know that the technician was just doing a job, and once it was done, it was gone and forgotten.

As in the past, Grandpa took us to the city. It was fun to have him along for company, and fun to stop somewhere to eat on the way home. I did not go home as tired from this visit as I had been a few years back. I went home with some hope. At least it looked as if things were being done correctly in this place, and that gave me a good deal of hope for Kelley's future.

We didn't do much talking at home about how we were dealing with this problem, or how we were going to deal with it. We simply did it. I did not like the idea that Kelley was missing so much time from school, and neither did Bob, but we accepted it. We were aware that we were devoting much more time to this child than most parents do with one child, and we tried very hard not to overlook the needs of the other children. We did not want them to think that the best way to get attention was to have to go to the hospital. We tried to grant them equal time, whenever possible.

We always made a special effort to treat each child as an individual, and to lead as normal and active life as possible, under the circumstances. I often ran into people who asked, "How do you cope?" They said, "I'm so thankful I have healthy children."

They didn't understand that we were as thankful for Kelley as we were for our "healthy" children. I remember sitting in the hospital waiting room with Grandpa one day, looking at the kids who were learning early in life how to cope with problems, and saying, "They may be losing some time from the classrooms, but these kids are learning some valuable lessons about building character."

There is no pat answer as to how we coped and handled the situation. We didn't waste time or energy feeling sorry for her or us. We simply did the best we could. I prayed for guidance, and believed guidance would come. It always did.

When I was a youngster, I heard a story about a man who went to God and complained about the cross he had to carry through life, so God took him to a big field filled with crosses. What a variety! Each cross was different from the rest. What an imagination God has! He told that man to take as much time as he needed to choose the cross he liked best. The man spent hours upon hours trying one cross after another, in an attempt to find the one that fit just right. He finally found it, and he returned to God jubilant about his find. "If I have to carry a cross through life," he said, "this is the one I want."

"Good," God replied, "that's the one you came in with."

I knew that God's wisdom is infinitely superior to mine, and that He would give us the strength to carry whatever crosses we had to carry. I have never heard of anyone getting any better by complaining, and I honestly do not believe we ever thought there was a reason to complain. Some people have trouble understanding this. They feel we should have experienced anger at God because such feelings are supposed to be normal. I am not too sure who decides what "normal" is supposed to be, but if that reaction is normal, I am glad God gave us the gift of being abnormal, in that instance.

The testing started. As each evaluation came in, our new specialist discussed it with us. Kelley was smaller than average for her age, and weighed less, too. We already knew that, but we had not known before that x-rays showed all her bones to be different from the norm. New light was being shed with each of the many visits. The day arrived when the specialist told us that the Rheumatoid factor in the blood was negative, and their belief was that Kelley never did have JRA.

My first question was, "Can we take her off the aspirin?"

I knew better than to ask what she did have. I was confident that they would tell me what they knew, when they knew it. Her x-rays had been sent to a doctor who had a large x-ray film registry for unusual skeletal problems. We waited for word from him.

I was warned to take her off the aspirin slowly, which I did. She experienced withdrawal symptoms, nevertheless. Through the years, Kelley had voiced numerous complaints of stomachaches. I attributed them, at least in part, to the quantity of aspirin she had been taking. She had a few days of being very sick, when the dosage was very low. Our chiropractor told us to give her eggnog when she was nauseated. It worked by causing her to vomit. After that, she felt fine.

She was still on medication for hyperactivity, which we felt we were not ready to give up, just yet, and we were still going to our nearby hospital for PT, twice a week.

Bingo! In March we had not one, but two possible diagnoses. What names!

It was thought that Kelley had either Mucopolysaccharidosis VI or Psuedo-Hurler Polydystrophy, and more study would be needed to see if she did have either one.

Naturally, I asked what it meant if she did have one or the other. The answers were that, right about that time, it did not mean a heck of a lot, but in time, perhaps it would, because the medical profession was working on it.

The next test they did consisted of taking a small piece of skin from Kelley's arm to grow in a lab for a few months. They would then do some testing on it, to help identify the problem. A presentation of her case was also scheduled to take place at a conference in that hospital in May.

While I have always enjoyed a mystery, I have enjoyed seeing the solution more. I loved doing math when I was a student, because I knew each problem would have an answer that could be proven. The only reason I have ever done a jigsaw puzzle has been to have the satisfaction of putting the last piece in place. It was difficult for me to be patient while waiting for this mystery to be solved, so we could go forth. I've always been an active person (Kelley had to inherit that hyperactivity from someone), and my own personal problem, at that time, was having a host of unanswered questions to which I was unable to find the answers, by myself. I knew there was no miracle cure for either of these diseases, but I did want to know which one I was supposed to call it. The approach that the doctors were using then was to rule out Mucopolysaccharidosis VI. All I could do was to pray for patience.

Around this time, we started noticing a problem with Kelley's eyes. It turned out to be a problem with her eye muscles, which was nicely corrected with the right glasses. Whew! The alternative would have been surgery.

Kelley looked darling in those first glasses. We picked out a pink frame, very much in style for little girls then. She wore pink often, as it went well with her blond hair and fair skin. She was happy to wear the glasses, as they put the world back together, and she stopped seeing double. They eye doctors were at the same big city hospital, which meant a few more trips a year, but we were able to get the prescription filled near home.

Neuropsychological testing was done on Kelley in April 1970. It took a full day to complete. The evaluation showed definite motor difficulties. They found Kelley to be cooperative, and approximately one year behind her chronological level at school. They questioned the possibility of overprotection. The doctor who asked me about this was trying to be tactful.

"Of course she has been overprotected," I answered, "We went seeking medical advice for her when she was three years old, and since then, up until a few months ago, we've been told that she had JRA. She needed frequent rest, and as little emotional turmoil as possible, because emotional reactions were, apparently, frequently the cause for flare-ups. We were, in essence, advised to handle her with kid gloves. Yes, I would say she has been overprotected!"

The doctor laughed and said, "Well, she doesn't have JRA now, so there is no need to overprotect anymore, but I do suggest you make the change slowly, or she won't be able to handle it."

It was very reassuring to be getting some concrete help for the whole child. I needed that advice, at that time. I had fallen into a pattern of overprotection with all of my children. A mother who stays home with her children most of the time, can sometimes fail to recognize the signals that they send her, indicating that they are ready to spread their wings a little. She is too close to the situation. I was grateful to have this pointed out to me.

God also intervened at this time in a unique fashion. He does have flair! He knew that after spending seven years at home, bringing up a family, this outgoing social child of His needed a change, so He sent me to work. That was the year that Industrial Engineers were laid off in droves. Bob was low man on the totem pole, since he had recently made a job change, so he found himself on a forced vacation. My response to this was to choose a practical course of action. The chiropractor had pronounced me healthy, a few months before, and he said, "You can do anything you want to now."

Wow! "Do you mean I can go back to nursing?" I asked.

"I don't know why not," he replied.

The day that Bob gave me the news that he was about to be laid off, I ran to the nearest hospital and applied for the job of nurse's aide, on the evening shift. The woman who interviewed me wanted me to go through a program, but I told her that I already knew enough from my background to handle the job.

She called me the next day, and told me to start the following week. I had to work on the day shift for two weeks of orientation, and I found out, during those two weeks, that there had been many changes in the twelve years I had been away. One of the biggest changes, that affected me, was that they were now giving aides much more responsibility than they had before.

Between my pay and Bob's unemployment, I knew we could make it financially, and he would not have to feel pressured to go to work at something for which he was ill suited. I later read that some psychologist said that a wife should not do what I did, as it would harm her husband's psyche. In our case, it turned out to be a very good situation for the whole family. I enjoyed going back to work in the hospital. It put a whole new energy into me and broadened my horizons. It also gave Bob an opportunity to really get to know the kids, and helped me to start to "let go" a bit. It was a positive growing experience for all of us. Bob learned how never-ending the job of running a home was, and I was given much more support from him in the future.

The hospital I worked in was fairly small, and I loved the atmosphere. Except for being "floated" on rare occasions, I worked on the same floor five evenings a week. This gave me the opportunity to know some of the patients very well. I allowed myself to become attached to some who were dying or suffering with long-term illnesses, even though some people cautioned me that that was not considered wise. I have never been afraid to go out on a limb, probably because I know God is there with me. I do believe that God is in everyone, and I always looked for this in my patients, especially the ones who were considered difficult.

I was able to use the hospital library, to look up the various diseases we were working on with Kelley. There was some information on the first possible diagnosis, and I studied it. With that disease, she should have been getting progressively worse, and it would have been fatal by the age of twenty. Since she was not getting worse, as far as I could see, I decided to adopt the attitude that she would live. The temptation to overindulge her, if she was going to die young, would have been great, and if she lived longer, she would have ended up being a spoiled brat. I reasoned that since no one wanted to associate with a spoiled brat, that was not a good idea. I decided to keep this information to myself, at that time, and continue to treat her as I did the other children.

When May came, Kelley was presented at a large conference of world-renowned physicians. Her doctor was hopeful that some other doctor would be able to shed more light on the condition. We felt fortunate to be able to tap into their knowledge and experience in this way. The thousands of dollars it would cost to travel throughout the world to see them all for consultation was way beyond our means.

We were pleased that Bob was able to go with us for that visit. The doctors had many questions for us, and the consensus from them was that we were on the right track. Some of her clinical work up didn't fall all the way into the pattern of MPS VI, but since no one had an alternative suggestion, the decision was made to follow the path on which we had started.

Although that summer was uneventful in the study of Kelley's disease, for our family it was a wonderful one. Bob was still looking for a job and doing many jobs around the house, and we went camping just about every other weekend. Because the hospital gave employees a day off, other than on the regular holiday, we managed a few three and four day weekends. It was a rainy summer. We started out in the rain, set up in the rain, ran around in the rain, laughed at the other fools that were camping in the rain, got ourselves and all our belongings wet, and dried out when we got home. It was fun!

Working in the hospital gave me a closer look at the medical profession, to which I once again belonged. The aides in that hospital wore white uniforms, just as the nurses did. The only way a patient could identify a nurse's position, was by the color of the stripe on the cap, or the initials on the pin. I soon discovered that my earlier observation of the general public, being in awe of the medical profession, was accurate. Patients and visitors alike tend to talk to doctors and nurses with a sort of reverence, and many of the doctors and nurses, with whom I worked, expected this kind of reaction. Occasionally, on the way to work, I would stop at a gas station or the post office, or run into a store to pick up something. The people in those places were friendlier and more helpful to me when I wore the white uniform than when I was simply in street clothes. I had stopped, on numerous occasions, at one particular store, that was run by a family who had always been pleasant to me, but now, they were really interested in me, a nurse! Wow! There was an obvious admiration for the uniform. It did feel nice to be given special attention. I suppose if my ego ever has a really down day, all I would have to do is to don that uniform and parade around town. People would be friendly and treat me with the kind of respect we really should accord each other, anyway. Nurses are people, just like the rest of the human race. They have definite needs, in most cases, I suspect, it is a need to be needed. I think the clerk at the grocery store has the same need.

I have always been a very interested observer of human behavior, believing there is nothing more exciting or challenging to study. A few structured courses and a good deal of independent reading added to my observations. I learned even more from watching the doctor-nurse, doctor-patient, patient-nurse, and patient-doctor relationships. As I watched, I was more able to understand the why and wherefore of my own handling of the situation with Kelley. This experience was invaluable to my growth and my ability to deal, more effectively, with Kelley's development, which, out of necessity, included the medical profession.

Many patients are intimidated, to one degree or another, by doctors, nurses, therapists and lab technicians. They do feel much more at ease; however, telling nurses what is on their mind and asking nurses questions, rather than bothering the busy doctors. When a doctor enters a patient's room and stands by the bed, chart in one arm, pen poised in the other hand, and one foot heading toward the door, the patient, understandably, feels ill at ease. They must state their symptoms quickly and wait, with bated breath, for this wise one's verdict of their prognosis, as though the doctor were master of their fate!

While working there, I enjoyed observing a doctor who was one of the best diagnosticians I've ever met, not because he had any more intelligence or experience than his colleagues, but because he really listened to his patients. He walked into the patient's room, pulled up a chair, and propped up his feet, looking, for all intent and purpose, as if he was going to spend the day — or night. I saw him do this as late as 10 PM. He would make some opening remark about how if he worked a little harder, he would get through sooner, and then he would ask, "How are you doing today?"

The patient would be relaxed, and would respond easily and thoroughly. He never gave the impression that he was someone superior. They (he and the patient) were simply two people trying to solve a problem. Funny thing was, he usually spent only five to ten minutes with each patient, and accomplished more in this time than the other doctors did with all their elaborate tests, attempting to find out what was wrong and what to do about it. This doctor was very relaxed because he knew and accepted his limitations as a human being.

We had one patient with a strange illness that had everyone stumped. Many doctors were in on this one. Test after test was done, as the patient drew closer and closer to death. It is strange when modern medicine can't figure out a solution! Most of the doctors involved in this one appeared to be very frustrated at their own inability (with all that knowledge and experience behind them) to diagnose and cure this man.

This doctor said, "He is going to die from this, and we will probably never know what it was that killed him." There was an acceptance in his sadness. He knew it was really in God's hands. We do what we can as humans, but ultimately, God is running the show. I often wished some of the other doctors could study and employ this man's techniques. I don't know if he came by them naturally, or if it was practiced. I do know it was most effective!

Then, there was the surgeon who should have been kept in surgery, and never been allowed to have a conversation with a patient. He was brilliant with a knife, but utterly incompetent with his tongue. I think we were all thankful that he had chosen surgery rather than psychiatry, as a profession. I helped dry the tears of quite a few patients, not to mention nurses, after he had left the room. The only patient I ever saw who had the nerve to put this man in his place, was a very mild mannered priest. It was beautiful! Word of that encounter traveled around the hospital very quickly.

Most of the people, with whom I worked, liked their work, and were truly interested in their patients. If it had not been that way, I would not have stayed there. There was an occasional doctor or nurse who probably would have felt more at home working as a librarian or a mechanic. Patients and colleagues alike wished that those people had gone into other fields.

It was not uncommon for a nurse to arrive early for work, in order to find out how a particular patient was doing; also most of the cafeteria conversation was shoptalk.

After spending so much time with medical people, I started to adopt some of their prevailing attitudes, to a certain degree. There is a certain superior feeling predominant among some professionals. When I realized that I was starting to think that way, I became grateful that I never did finish nurse's training.

My favorite part of the job was giving back rubs, and settling people for the night. I felt much better about doing that than I would have passing out medication. I had a great deal of empathy for my patients. In discussing the vulnerability of patients with another nurse one evening, I remarked, "After all, they are at our mercy."

She became a patient herself a few months later. The first thing she said, when I walked into her room, was, "I'm at your mercy!"

"Aren't you glad we are friends?" I joked.

I was surprised and somewhat upset by some of the prejudice I heard from some nurses — not against the poor foreigner who spoke broken

English, but against the wealthy woman, who had as much right to receive medical care as anyone else did. One particular woman was being admitted through the emergency room one evening. Presumably, she would be having private duty nurses, but for that evening, she was on her way to our floor, to be taken care of by us. The discussion that ensued, before she arrived on the floor, was one of total pre-judgment. I said something like, "You guys have a case of reverse snobbery! You've already decided what she's going to be like, and you haven't even met her yet! Well, I intend to treat her like any other patient. She may be 'Mrs. Somebody' to you, but she is a sick woman in need of care to me!"

I did not win any popularity contests, when I got outspoken like that, but I spoke my mind, anyway. As it turned out, she did not have private duty nurses, and she was a honey of a patient, with few demands and many gracious words of thanks. It seems to me that people who feel inferior often try to find fault with those they imagine feel superior. I dare say, I do believe some of those nurses missed the chance of getting to know that woman because they did not allow themselves to accept her for herself.

I saw many good works done in that hospital. I also saw some covered-up mistakes. Nurses and doctors are very human.

We sometimes had a patient who needed a particular type of lab work done, in which the urine was to be collected for twenty-four hours. It was difficult to remember not to discard the urine when emptying the bedpan. One night I forgot. As soon as I emptied the pan, I realized what I did. I knew this woman was waiting for this one last test to be completed before she was discharged, and I was under the impression that it was most important to have every drop she voided for the test. I felt terrible about making such a mistake, and I really told myself off! Then, I told the nurse, who was my supervisor, what I had done.

"Well, if you don't tell anyone, they will never know," she said.

"But I can't do that!" I said, looking at her in disbelief.

"Why not?" she asked.

We were too busy that night for me to give her a complete synopsis of my moral standards, so I walked away from her. Then, when the patient's doctor showed up, I approached him, before he went into her room, and told him what had happened.

The doctor, who was frequently on our floor, and knew me fairly well by then, put his arm around my shoulder and said, "Don't worry about it. With this particular test, I'll get all the answers I need, and she'll be able to go home tomorrow."

Whew! The nurse in question still thought I was a real dope to tell him that, but a very funny thing happened that I never mentioned to her. That doctor seemed to have a lot more confidence in me, and a greater respect for my opinions and judgment, after that incident.

While on that job, I learned by listening, reading charts, observing, and asking questions. Most of the professionals, with whom I worked, were happy to answer my questions, and my understanding of the workings of the human body became clearer.

The working of the human mind intrigued me even more, and it appeared to me that the old saying, "A healthy mind is a healthy body" must have originated with someone who also noticed the same things that I did. I was not alone in my observations. Others talked about it, too. I became more convinced than ever that attitude was a very important factor in recovery. We seemed to have some patients who came back on a regular basis (we called them our summer reruns), with one ailment or another, when their life became too difficult.

Very often, although certainly not always, a physical ailment can be caused by an inner conflict. Some of the doctors wouldn't listen to that idea at all. However, the doctor who had understood me, when I had made a mistake, was also the one most likely to listen, when I told him something that I had learned about a patient's emotional life.

The opportunity I had to look at the medical field, from this angle, proved to be most beneficial, as I helped Kelley travel along on her journey.

# CHAPTER SIX

In August 1970, a report was sent to the school with the results of Kelley's neuropsychological testing, and suggestions for special help when she entered the second grade.

That September, all three children went to school. Kelley was in the second grade, and Susan in the first, so we sent David to a private Kindergarten. He had always had a playmate at home, and now, with both sisters in school, he needed a little more outside companionship. He did have a pal in the neighborhood who was a little younger, but a good playmate at times, nevertheless. How David wished for a brother! There were times when I thought about adopting a boy David's age. The closest he had to a brother was his cousin, Michael, who unfortunately lived about two hundred miles away. My sister Hilary and I had them visit each other as often as we could, but David still found it necessary to invent an imaginary friend. Steven was with us for quite awhile. When we were camping on one mountain, he was camping on the next. David told us of many of Steven's adventures, and we were impressed with our son's imagination. Steven was a good guy. He never caused any trouble, and we were glad he kept David company some of the time. School was good for David, and he loved it. He was able to play with real boys there.

When they were all very small, and I complained about them being early risers, my mother said, "Wait until they start school, then they will want to sleep late."

She was right! However, we were lucky to be located on a dead-end road. The bus passed the house and went down to the end to turn around before picking up the girls. We always had a two-minute warning. It did take me some time to get that morning routine down to a science. I needed to do PT before school, or we never would have fit it in twice in a day. I set the breakfast table before I went to bed, and I found a system for their clothes. On the weekends, I prepared for the coming week by attaching, with clothespins, the socks and undies to each of five dresses for each girl. That way, they had their choice to some extent, and we did not have to go on a last minute hunt for matching clothes. In 1970, little girls still wore dresses, and it was important that the socks match! I really enjoyed making some cute dresses for them.

Susan was the next to get glasses. They had blue rims to match her beautiful blue eyes, and they corrected her nearsighted problem.

When we visited Kelley's doctors that September, they said they had come to the conclusion that her problem was genetic, and that both Bob and

47

I were carriers of a rare gene. It was explained that statistically, one of four of our children would have the problem, but these things didn't always follow the statistical probabilities. I did not want to imagine what it would have been like to have two or three of them in traction at the same time!

Bob was still looking for a job during this time, and I kept saying, "God will take care of us."

By Thanksgiving time, I could not keep our little secret a secret any longer. I had experienced two miscarriages in the years since David was born, so I didn't want to get the whole family excited about a new baby until I was past the first few months. Besides, my sister Mary Lou was expecting her first child, and I did not want to steal any of her thunder. Our new addition was due to arrive in May.

Pantsuits for nurses were just catching on at that time, and I had the unusual distinction of being the first to wear a maternity pantsuit uniform in that hospital. I also ran into a good deal of prejudice. Attitudes really had changed in a short time. I always believed a new life was a reason to rejoice! It surprised me when friends asked how I dared to become pregnant, when my husband was out of work. We certainly did not expect him to be out of work forever!

A patient had the nerve to tell me that I had no right to bring another child into the world. I informed him that it was God's world, and God's child, and there was no doubt in my mind that God knew how to plan things better than he or I did.

Some of Kelley's specialists appeared to be shocked when they saw me in maternity clothes. The age had dawned when women were being tested in the early months of pregnancy to decide to get rid of the fetus if it was not going to be perfect. Our love for our children had nothing to do with any particular physical attributes, or lack of such. I figured if we had another child with the same problem, I would want to move closer to the big city, so we would not have to spend so much time traveling.

It was disappointing to learn that our family doctor was not taking any more obstetrical cases. I decided to see an obstetrician who was respected at the hospital in which I worked. When I was in the seventh month of my pregnancy, he told me that I should think about this being my last baby. This took me by surprise, and I spent the next month wondering what was wrong with me physically. I worked up my courage to ask him at my next visit, and he got on his soapbox, and preached to me for the next half hour about the population explosion. This was a man who had been educated in Catholic schools, and was sending his children to Catholic schools! As I listened, I thought about the women who were sitting in his waiting room, waiting for some time and wisdom from this self-appointed god. When he finished, all I could say was, "Oh, ye of little faith!"

God came through. I knew he would. He sent Bob back to work in December. That meant I had less help at home. Taking care of three children at home, and working while I was pregnant, caught up with me quickly. I was sick through the Christmas holidays with a strep throat. I did manage to stay at work through January. However, the weight of the baby and eight hours on my feet at work, plus keeping house, caused very painful varicose veins, despite my special stockings for support. When February arrived, the doctor recommended I start my leave of absence.

I had put off many things that needed to be done at home, as well as things like doctor and dentist appointments for the kids, until my leave. While making the appointments for February and March, I one day called the catalogue store, so I could order some household items, and I asked for an appointment. The voice on the other end told me that I didn't need to make an appointment to place an order. I was more tired than I had realized!

Bob was glad to get back to work. I was glad to have a break from it, under the circumstances, but I was also grateful that I had been able work to help keep us above water financially. Bob was also much more understanding of the demands of my job at home once he had done it, and supplied more empathy and help in the future.

Being already crowded into a small house, we would need some more room with another member added to the family. We made plans to add a room to the house. It was something we had wanted, and now decided the time had come. It was really a fun project.

Kelley was doing well going to school full time. She seemed to have some more stamina since she stopped taking the aspirin. She was still on medication for hyperactivity. I questioned the doctors as to whether others with her disorder were also hyperactive. They said there were no reports to indicate so. Her teacher that year was a very sweet and patient woman, who was very sympathetic toward Kelley. When I went in for a conference during the winter, I discovered that Kelley had charmed this woman into putting on her snowsuit for her, so she would be ready for the bus on time. I carefully explained to this sweet lady that sympathy was not at all what Kelley needed. I said, "She can put on her snowsuit by herself if you give her enough time. She does it every morning. At times she has whined, and I have told her that it was a long walk to school if she wasn't ready when the bus arrived. Just tell her that you know that she can do it, and give her a head start."

I told her that we expected Kelley to do at school as she did at home. It was then that I decided that in the future I had better talk to her teachers at the beginning of the school year, in hopes of avoiding that problem again.

Kelley's charm also included always knowing when to be extra good. Whenever her parents were displeased with any child's behavior, she tried very hard to please us. She never liked to see either of us upset.

From the time I left work, until the new baby arrived in May, there was much excitement and expectation in our home. We had a wonderful time discussing names for the baby, and the ones we finally chose were pleasing to the whole family. The new room we were adding was a master bedroom for Bob and me. We chose a wonderful large window overlooking the water. It was supposed to be done by the time the baby arrived at the end of May.

On the morning of May 18, I knew the time had come. My babies all came ahead of schedule. I told Bob to go to work, as I would have my mother take me to the hospital. Husbands were not yet allowed in the labor or delivery room. I called Mom early, and told her not to go anywhere.

My dad took David to his school, and I got the girls on the bus. Then Nana arrived. It was around 9 AM, and I was ready to go.

The men were working on the addition. They did not see us put the suitcase in the car. They did notice, however, that Nana had difficulty in getting the car started. One of the young men came to our aid, and promptly started the car.

"Thanks," I said to him, "now I can go to the hospital to have my baby."

"You mean?" he asked, looking shocked.

I laughed and pointed to my suitcase in the back. He wiped his brow!

Just after lunch, Mom reported to them that our little girl had arrived. It was okay with me that the room was not finished. It was more important to me at that point that Kelley was going to make her First Communion on the 23rd, and I wanted very much to be there.

There has been nothing more important for me to do for my children than to help them to have a personal relationship with Jesus. Such a relationship sustains you through anything you have to face in life. When you choose to walk with the Lord, He gives you the grace you need to accept His will. I knew that I would not always be able to be there for my children. I hoped they would all learn to rely on God.

In those days doctors were of the mind set that mothers needed five days in the hospital following a normal delivery. I had other ideas. As soon as I saw my doctor after the delivery, I started begging to go home. By the third day, he relented, although he said he was afraid I wouldn't get enough rest at home. I knew I would be much better off in my own home, where the baby could sleep and nurse on her own schedule.

Nana and Grandpa picked David up at school, at noon, on that Friday, and they all came to the hospital. Getting into the back seat of the car with David, I put Peggy in his arms. Even though he had wanted a brother, this precious bundle won him over instantly!

By now, David was a tall as Kelley, and ready to pass her in height. Kelley's first remark when she saw Peggy was, "Well, it will take awhile for HER to pass me by!"

When I went to church on the 23rd, my mother, who thought I was overdoing it, remarked, "They wouldn't even let us out of bed for ten days when you were born!"

Since I had felt run down during the pregnancy, by contrast, I now felt wonderful. The time of year helped, also.

Peggy learned very early to sleep through noise, and she was a very easy baby to care for. Part of that was probably my perspective. Experience was a wonderful advantage. I had been pretty relaxed with the others, but this one, I truly enjoyed. Sharing it with the three older children magnified the joy.

At the suggestion of the big city doctors, I took Peggy to them for a checkup when she was six weeks old. They decided that she did not have the same disorder as Kelley, so I guess it then became okay that I did not abort her. I have never understood how members of the medical profession can go along with the idea of abortion. They spend years learning to help people sustain life. Denying that a fetus is life becomes a contradiction when you see it as something that you need to get rid of so it won't be born alive.

On my leave of absence from work, I was content at home, and reluctant to return, but I had received an employee discount on the hospital bill, so I believed I owed it to them. I spoke to the evening supervisor to ask if I could work just part-time. She said if that were the case, I would not be permanently assigned to a floor, but would have to work as a "float." We were still paying for that new bedroom, so I determined to make the best of it. The second evening I was back, they floated me to pediatrics. My idea of a break in the routine of caring for four kids did not include working on pediatrics! The nurses there didn't like me picking up the crying babies. They said I would spoil them. I didn't like being there, because I kept identifying all those kids with the ones I had at home. I went home that night with a heavy heart.

Two nights later, someone came to the floor I was on and told me to go to pediatrics. Seeking out the supervisor instead, I told her I was ineffective on pediatrics, and there must be someone else in the hospital better suited to the job. I said that if she insisted in sending me there, I would quit on the spot. She did not like it. I did not expect that she would. She did understand, however. I never was floated to pediatrics again.

I discovered that floating was not difficult if I got to the floor in time for report and took plenty of notes. It's helpful to know a patient's diagnosis when you walk into their room. I also learned to look in the most likely places for supplies. Once I had made the rounds to the various floors in the hospital, I was comfortable going back, and actually liked being a float. It was probably also very good for me at the time. I didn't have the opportunity to become attached to any of the patients, and with such a busy home life, that was good.

When our room was completed, we moved into it, and redecorated our old bedroom for David. He was thrilled to have his own room! Susan enjoyed having Peggy in with the girls, because playing mother was one of her favorite pastimes.

My sister Mary Lou's baby girl was three months old when Peggy was born. We were both pleased that our little girls would be able to grow up together. Mary Lou and her husband Bob were happy parents. Happy and relieved! Mary Lou had undergone major emergency surgery at the beginning of the pregnancy. She didn't even know that she was pregnant at the time, or for many more months, either. When Jean Marie was born, they told her pediatrician of their concerns. He said the baby was fine. We all breathed sighs of relief.

That baby had as many photos taken of her as a princess would. She was their little princess. She was healthy too, until the time she got a cold that she couldn't fight.

A rush trip to the local hospital when her breathing became difficult was followed by an immediate transfer to the big city. Jean Marie was in a serious condition. In time Mary Lou and Bob learned that the optimism of the original pediatrician was erroneous. Jean Marie had severe lung and heart defects. The experts in the city said they could try to make surgical repairs at the age of two, if she lived that long. They advised that surgery before that age would most likely cause brain damage. In the interim, the concerned parents were instructed to keep Jean Marie away from other children, so she could avoid germs. Crying was not good for her, so they had to try to limit that. If she did cry, she needed to be held upright.

After they took her home from the hospital, with instruction for her care, I spoke to Mary Lou on the phone one morning, and thought she sounded exhausted. I left my baby with her grandparents, and went to Mary Lou's house, which was about an hour away. She was walking around with the crying baby, patting her on the back, and trying to comfort her, when I arrived. I took the baby, so Mary Lou could have some breakfast. After Jean Marie quieted down, we discussed the situation. Mary Lou had been given instructions to do a type of therapy with Jean Marie to keep her only lung clear. It was the same kind that was being used for babies with Cystic Fibrosis. The baby was placed across her lap, chest down, so her mother could gently hit her on the back of the chest, to help breakup and release any fluid.

I looked around and thought about all the things that needed to be done for a baby in general, and all the extras that needed to be done for Jean Marie. I wondered where Mary Lou would find the energy. There was no one nearby to help her. When she went to take a shower, I called our mother. Next, I started taking the crib apart, to load in the back of my station wagon.

When Mary Lou emerged, dressed for the day, I told her to pack her clothes, because I had almost everything else packed.

"What do you mean?" she asked.

"You live too far away for us to be of much help. You and the baby are going to stay with Mom and Dad for awhile."

She was so tired, both physically and emotionally, she could only say, "Oh."

Her husband thought the arrangement was a good idea, and in a short time, he put their house up for sale, and found one to buy much closer to ours.

Once they were settled in their new home, we could all take turns helping her. Jean Marie was beautiful, and as she grew, it became apparent she was as bright as she could be. I found it a joy to have a turn to take care of her now and then — when someone else was taking care of my children. Unfortunately, they could only see her through a glass door.

Jean Marie had numerous tests and hospitalizations. The last was in the summer of her second year. She contracted an infection that her body was unable to fight. My sister called me from the city to say that it looked as if the end was near. She said they had taken a room at the nearby Inn so they could take turns sleeping and sitting by the baby.

I had Bob take me to the city to be with them. That darling little baby looked so small on the large bed in the intensive care unit, with lines and tubes connecting her to machines and medicines. It was a heartbreaking sight.

Mary Lou and Bob were as prepared as anyone could be for the inevitable. Bob stayed with the baby so his wife and I could go to the Inn for her to get refreshed.

As we sat in the room at the Inn, she said, "I don't know how I'm going to be when the end comes, so I want you to be sure that they have me sign the papers for an autopsy. I want them to learn anything they can to help another child."

I assured her I would. It was good I could be there. We had been raised to understand the value of sharing. Usually that meant to share our possessions and good times. When facing a difficult situation, who better to share it with than someone who had already been there through many of life's experiences? I could only imagine what a trauma this was for Mary Lou. Her only child was near death. Everything humans could do was being done. We sat on the bed talking until the phone rang.

I answered.

"Better get over here," my brother in-law said.

We were there in a matter of minutes, to be met at the elevator by Bob and the doctors.

Mary Lou and Bob held each other. One of the doctors said, "I'm sorry."

The grieving couple then went on to console the doctors, saying that they knew they had done everything they could, and that they knew their baby had gone home to God. The doctors seemed so young, and so disappointed. They wanted to save Jean Marie's life. They failed. Mary Lou and Bob understood.

They signed the autopsy papers. Then Mary Lou asked me to go with her to a closet where some of Jean Marie's things had been stored. Her favorite stuffed animal was a "Tony the Tiger" with a music box enclosed. Mary Lou took that. She gave some of the audiotapes and books to a nurse, in case another child would like them.

We went back to the Inn and packed. It was about 2 AM when we were at the checkout desk, and the clerk asked if we were leaving because something was wrong.

"Yes," Bob answered, "our daughter just died."

I could not believe the man had asked! Why else would we be checking out at that time? This Inn was attached to the hospital. People stay there when their children are in the hospital. I don't know how Bob managed to answer that stupid question so soon after it had happened. They did know for a long time that it was a possibility, but there was always hope. She had been a bright and beautiful baby, who required so much care, that all of their time had been devoted to her for over a year. There was some relief that she was no longer suffering, but the loss was terrible.

We got into Bob's car to drive home in the wee hours of the morning. In his typical fashion of finding something quirky to say, no matter what, Bob quipped, "Gee, I wonder if the funeral parlor will take Master Card."

I had a long list of mutual friends to call with the news. Some of them knew immediately when they heard my voice early on a Sunday morning. It took me hours to get all the calls made. Every time one of them cried, I cried with them.

Tony the Tiger was buried with Jean Marie.

One of the saddest experiences I have ever had took place the day, sometime after Jean Marie's death, that Mary Lou called me to say she was ready. I left Peggy with my folks, and went to my sister's house. Together, we took apart the crib and folded up the baby blankets. We took down the Raggedy Ann curtains and packed away all the things that Jean Marie had used. She no longer needed them.

Months later, Mary Lou suddenly burst into tears one day when she was helping me with some painting at my house. We later realized that the fact that women sometimes tend to get weepy with they are pregnant, played a part in her crying. Their son, Jimmy was born the following September.

The rest of that summer raced by, and the children went back to school. Now, all three older children had to be ready for the same bus each morning, so I had to have a system. Many mornings, Peggy was in one arm while I served breakfast with the other.

Kelley needed to repeat the second grade, as there was some question about her ability to handle the third grade. Because Susan was now in the second grade, she had the sweet grandmotherly teacher Kelley had the previous year, and Kelley had one with a completely opposite personality. She was young, inexperienced and high strung. She frequently yelled at the children, and Kelley found this very upsetting. I think all she really learned during that year, was that staying out sick was preferable to being in that room!

In October, she started experiencing severe abdominal cramps, for which she was put through a complete GI series. Convincing her to drink the chalky stuff was, indeed, a challenge. There was nothing conclusive from that testing, and the decision was made that perhaps the medication for hyperactivity was causing the problems, so we slowly discontinued that little pill.

She also developed a cough that kept her home from school frequently. It was a very hoarse sounding cough, surprisingly loud from such a small child. We became accustomed to it, but it appeared to alarm anyone else who heard it. The people at school seemed to be just as glad to have her stay home. We did not worry about her absences, since she was repeating the grade, anyway.

An unexpected development that year was that Kelley had a noticeable improvement with mobility. No one in the medical profession knew why. I mentioned Kelley's visits with the chiropractor to the doctors in the city, but they refused to believe that could have been the reason. I believed differently, and kept taking her regularly to the chiropractor.

David, now in the first grade, was also wearing glasses. It seemed strange to us that all three needed glasses (for three different reasons), although, at that time, neither Bob nor I did.

David did not particularly like his teacher. She was rather gruff. The fact that he was able to make new friends at school made up for it, though. It was the first year that he knew enough boys his age to have a real all-boy birthday party. David was a natural student, and he did well in school.

Susan also made new friends, and she and Kelley were able to each cultivate their own friends, independent of each other, which I thought was healthy.

By the time that school year had passed, there was nothing new about Kelley's problem, but the school had decided she could use some extra help, so that was arranged for the following year.

We went camping again during the summer after Peggy's first birthday. She thoroughly enjoyed having us all in the tent, and kept us all awake at night, and up early in the morning. We all decided to join her at naptime.

# CHAPTER SEVEN

By September 1972, the three older children had advanced a grade, and Peggy had become adept at keeping me on my toes. The older ones presented new challenges.

They came bounding in from the school bus one day saying, "Tell us some swear words."

We were at the kitchen table, where we had many interesting chats, while they had their usual afternoon snack. This one started off in a pretty lively way.

"What?" I squeaked.

"Tell us some swear words," one of them repeated.

"We heard some words on the bus, and we want to know if they are swears."

Now, I did not intend to spout off all the swear words I had ever heard, especially for my children.

"Tell, you what," I said, "Here's a good way to know. If it is something you don't hear in this house, it is probably not a good one to use."

"You won't tell us any swear words?" one of them asked.

"No, kids. You know I don't use those words. There are plenty of good words in the English language that we can use to express ourselves. People who use swear words are just showing how little they know. Really clever people build up a vocabulary. That way they don't have to use swears," I explained.

They were disappointed.

Kelley's hyperactivity had calmed down somewhat (or we were used to it by then), and she was more cooperative with PT (or she had resigned herself to it), by this time. She was able to do a lot more for herself, even though the joints in her hands were still very tight.

That fall we received the shocking news that the company, for which Bob worked, was going to close the plant where he was employed. The area in which we lived offered little opportunity for an industrial engineer, so when they offered him a transfer, he accepted.

When he started in the new location, he traveled. It was a ninety-minute drive each way, when road conditions were good. The children were only able to see him on weekends, as he was gone in the morning before they were up, and very often home after their bedtime. I loved where we lived, but I had to be realistic about how that arrangement was affecting family life. Reluctantly, we made the decision to sell the house and find one closer to where he was working.

House hunting, from that distance, was not the easiest chore. Sometimes Peggy and I went with Bob to work, early in the morning, kept the car for the day, to make the rounds, and picked Bob up at the end of the day. They were long days, but Peggy loved to travel, and I suspect, she liked having her mom to herself. My folks took care of the others, when they returned from school. On occasion, Bob and I did some house hunting on a weekend. It all worked out somehow. I was reluctant to give up my job, but commuting that distance, for the kind of pay I made, was unthinkable.

We found a house that we liked well enough, though it was not right on the water. It was across the street from a lake, where we did have access to a beach. Shortly before Peggy's birthday, we moved. That was fun.

Because it was a company transfer, they paid for the movers. It was a treat to have the movers pack for us! The first thing they did, when they arrived, was to locate the stereo and start the music. It was the last thing they packed.

Shortly before I left, I received a call from the lawyer who had handled the transaction on the house we bought. He told me that the people, from whom we had bought the house, had not moved out yet. Furthermore, he had anticipated trouble, and therefore, had not released the full payment to them yet. He told me to expect them to give me a sob story about having a sick kid, and no place to go. He said not to fall for it, because he knew better. He advised me to go there in the morning and ask to use their phone. Once inside, I should call him and let him know that I was in possession. Then, he would release the remainder of the money to them. I thanked him for the call, and checked to see that the movers were just about finished.

After packing four kids, two cats, a large dog, and our suitcases into the station wagon, we said our good-byes to my folks and the neighbors. We set out for the motel near Bob's work, where we would meet him, and spend the night. Before checking into the motel, we left the animals at a nearby kennel.

In the morning, Bob left for work, and I took the children for breakfast in the motel dining room. My plans were to meet the movers at the house, and have Bob meet us there, after work. I had not thought to tell him about the call from the lawyer, since I knew what I needed to do.

While we were eating breakfast, I was surprised to see Bob walk in, looking for us. He said that he had received a strange call at work from the moving company. The woman who sold us the house called our old house, just after I left the day before, and the movers answered the phone. She told them not to deliver the furniture the next day, because she would not let them enter the house. They, in turn, called Bob at work in the morning to ask when they should deliver.

I never imagined that she would have called the movers, and that they would have listened to her. We were the ones who had hired them! When I explained to Bob about the call from the lawyer the night before, he decided to take the day off from work, and go with me to the new house. He felt he should be with me if they gave me any trouble. I was glad we had boarded the animals for two nights.

When we arrived at the new house, the woman said she would not let me in until she was paid, and that her husband was at the lawyers waiting to get the money. I informed her that the lawyer would not release the money until I called him, so it would be a good idea for her to let me use her phone.

I was in! I called the lawyer and he said, "It's your house, so don't leave. Tell them they have to. You now have possession, and I will release the rest of the money."

Next, I called the movers. They said that the crew was off on another assignment, and they didn't know when they could deliver. I told them to find someone to deliver, because they never should have taken direction from anyone else regarding the delivery. They agreed to have the truck there by 1 PM.

"This is my house now," I said to the former owner, "and my family and I are going to sleep here tonight. I suggest you get your things out of here before the movers come with our things."

As my family was entering the house, she was complaining about one of her kids being sick. As if on cue, our Susan got sick, and ran to the bathroom to vomit.

They did not have all of their belongings out before the movers arrived, because they were using pickup trucks, so our movers helped them to remove some of the large items. I shivered to imagine how that day would have gone if the lawyer had not thought to protect us!

Once we were settled, we started sprucing up, inside and outside. The neighbors stopped by to welcome us when they saw us removing the junk from the yard. We also replaced broken windows and painted the trim, which was a mess. There were plenty of kids in the neighborhood, including a two-year-old next door, called Peggy. "The Peggys" became fast friends!

Right after we moved, there was another conference to attend in the city. This one was put on by the March of Dimes for the National Birth Defects Foundation, and was much larger than the one we had attended previously.

Bob was not able to join us this time, and I no longer had Dad next door to take Kelley and me, or Mom to baby-sit for the older children. I had to find a baby-sitter quickly, and find my way into the city from a different direction. We were still an hour away from the city, but from the North rather than the South.

The presentation was very interesting. Kelley and I sat up on a stage, in front of the audience. Her x-rays were shown on a large screen. One of the doctors pointed out a variety of abnormalities with her bones and joints, and ran off a list of results of various lab reports from blood samples. All of the other children presented that day were babies, but Kelley was almost ten years old, and the doctors had many questions for us. One of our doctors took Kelley into the audience for the others to see her up close. We were later approached by a doctor who said he had seen hands like hers before, and he would be able to suggest some more tests. I had not expected anyone to come up with an instant cure that day, but I had hoped for a little more than a recommendation of more tests. Nevertheless, I knew we had been exposed to some of the world's most informed physicians, so there was nothing more that could be done than we were doing.

As soon as we moved in at our new location, I enrolled the older children in their new school, and set out to find a new family doctor. I was pleased, the next month, that I had done so. Kelley had contracted a cold that suddenly turned into bronchitis. She spiked a high temperature. I called the doctor, and he said I should meet him at the local hospital with her. I needed to get directions from a neighbor. Kelley was so sick, that I had to carry her in to the building. Every time I have had to carry her, I have been thankful that she is small!

The care she got in that hospital was terrific! She was in a "tent" for five days, right next to the nurse's station, and they took care of her as though she was their own child. They loved the girl! She had no energy, so she went along with anything they said. I learned a lot during that time to help her ward off such an attack again. Two days after she returned home, she suddenly had a crying spell that had me perplexed, as she was a child who did not cry easily. It turned out that she missed the nurses! I let her call them that day, and I took her in to visit them a few days later. I did not want her to think that she needed to get sick to see them again.

The children spent a very short time in their new school, and then they were on their summer vacation.

Our house was just about equidistant from two different Catholic churches. For a while we alternated week to week. After a discussion with the children as to which one we liked best, we stopped in the sacristy after Mass to tell the priest we wanted to sign up as members. He asked where we lived, and when I told him, he said that we really were supposed to belong to the other church.

I said to him, "But Father, the children pay more attention here, and besides," I added, knowing it would make a difference, "I'm a CCD teacher."

He burst into laughter, and signed us up right away. We were very comfortable in that parish. That priest had a wonderful way of running teacher's meetings. He always had an agenda, and he had a knack of keeping us all on the topic at hand. He finished the meeting on time. He had the best attendance I've ever seen at that type of meeting. Most of us felt they were very worthwhile.

It was while we were living in that house that Peggy adopted some imaginary squirrels. There were two of them. She had fun with them, and we all thought it to be very cute when she set up places for them to join us at the table for dinner. Everyone accepted the little creatures until she started to blame them for everything that went wrong.

"Does anyone know how the powder got spilled in the bathroom?"

"Squirrels did it," Peggy told us.

"Has anyone seen the scotch tape?"

"The squirrels must have it," we heard.

"Who tracked all that mud into the house?" silly question!

"The squirrels," Peggy obliged us, with answers for everything. Those little creatures became a problem. I didn't want to squelch the child's imagination, but I couldn't let her get away with blaming them for everything. The next time she used the excuse, I was ready.

"Gee, Peggy," I started, "I'm afraid those squirrels of yours are causing a lot of trouble around here."

She scowled, as if to indicate that she knew that they had been naughty.

"Since they are your animals," I continued, "I think from now on, you are going to have to take responsibility for anything they do wrong."

Her scowl turned into a startled expression of fear. She was about to lose her best excuse yet!

Many months later, I casually said to her, "I haven't heard anything about those squirrels of yours for a long time. What happened to them?"

"They couldn't behave themselves," she responded just as casually, "so I sent them away. They live in New York now."

Our next visits to the big city were made complicated by the fact that our second car quit on us shortly after we moved. I had to add dropping Bob at work in the morning and picking him up after work to my running around. The doctors decided that summer that Kelley should use the night splints for her arms again, and braces for her hands in the day.

In the fall of that year, Kelley was scheduled for another day of neuropsychological testing in the city. It meant I had hours to wait for her. Happily, I met another mother in the waiting room in the same situation. The two of us had a great time, sharing a walking tour of the city. It was a lovely day, and I felt like a tourist on vacation. Probably it was all the more fun, because it was unexpected! When we received the results of the testing, they assisted us in giving the school personnel a better idea of what they could realistically expect from Kelley.

Also in the fall of that year, my Dad, who had been quite healthy most of his life, was admitted to the hospital. By Christmas, it was obvious that he was suffering from congestive heart failure, and we were probably going to be celebrating Christmas with him for the last time. It really happened rather quickly. At the age of seventy-five, he was still ice-skating—indeed, teaching others to skate, and before his seventy-fifth year was over, he was gone. We were fortunate, however, that we all had enough time to prepare, and to say good-by.

It has turned out, though, that in many ways, he is not gone. He was such a wonderful man, who shared so much of himself with us that his spirit has stayed with us all. A short time after his death, I was involved in a minor traffic accident. I was rather annoyed at the man who hit my little car with his big one. His did not have a scratch. Eight-year-old David helped me put it all in perspective when he asked, "What would Grandpa do?"

Of course, Grandpa would have laughed, and said, "As long as no one got hurt, it's okay."

People always said that you knew when Fred Kelley was around, because you could hear him laughing. Could there be a better legacy?

Kelley was in the fourth grade, and blessed with a wonderful teacher! We did have the neuropsychological report sent to the school, but by that time, this teacher had already figured out the best way to get Kelley to perform at her best. She was the one who told me that Kelley could do as much as the other students if she just gave her a little at a time. Otherwise, Kelley felt overwhelmed and thought she couldn't do the work, so she wouldn't even try. It really made sense to me, because that was the way Kelley often ate. If I gave her a plate full of food, she barely touched it, but if I gave her just a little, she would eat it, and often ask for more. It was such a good school year for Kelley, and I was so grateful, that when I learned the teacher was pregnant, I organized a shower for her at my house. Most of the mothers of other students in her class were happy to attend.

After all the new testing had been accomplished, we were told that Mucopolysaccharidosis had been ruled out, and that Kelley's condition was called Pseudo-Hurler Polydystrophy, also termed Mucolipidosis III (ML III). What this meant was that she probably would not die before the age of twenty, but there was really not enough information on the condition for them to give us any kind of prognosis. All we could do would be to treat whatever problems she had as they appeared. She had some periods of very painful swollen joints, and other times when they did not bother her at all.

When she was pain free, she did just about everything the other kids did, plus physical therapy. Occasionally, when we were in the city, they also had her see an occupational therapist.

The one she saw in September 1974 seemed to think it was most important to have Kelley use her hands in the conventional way. I watched silently for a while, as she and Kelley were both getting very frustrated, because Kelley could not pick up a piece of paper between her thumb and forefinger. When I could stay silent no longer, I intervened saying, "Kelley, show me how you would move that paper to the other table."

She promptly picked the paper up between her first two fingers and moved it to the other table.

"If the object is to move the paper from point A to point B," I said, addressing the therapist, "who cares what method one uses to get it there? Trying to make her do it the way you and I would, only frustrates her. Accept her the way she is, and let her do it her own way!" I think I came on a little strong.

The therapist simply said, "Okay."

I hoped I was also giving a message to Kelley that, just because I do something one way, it does not mean it is the only way or the right way it should be done. Kelley had, after all, reached a point of independence where the only thing she could not do for herself was to tie her shoes, and that was because she could not reach her feet! Her arms were short, and her elbows had a permanent bend. Somehow, she had taught herself to tie a bow by observing others. She does not do it the way most of us do. As a matter of fact, I am not sure just how she does it, but she does it! I don't know why it should matter to anyone how she does it.

I felt a need to earn some money to buy another second car, but I did not want to be away from my children. It was okay when I worked in the hospital on the evening shift, and my folks could watch the children for the short time between my leaving for work, and Bob getting home. However, I did not want to have to leave them with baby-sitters all the time. I also liked the idea of being home with Peggy all day, and of being there when the kids got in from school in the afternoon.

The solution was to provide day-care in my own home. I cared for a family of three little girls, whose mother dropped them off each morning, and picked them up in the evening. One was in kindergarten, and the others were preschool age. I also had another, older child after school, until her mother was home from work. Bob was in a car-pool at that time, so I had the use of a car a few days a week, which was very beneficial. I tried to make the appointments with Kelley's doctors during school vacations, so she would not have to take any more time out of school than necessary.

Since I had a very large family to take along on visits to the city, I turned the occasions into field trips. We took picnics and stopped to have lunch in a park, or we went window-shopping in the city, or visited various attractions.

Sometimes I had an extra child or two for a short time. One day, when I was expecting a father of four to drop off his baby, we had a snowstorm. School was canceled. This father had recently been left alone with the four kids, and it occurred to me that he might not have anywhere to leave the other three. I called him early to tell him that he could leave them with me for the day. He was glad to hear from me, because he was not even aware that there was no school. So, that day, I had my four, his four, my usual three, and my usual after schoolgirl. With a dozen children, I spent most of the day either feeding them or taking boots on and off, and drying mittens and hats in the dryer. I lasted about a year at that job, before I decided to find another way. I started to feel that, even though I was there for my children, I was spending so much time caring for the others; I really wasn't as "there" as I wanted to be. I did, however, have enough saved for a down payment on another car.

My next solution was to work three nights in a nursing home, as an aide.

Two of Peggy's playmates were attending nursery school mornings, so I decided to send her, and we car-pooled for that. That allowed me a few hours of catch-up sleep. I also took a nap before work on the nights that I worked.

The job was not easy. Contrary to what people think of the night shift, this was not the kind of job where one could catch up on sleep while at work. We were busy just about all the time. I liked the people I worked with, and I did like picking up the paycheck, but I did not like constantly being pressured by them to work extra nights. I especially did not like them calling me at midnight on the nights I was sleeping to ask me to go in because someone had called in sick. I fell for the "emergency" line a few times. When it became too frequent, I decided they had a problem that could have been handled by adding some staff, and I learned to say no to all the extra requests. The job did help me to make car payments. Thus, I was able to take Kelley to the city when necessary, and to be there for various school activities the children wanted to attend.

# CHAPTER EIGHT

It was spring 1975, when I discussed, with Kelley's doctors, the difficulty I was having in getting PT done with Kelley. We both disliked doing it, and I found it difficult to be the one to push her all the time. She was never disrespectful. However, she would attempt to be funny, or be silly and try to distract me, to get me to skip part of the routine, saying things like, "Oh, yeah, we did that one already, don't you remember?"

She was very cute about it, which in some ways made it more annoying. As her mother, I was the one who most often had to discipline her in all other matters. When I requested suggestions from the doctors, they asked if I would be able to take her to a local hospital for PT. Now that I had a car again, that was possible, so they wrote up an order for her to have it done by a therapist three times a week. What a relief that was! Three times a week, I picked her up after school, took her to the PT room at the local hospital, and left her with them. Sometimes she gave them a really hard time, just as she did with me. However, I figured that was their problem. They chose to be physical therapists. I never would have chosen that job for myself. Making someone do something that hurts is not my idea of a good time. I know the reasons are worthy, but I just don't want to be the one to enforce them — especially with my own daughter. As it was, I frequently had to help her handle the pain of swollen joints, and the pain of being different.

Kelley could not make a fist, and her fingers were all curved and stiff. Other kids called her 'lobster claws' when they wanted to tease her. I told her that all kids teased other kids for all sorts of reasons. They called each other fat, skinny, shrimp, beanpole, or they teased them about where they lived or what their name was. More often than not, I explained, it was a way some people had of trying to cope with something they didn't understand. I am sure the teasing still hurt. Even though all of her joints had been affected, it was her hands that people noticed. I also told her that she had a great smile, and if she used it enough, people would not notice her hands as much. Kelley was also very short. At the age of eleven, she weighed 57 pounds, and was just 4'2" tall.

Kelley never had a simple cold. It was always a severe one. She missed many days from school, and I tried to help her keep up, but when one is really sick, and in pain it is difficult to concentrate on homework. She was getting extra help at school for special needs. In May of that year, we received a report, from that school, that made us wonder on whom they did their evaluation. We simply did not see the same child! They apparently had expectations of her based on who they thought she should be. We never had any such expectations of any of our children. Each person is unique, and needs to be allowed to be themselves. We expected them to behave nicely towards others, but that was about it. Kelley was never openly defiant (as I was in childhood), but she internalized the pressure they put on her to conform to some standards they set.

Basically, we had a typical household for a family of six. The kids were growing up and experiencing all the challenges and joys of doing so. We went through the usual chicken pox, poison ivy, sprains, cuts, arguments, talking back, telling lies, blaming each other, and of course, covering up for each other. Typical of that was the time that no one broke the lamp. The baby-sitter did not know how it happened, but *no one* did it!

"Honest, Mom." "Honest, Dad!"

We still do not know how it happened.

Kelley had some extra problems to deal with, and we were trying to teach her to do the best she could with what she had. The pressure of wearing braces on her hands, splints on her arms, doing daily PT, seeing doctors all the time, plus always having to have blood drawn was enough!

However, the people at school indicated they thought we were doing nothing at home to help her! Because of her difficulty using a pencil, I was teaching her to use an electric typewriter. She also had a pen pal in Canada, and wrote (on her own) letters to her cousins and grandparents.

They thought she didn't have friends. While she found it difficult to make friends at school, because she was absent so often, she did have friends in the neighborhood. Mostly, she played with the boys.

They also thought she had no social interests or hobbies. In fact, she often did her own craft projects, somehow figuring out her own way of accomplishing these things. She made little gifts and cards for friends and relatives, and even had me take things in to the patients at the nursing home. I took her with the other children to the "Y" for swimming lessons, and we often went as a family for the family swim time. When Kelley was laid up, she liked to read.

Finally, the educators thought that she was not working up to her potential. I, in turn, thought she was having increased headaches and stomachaches again due to the pressure they were putting on her. I wanted them to let up a bit. I reasoned if they would not listen to me, they probably would listen to our friends, the big city experts. Her primary doctor at the medical center set up a meeting for us to see a child psychologist to discuss these issues.

We received even more than I expected. The psychologist sent a report to the school stating that Kelley had no psychiatric difficulty, and that she was in fact doing a remarkably good job of trying to adjust to a difficult situation. The recommendation was for those in authority to respond to the social consequences of her disease by giving more positive reinforcement about what she did, and less negative reinforcement about what she did not do. Praise God! Thank you, Doctor!

The school personnel modified their plans and pressure, and were even willing to listen to the suggestions that I had learned from the fourth grade teacher. Just about the same time, I started seeing a chiropractor once more, as my back was causing me some trouble again. I also started taking Kelley.

Her headaches and stomachaches decreased. I guess we will never know if it was because there was less pressure at school, or if it was because of the chiropractor's adjustments. Perhaps it was a combination of both.

That fall, Kelley was also referred to an orthopedic specialist at the medical center, to determine if she had carpal tunnel syndrome. The answer was yes, and surgery was recommended.

This doctor was not only an orthopedic surgeon, but also a natural teacher. We asked questions about the procedure, and he answered thoroughly, including drawing pictures for us, showing how the nerve was enclosed in a tunnel. Because this nerve was being pinched, Kelley had lost feeling in the tips of her fingers. She never complained about it, because she didn't know that it wasn't normal. She could not remember if she ever had feeling in them. That helped us to understand why she often dropped things, and why she sometimes had cuts in her fingers, and bled profusely before being aware that she had been cut.

The surgeon said that he didn't expect that the feeling would return as a result of the surgery, but the situation would progress, if she didn't have the surgery. He also said that he did not think it was fair, to a child, to do both hands at once, so he would do one, and let that heal completely, before doing the other.

There was one more surprise. She needed to have a test called an EMG. During this test, needles are stuck in the ends of fingers to send electrical impulses up the fingers. The purpose of this was to determine how much feeling was still present, and how much was missing. They sedated Kelley ahead of time. Nevertheless, it was a very nasty test for a little kid to have to endure. I had not been able to prepare her first, because I didn't know what it was like. I thought it would be painless, like an EKG or an EEG. Worse than that, I was out in the hall, rather than with her when she was going through it. Had I known that she was going to feel a shock every time they sent an electric impulse through each finger, I would have at least been in the room with her.

I was able to prepare her for the surgery. My own experience with surgery, plus my hospital experience helped me to let her know what to expect. I believe that people can cope better when they are prepared by being told the truth. When someone says to a child, "This won't hurt," before giving a shot, all they do is create distrust!

We left Kelley at the hospital on a Sunday night. This was before the time that parents were encouraged to stay with their children. The staff really did not want to have parents around. We were *tolerated* during visiting hours! The surgeon said he would call me at home when the operation was done, and I could head into the hospital while she was in recovery.

Since this was Kelley's first operation, the wait seemed very long. In retrospect, it was a relatively short time. The surgeon called to say it went well, and he took "a lot of junk" out of there.

Kelley did very well post-op. We thought her attitude was remarkable for a child her age. In fact, it would have been remarkable for an adult! She was home from the hospital by the end of the week, with her arm in a bandage and a sling. After a few more days of recovery at home, she returned to school with a note from her doctor for her gym teacher, asking her to be excused from participating in gym class while still using the sling.

That afternoon, a very upset girl came home from school. When she told me that the gym teacher thought that doing jumping jacks would be good for her, I could barely believe it!

I went straight to the school principal's office the next morning, and told him that I would get a doctor's note to keep her out of gym for the rest of the year if necessary. I advised him that my father had been an excellent gym teacher, and he never would have ignored a doctor's order. He assured me that such an incident would never occur again.

I also told Kelley that it was not only okay, but it was necessary for her to say "NO!" to any teacher, or any other person who asked her to do something that wasn't good for her.

In December, Kelley had the operation for her left hand. I had worked on Saturday night, and was off until Wednesday night. Everyone at work knew that my daughter was scheduled for surgery on Monday. We left her at the hospital on Sunday night and went home to bed, knowing that she was in a good place, and God was with her. The ringing phone jolted us out of our sleep at 11:30 PM. The nursing home supervisor wanted me to go to work that night. That was upsetting. It took awhile to go back to sleep.

The surgery went well, and Kelley was discharged on Thursday. The staff at the hospital was shocked to see me there by 8 AM. I went in to pick her up after working at night, reasoning that if I had gone home to sleep first, I would have taken a long time to get there. I knew Kelley was eager to go home. Her recovery from this operation went very well. She had few complaints, and no problems with the gym teacher.

A few months later, the surgeon wanted to do another EMG for a comparison with the one done before surgery. Kelley knew from that experience what she was in for, and was very nervous on the way in to the hospital. They gave her some sedation, and I insisted on being in the room with her this time. I was told they didn't usually allow that, and I said if they wanted to do the test, they were going to have to put up with me. While the test was taking place, I did what I could to make it less traumatic by talking to her as much as possible, without interfering with the testing. Since we usually stopped at different places to eat on the way home, I started by asking her where she wanted to stop. She mentioned a particular mall. There was a restaurant there with a waitress who seemed to delight in taking care of Kelley. I said that was a great idea, and we chatted about that waitress. Then I noticed that her purse had become rather worn, so I suggested we would shop at the mall to find her a new purse. We talked about what it would look like, in between the electric shocks. Next, she brought up the idea of shoes, and we discussed the possibility of buying those. I was relieved that the test did not last any longer. It turned out to be a very expensive one for me, but not as upsetting for her as the first one had been. I thought that the doctor decided that having me there was not such a bad idea, after all. Kelley was very cooperative with the doctor and technicians during the procedure.

Shoes were becoming more and more of a problem to find. Kelley's feet were short and wide, and the right foot kept getting wider, as a bunion type problem progressed, and the large toe started to cross over the next toe. The surgeon said that she would need an operation on that at some point, and we needed to see him for regular checks.

My preference has always been for early morning appointments. It is easier to travel with the experienced drivers who know where they are going. By and large, they are good drivers. In the city, I never expect other drivers to do things the way I want them to. They are there for their own purposes, and my concerns are of little interest to them. Since I do not have any expectations, when another driver is polite, I am pleasantly surprised. I experimented with different ways of driving out of the city, so, if the day came, when there was a bad traffic tie-up, where I usually traveled, I could easily find another way in or out of the city.

The highway is the most efficient way to access city streets, but in bad weather, I travel on back roads. It does take a little longer, but I know that, if we run into problems, there is, usually, a house or a business to which we can walk. On the highway, one can be miles away from everything. It's not a good place to be stuck in a snowstorm. People have been stranded out there, after a truck has jackknifed and blocked an off ramp.

My parents taught me very well the fine art of being punctual. It has been internalized. Knowing that there are often traffic tie-ups going in to the city, we always plan to get to our appointments ahead of time. Often, we arrive in plenty of time to stop for a cup of coffee or snack. We have spent many hours sitting in waiting rooms, so we always take books and snacks with us. This waiting became much easier when Kelley was old enough to read. There are now televisions in some of the waiting rooms. Usually they are suspended from the ceilings, and those doing the waiting have no control over the choice of programming. We prefer our books!

The only time we were ever late getting to an appointment was for a checkup with the orthopedic surgeon. We were traveling down the highway, out in the third lane of a four-lane road on a rainy morning. The trucks travel in the first two lanes, and I usually try to stay out of their way. I had a small car at that time. The rain became very heavy, and an eighteen-wheeler in the second lane passed me with such speed, that the rainwater splashed up under my hood. In a very short time, I realized my car's wires had become wet. The engine quit. I put on my hazard lights and pumped my brakes to let those behind me know I would be stopping. I had no choice. The cars right behind me dispersed. Whew! There I was, stopped in the third lane at 8 AM, unable to move! I closed my eyes for a brief moment, and silently prayed, "Lord, what do I do now?"

I was jolted, out of this thought, by a knock at my window. There was a man standing there asking me if he could push me over to the breakdown lane. I was amazed! He was taking a big chance with the traffic the way it was on such a rainy morning. I quickly agreed to his proposal. Somehow, he maneuvered me over there, dodging the trucks. Then he got out of his car again, and came to my window to tell me to wait for about twenty minutes and try it again. I thanked him, and he was gone.

I asked Kelley to join me in saying a prayer of thanks, and to ask God to bless that man with a very good day. Perhaps there are angels among us!

A year of working nights in a nursing home convinced me to find some other way to earn money. I took a course to prepare for the state Real Estate exam, took the test, and passed.

Before embarking on my new career, I sat down with the children to discuss the effects my job would have upon all of us. I explained to them that I could do most of my work on weekends and in the evening, when their Dad would be with them, but there would be some daytime, too. We had already started leaving them for short periods of time, with one of the older ones in charge of Peggy while we ran errands, or went for a ride, and

70

discovered that they did just fine. At this time, Peggy was five, and soon to be going to kindergarten. The others were going on eleven, twelve and thirteen.

I told the children that I wouldn't have as much time to do all the things that needed to be done in the house, plus be able to chauffeur them to all the places they wanted to go. I appealed to their reasoning by asking if they had any suggestions as to how we should handle it, since we would all benefit from the money I made.

Their suggestions were great! They volunteered to do more housework (they did already have some chores), including cooking. We worked it out so they each did the chores they liked best, and the few things no one wanted to do, were assigned on a rotating basis.

I started my new career, and somehow, for the next three years, I managed to sell Real Estate and have enough time for my children. The older ones learned a lot about responsibility, as well as acquiring culinary skills! They were thrilled, when I received my first commission check, and they all were given new bikes, as a reward for their cooperation.

Buying the bike for Kelley did cause me some momentary regrets the day she came home covered with blood, after taking a nasty spill. I didn't know quite where to start the cleaning process! I put her in the tub, clothes and all, to wash off the blood and to see just how bad it was. Thankfully, her many wounds were superficial. She limped around for a few days, and I had to remind myself that many kids take such spills, and if she wanted to ride the bike again, it would have to be all right with me. Her main concern was not the cuts and bruises, but the fact that she smashed up her new wristwatch.

Sometime after that, Kelley had a flare-up in a knee that was so severe; I took her to the local hospital emergency room. They took x-rays and said they didn't know what to do. I called the orthopedic surgeon who had operated on her, and he said to bring her right in to see him.

He took x-rays, and showed them to me, pointing out how the ends of the bones, that were supposed to be rounded, were jagged. He could see where some little pieces of the bones had splintered off, causing an irritation, which in turn caused the fluid to accumulate in the joint. The small needle he put in Kelley's knee, to numb it, really hurt, but the large one, which he used to aspirate the fluid, didn't. It just looked threatening! He then put her leg in a splint, to immobilize it, and gave her Tylenol and codeine, for the pain. That was the day we discovered that Kelley became very ill from that medication! It was awful. By the time we arrived at home, the pain was worse, the room was swimming around on her, and she was vomiting and shivering! No more codeine for Kelley! When she recovered

71

from that reaction, she did experience some relief, as a result of the aspiration, and was in good shape to go camping that summer.

Besides our usual family camping trip, the three older children were each able to go away to an overnight camp for kids.

Kelley's knee did not act up again until April 1977. This time the doctor hospitalized her to try a little traction. She was in a room with three other girls, one of whom was a real whiner and complainer. I hoped this attitude would not be picked up by Kelley, but it finally was.

I walked into her room one afternoon, to be greeted by that kind of attitude, from my daughter, as soon as I took off my coat and kissed her hello. I can be a very empathetic person, but I am of the belief that pity leads to self-pity, which is destructive. Feeling sorry for oneself hampers recovery.

When someone had to deal with as many problems as Kelley, that kind of thinking needed to be stopped. Just because I believed this, it did not make it easy for me to do what I knew I had to do.

I started to put my coat back on, and headed for the door saying, "I didn't drive all the way in here today to visit with someone who was going to use up all their energy on whining, so I'll go home. Maybe you'll be in a better frame of mind when your Dad gets here tonight."

"Wait," she yelled as I reached the door, "I won't do it anymore. Please stay."

I was relieved! We worked on counting blessings.

Bob and I always had confusing schedules when the children were young, and Kelley was in the hospital. He had to be at work daily during the week, so I went in to see her during that time, as much as possible, and I had to take jobs that would allow me some flexibility. Bob usually went to the hospital after work, while I was on my way home, to be with the other children. On the weekends, we went in together, if we could. Sometimes, we were able to take one of the other kids with us, when they were old enough.

It was always a balancing act to keep up with all the needs of the other children, when Kelley was hospitalized. We didn't have much of a chance to discuss what was going on, or how we were feeling about it. We were too busy doing what had to be done. We were both aware that I was more comfortable with the hospital atmosphere than Bob was, and I usually handled the conferences with the doctors. I also knew my way around, and could get Kelley what she needed. The only thing I had to ask for was medication. Sometimes the nurses thought I was infringing on their territory, but when they discovered I was helpful, they welcomed me. I had learned that by acting as if I belonged, I could ignore the visiting hours, and go to the hospital whenever I was able. Once I learned my way around, no one bothered me. I brought in food from home that Kelley liked, so she would eat, and we didn't have to complain about the hospital food. It is, after all, impossible for them to please everyone.

While I was sitting in Kelley's room one day, checking out the Real Estate section of the paper, a physical therapist, whom we had not previously met, came to work with Kelley.

"Are you looking for a house, too?" she asked.

When I told her that I was a Real Estate agent, she told me about her search for a house. The agent, with whom she and her husband had been looking at homes, had taken them into all sorts of places that they had told him they didn't like. Most likely, he was trying to get them to buy one of his listings. They were looking in a town close to where I worked, so I asked what she wanted in a home.

"I can find that for you," I assured her after she gave me their particulars.

They bought the first house I showed them. In addition to this, she was the best physical therapist Kelley had ever met. She had a way about her that Kelley responded to very well. If she asked Kelley to do something she said she didn't like, this woman would say, "Okay, we'll get back to it later."

Her method apparently made Kelley feel as if she had more control over the situation, and she cooperated with this therapist more than she ever had with any other.

After getting some relief from the pain, and learning to walk with crutches, Kelley was discharged. Her doctor instructed her to use the crutches any time her knee started to bother her. His opinion was that, as long as her bones were still growing, she would be apt to have such problems.

She also had a special needs teacher, that year, who really understood her. Her end of the year report read in part, "Kelley manages extremely well despite physical problems. For such a young person, she has incredible emotional strength. She and her family have a positive attitude toward her disability. When Kelley lacks motivation in school, it may well be that she is not feeling well, but is not making a fuss about it. She tunes in easily to other people, and is sensitive to their feelings and problems. She tries to help others. Kelley is a concrete learner and has sound common sense."

It was good to know that those comments about the real Kelley would go on her permanent record.

While I was out selling houses, I started to realize that we could probably find something larger for our family, if we sold ours, so we put ours on the market. It sold in time for us to get the absolutely right house for us. We moved at the end of the school year into a charming big old house, where the children each had their own bedroom. During the years we lived there, we often remarked about how lucky we were to have found that house. Our old neighbors (with Peggy's friend, Peggy) had moved previously into that same neighborhood, so "the Peggys" were able to walk together to elementary school. They were delighted about that!

# CHAPTER NINE

Shortly after Kelley's fourteenth birthday, the bone in her foot was causing her so much trouble that the only avenue to travel was surgery. The orthopedic surgeon said it was not a bad operation. She would spend about five days in the hospital, a month with a cast and crutches, and a month in a walking cast after that. I asked if it could possibly be done just before Thanksgiving, so her recuperation would include Thanksgiving vacation from school. We were always aware of the school time she was missing.

The doctor said that his schedule was very full, but he would see what he could do. A few days later, we received notice that the surgery was scheduled for the next week, over a month before Thanksgiving!

"So soon?" Kelley asked apprehensively.

"That way you won't have too much time to think about it first," I cheerfully said, forgetting that I am a person who processes things quickly, and she is a person who needs time to prepare herself.

We talked about it a few times during the week, and I thought she had accepted it. She appeared well, and only slightly apprehensive. I thought all was fine. How little I knew!

The morning Kelley was to be admitted to the hospital, she walked into the kitchen, and mother's instinct made me feel her forehead. I whipped out the thermometer. Her temperature was 100.6 degrees. I knew it was going to rise, so I called the doctor and told him that I didn't want her to be admitted, only to be sent home again. He said that, if I brought her in, he would have the anesthetist see her before admitting her, to make a judgment. Kelley had never had a fever for just a few hours, to my knowledge, but I decided to let them see for themselves. She was not too feverish when we arrived there, and the anesthetist said her lungs sounded fine. He didn't think the sore throat, about which she had told him, was of any concern, so she was admitted and kept on the OR schedule.

After the admittance visit to the lab, we stopped for food. When we entered Kelley's room, she was finishing an ice cream cone. The admitting nurse took her temperature, anyway, and of course it wasn't elevated. An hour later, I took Kelley's temperature. It had risen. I showed the thermometer to a nurse. Nevertheless, the standard routine with the medical students took place. Each time I responded to their many questions, I wished I had made a recording. I don't think any of them had any idea how many times we had been asked the same questions. Although they were all working under the assumption that Kelley would be having surgery in the morning, by 4 PM I was sure there would be no surgery the next day. Her fever was not going to go away.

Now the orthopedic surgeons found themselves with a real dilemma. They wanted a patient on whom to operate, so they could fix her bones, but they did not want a sick one. What can a surgeon do about a fever? They called the medical team, who knew what tests to order to diagnose what was causing the fever.

Now, this was a big city hospital, a teaching hospital, where they are always looking at the different and the rare. How could I, a mother, tell them that Kelley was coming down with a cold? Would anyone have listened?

"Don't worry honey," I said to Kelley before I left that evening, "There won't be any surgery for you tomorrow."

In the morning the surgeon called me to say, "Kelley seems to have a cold. I guess you should take her home today, and we'll reschedule."

I laughed.

"I know." he said, sounding contrite, "My mother has tried to tell me that I should listen to a mother's intuition. You were right yesterday!"

The surgeon had, to his knowledge, released her to the medical team, who were still waiting for results from some of her tests. After I arrived at the hospital, I was told one of the medical men would be there to see me soon. Some people have no idea of the true definition of that word. It was 1 PM when they told me that their tests indicated that Kelley probably had a cold. Bye-bye.

We started packing up Kelley's things, and a nurse told us to wait. No one had written a discharge order. Great! Medical had figured that the surgeon had done it, and he figured medical would do it, and there we sat until 4 PM, waiting for someone to come back and write the discharge order. We were just in time to travel out of the city in the rush hour traffic!

I thanked God that the cold symptoms hit when they did, rather than a day later. She would have had one heck of a time trying to recuperate from the anesthesia with a cold.

Kelley seemed relieved and relaxed when we were home. She spent quite a few days battling a very bad cold. She also felt embarrassed about going back to school without the cast she had told them she would be wearing.

Having previously observed that emotions can play a large part in one's general health, and having done some reading on the subject, I gave the whole situation some serious thought that week.

Sitting down with Kelley one day I said, "You seem to have some way of psyching yourself up to handle things like operations, and you seem to need time to do it. When you had the carpal tunnel operations, you had time to think about it, talk about it, and ask all the questions you needed to ask. When the time came for the surgery, you were ready. This time, I think you had already started psyching yourself up for November, and suddenly it was sprung on you a month ahead of time. I thought you were ready for that surgery, but now I believe you weren't. Your inner mind took over, and, in essence, took you out of a rotten situation — one you weren't ready to cope with yet. It allowed your defenses to let down, so you caught a cold, and got out of the operation for now. Do you follow?"

"Yeah, I think I know what you mean," she responded, "and it's true that I wasn't ready."

"Hey!" I said, "I think we have learned something! If I had been aware of this before, and I had been able to have the courage of my convictions, and if you had told me that you wouldn't be ready emotionally by that date, I would have been able to tell the doctor, when we first got that letter, to change the date. He probably wouldn't have liked it, but I bet we would have saved you a week of being sick!"

These theories and thoughts, that took me thirty-eight years to conclude, were readily understood by my fourteen-year-old daughter, who simply said, "You're right."

"Well girl," I said, "let's try, from here on in, to get in touch with those emotions. If you'll let me know what's going on inside that head, I'll do my best to understand, and stick by you, no matter if I am unpopular with some doctors."

A new surgery date was set for November. Kelley was ready then. It turned out to be a more extensive operation than we had anticipated, with a longer hospital stay.

The surgeon chiseled off some of the protruding bone and attempted to straighten out two toes by putting pins in them. Kelley's foot was then placed in a cast. The anesthesia had caused some breathing difficulties, a fact of which Kelley was not aware.

She had an order for a strong medication for the first few days post-op. Nevertheless, there was often a long wait from the time Kelley requested it, until the time it was given to her, even though I was there to advocate for her. It was very frustrating. A while after receiving the medication, Kelley could relax, and drift into sleep, only to awaken with a scream, when the medication wore off, a few hours later. I winced every time she screamed, wishing I could trade places. It would have been easier to feel the pain myself than to witness her suffering. A request for medication sometimes had to be repeated two or three times. To make matters worse, the nurses and residents kept trying to tell me that Kelley had a low threshold for pain. When I argued the point, I got the "You're just a mother" routine.

Because of the way Kelley screamed about her foot, with it waking her from a drug-induced sleep, I was convinced something was terribly wrong. I wanted them to remove the cast, and look at her foot, but the operation had been on a Friday, and her surgeon was away for the weekend. The residents were in charge. They did not know Kelley, they did not know me, and they would not listen. The weekend was horrendous!

By Monday, when the surgeon was back, the severity of the pain had lessened, so it was at least tolerable, with the help of medication. However, there were some nurses on that floor that were either overworked or uncaring. They appeared to be rather judgmental. Because I was really concerned about the kind of care that Kelley would receive, when I wasn't there, I told her about the squeaky wheel getting oiled. She was not a complainer, nor was she demanding. I knew that, with the crew on that floor, this usually polite and compliant girl would be almost ignored. Under the circumstances, I decided it would be okay for them to judge her to be a nuisance, if that was how she would get her medication.

"Kelley," I advised, "if ever I'm not here, to get what you need for you, and they make you wait a long time, you just holler and put up a fuss. They'll probably complain, but they will get you what you need."

She seemed very surprised. That advice was contrary to the way we did things in our home, or what we would normally approve of, but these were unusual circumstances.

Later that week, upon my arrival one afternoon, I checked the chart on her door, and noticed her blood pressure and pulse were elevated at 11 AM.

"Kelley, what happened at eleven this morning?" I asked.

"They wanted me to get out of bed, and I told them I wanted my pain medication first. They weren't going to give it to me, so I yelled 'til they did."

I suppressed a laugh. It was a relief to know she really would do it!

Getting out of bed proved to be a distressing task. When Kelley first lowered her foot, she suffered intense pain. The staff thought she was exaggerating, but I believed her. I knew her. When I was there, I helped her to get up at her own speed. I had the time to wait.

In order to be able to walk with crutches, Kelley started daily visits to the Physical Therapy room. I arrived one day as she was telling the therapist that she did not want to go. The therapist and the nurse were urging her to start walking, so she could be discharged.

"I'll go with you to PT," I volunteered.

"Visitors are not allowed in there," the therapist said.

"I am not a visitor, I am her mother," I said, "She will go if I am with her."

Once in the PT room, we saw the good therapist that we had met when Kelley's knee was bothering her. She came over to talk to us, and I gave her a brief description of what was happening.

She became involved, and the session was much better. She allowed Kelley to take her time, and she acknowledged Kelley's fear of pain. I hoped the other therapist was learning something from her method. The next day, she was not around, and the pressure was on again. Everyone kept telling Kelley that if she didn't start walking, she wouldn't be home for Thanksgiving. I became caught up in it with them, even though she complained, "But it hurts too much."

Sometimes it was very good to have a long drive home. It gave me time to think about things. That night, on my way home, I started looking at what a negative experience this one was. It had not been this bad since way back at that first hospital. It was helpful that she was older now, and better able to understand. We had even started playing a game of trying to get that surly resident to smile, at least once, before we left. I actually bought a little plaque to put by her bed. It read, "If you see someone without a smile, give them one of yours." We both said some very silly things to him, trying to find his sense of humor.

As I talked to myself on that ride home, I came to realize that, even after I told her I would listen to her and respect her wishes and needs, I had joined in with them, singing the "You gotta get home for Thanksgiving" song. What a fool! Who cares if she is home for Thanksgiving or not, if she is just going to be miserable trying to get there? We'll all go to the hospital if she's not home. It will still be Thanksgiving, and we'll still be together, so what does it matter where we are?

Once home, I called her. "Kelley," I said, "I have to apologize to you. I became caught up in the pressure they were applying, and I was wrong. From here on, you just tell them that you will go at your own pace. It doesn't matter if you're home for Thanksgiving or not! We'll bring it to you, if you're still there."

"Oh, okay, Mom," she replied, sounding weary.

"And one more thing, Kelley. When your doctor comes in tomorrow morning, tell him I want him to call me. Tell him it's important."

"How come?" she asked.

"I'm going to tell him to get all those people to back off," I said. She giggled a little, and we said our good nights.

When the doctor did call in the morning, I told him about the pressure everyone had been putting on Kelley, as well as my ideas about Thanksgiving. I said that I thought her emotional health was every bit as important as her physical health. I asked him to please have them all back off.

"Oh," he said, sounding surprised, "Well, I'll tell you what," he paused, "Kelley does know how to walk on crutches, doesn't she?"

"Yes, she does."

"Suppose you just take her home today, then. Her progress is fine, and I know Kelley. It's just a matter of time until she is up and about."

"Oh thank you!" was my breathless response, "You'll write a discharge order now, then?" I was not taking any chances.

"Right now, and my office will notify you of the time next month to have the cast removed."

When I reached the hospital about an hour later, no one had told Kelley she was going home. I don't think anyone had seen the order yet. She was about to go to PT, and I told her she didn't have to go.

"But there is an order," the therapist said.

"Go check the chart," I happily stated, "I think you will fine there is now an order for her to be discharged today."

Everyone was surprised. I guess the message got around quickly, and our favorite therapist came to see us and say, "Good for you. Most people don't speak up, and they think they have to put up with everything. I've never seen her doctor do anything like this, but I'm glad for you that he did!"

On the way home from the hospital, Kelley remarked, "It's a good thing it was me, and not anyone else in the family who had this."

"Why do you say that?" I asked.

"Because I know how to handle it." was her modest answer.

That left me pretty speechless.

The day before Thanksgiving, Kelley stood up, placed the crutches under her arms, and took six steps on her own. I called our favorite therapist at home that evening to tell her. She was delighted, and said she would be happy to tell everyone at the hospital.

The cast was large, heavy and cumbersome. Kelley was looking forward to having it removed before Christmas. When we received a notice, in the mail, that the appointment had been made for few days after Christmas, she was crushed. I called to discuss it with the doctor's secretary. She informed me that she couldn't change it. In response to my request, the doctor called me.

I explained to him that Kelley had been counting on four weeks, and that would fall well before Christmas. If he waited until after Christmas to remove the cast, it would be closer to six weeks. I said that all she wanted for Christmas was to get the cast off, and appealed to him to find the time somehow. He was not only a good surgeon, but a compassionate man as well. He found the time.

During the week before Christmas, the cast was removed. It was a surgical procedure, requiring anesthesia, but we were able to have it done on an outpatient basis. I took Kelley in, and waited while she was in surgery. After the procedure was completed, the surgeon came out to see me.

This man's presentation was usually factual, and he always courteously answered all of our questions. I felt confident with him.

He stood above where I was sitting, and reported, "Kelley is doing okay. She tolerated it well, and the cast is off. We did have some difficulty keeping the IV's going. You know how easily her veins shut down. She is in recovery now, and I'll let you go in to see her in just a minute."

That was a first! They had never allowed that before! I expected the doctor to walk away, when he suddenly sat down next to me. I must have given him a quizzical look, as he paused.

"There is one problem," he finally said, "there is an area on the side of her foot, about the size of my thumbnail," he illustrated by pointing to his thumbnail, "where the skin is missing."

"Missing?"

"Yes," another pause, "apparently she developed a blister, right after the surgery."

"So that was it!" I exclaimed, wide-eyed.

Now it was his turn to question, "Was what?"

"You did the surgery on a Friday, and you were away for the weekend," I explained, "that whole weekend, I argued with your resident and the nurses. Kelley had so much pain, I thought something was wrong, and I wanted them to take the cast off, but they kept telling me that she had a low pain threshold."

"No," he said, shaking his head and looking concerned, "she can tolerate a lot of pain. Why, it's even harder for her just to walk than it is for the rest of us."

"By the time you were back," I continued, "the worst had past, so I stopped complaining, but now, I also understand why she was reluctant to get up to walk! I guess when she put her foot down, that cast was hitting raw flesh!"

His anguished expression made me realize that I didn't need to say anymore. I was confident that the resident in question (the one without a smile) was about to learn a lesson, which, hopefully, would help other patients, in the future. I also silently vowed to myself that I would never again allow anyone to ignore what I knew was right for Kelley.

"So, what do we do about it?" I asked with trepidation.

"It is possible," he said cautiously, "that with the right care, the skin may grow back, but with her condition, I don't know what to expect. She might need a skin graft if it doesn't."

I swallowed hard as we rose. He took me to the recovery room. Kelley was looking pretty bright. A technician was trying to get an IV started.

"My veins haven't been behaving today," Kelley told me. She needed more fluid, and it was too soon for her to be taking anything by mouth. To my relief, the staff quickly realized that I would be more of a help than a hindrance.

Kelley was alert enough for me to say to her, "Now we know why you had so much pain right after the surgery, and why it hurt so much when you put your foot down to walk."

"What do you mean?" she asked.

"You had a blister for a few days. Once the blister broke, the pain wasn't so bad, but being all enclosed like that, the skin didn't grow back, so now you have a raw spot that we will have to heal," I said, hoping that I made it sound easy. I did not mention the idea of more surgery. Why worry her about something that may never happen?

"How big is it?"

"I haven't seen it yet. There's a bandage on it, but the doctor says it's about the size of his thumbnail." When I did see it, I decided the man had a rather large thumbnail.

Before we left, I was given instructions as to the procedure for cleaning the area, three times a day, with sterile saline and swabs, and changing the dressing. Since the cost of all those sterile supplies from the drug store was high, I only bought the pads for the dressings. I did the rest myself. The kids liked to joke about it by saying things like, "Looks like a good meal tonight. Mom's boiling cloths again."

I was absolutely faithful to the routine for those treatments. With each treatment, I said positive prayers, thanking God for healing the wound. We went to see the surgeon monthly.

By the third month, I was really anxious for him to see Kelley's foot. The skin had started to grow back from the outer part of the circle. The doctor looked at her foot, then looked at me with a wide smile.

"You win the nurse-of-the-year award, Mom," he said.

It was still a month before the area was completely healed. That was when I told Kelley how grateful I was that God had answered my prayers, and she didn't need another operation for that problem.

Kelley never complained about the issue, or tried to place any blame. She somehow knew, at that age, that you hurt only yourself, when you bear a grudge.

I realized, from this experience, that I had been expecting the communication, between the staff and doctor, to be taking place as it had in the hospital where I had previously worked as a nurse's aide. There was a difference. I worked in a small hospital, with a continuity of staff, and a close rapport between staff and attending physicians. This was a large city, teaching hospital, where the staff changed more frequently. I learned then that, in the future, I was going to have to keep the doctor informed myself, and not rely on the staff to do so.

During the time the cast was on, Kelley had a home tutor for her schoolwork. After Christmas vacation, she went back to school with a crutch, and a smaller "walking" cast, which was in a boot. Much of her time was spent in the resource room with one particular teacher. She was in the eighth grade, and needed special help to keep up with the class. I also helped her at home, as much as possible.

One afternoon, while I was at work, this teacher called me to tell me about an incident that had happened that day. We talked for quite awhile after he told me that Kelley had gotten upset when he accused her of cheating. It baffled me that anyone would accuse her of cheating. She never had a motivation to cheat. We never were very concerned with her grades, and neither was she. Naturally, we wanted her to learn, but with all the battles she had to fight in life, we were not going to worry about how soon she learned how much.

I questioned him as to why he thought she had cheated, and he said that she couldn't have done a particular assignment without cheating. I asked for specifics, which he supplied. I then patiently explained to him that she and I had, in fact, spent two hours the night before, at the kitchen table, working on that very concept, and before we were through, it clicked. She had it. That was the way she always learned. She could work on something for a long time, and it would look as if she was never going to get it. Then, suddenly one day, it would become clear, and she would have it for all time.

Amazingly, to my way of thinking, he didn't want to listen. It occurred to me that the reason he called was to give me his side of the story first, before Kelley complained to me. He said some things that truly astounded me about "all these kids cheating" and such. I thanked him for the call.

When Kelley and I were together that evening, and she had not yet brought up the subject, I asked her what happened in school that day. Apparently, she was going to let the incident pass. I might not have pursued it, if I had not heard him say some things that I never expected to hear from a special needs teacher.

"The usual," was her answer.

"Well, what about the math stuff we worked on last night?" I asked.

"Oh, yeah. I got it right the first time, and he thought I cheated."

"How did you feel?"

"I got mad. I told him I didn't cheat. I got it right! My friend got so mad that he accused me of cheating, that she yelled at him and stormed out of the room," she said matter-of-factly.

I laughed. I knew which friend she was talking about, and I could picture it. I asked, "Where did she go?"

"I followed her. We just went to the ladies room. I think he was afraid she was going to the principal's office, and he would get in trouble."

"So that's why he called me."

"He called you?" her eyes grew wide with surprise.

"He did. I think he wanted to give me his side of the story, like a little kid does, when they are afraid of getting into trouble."

"He's a jerk! He's always accusing someone of cheating. He says we have to prove to him that we can be trusted."

"Well, don't take it personally, honey. You and I and God know that you don't cheat, and that's all that matters," I tried to reassure her. I didn't tell her my plans.

The next day, I called the school and talked to the assistant principal. She was an excellent person for the job. She really knew her students, and when a mother had three kids in the same junior high, one of them with special needs, she knew that mother, too. She was a kind and understanding woman, but she made no allowances for nonsense. Everyone respected her. I didn't think it would be a good idea for me to do a "he said, I said" routine. Instead, I asked for a meeting with her and the teacher — just the three of us. I knew she thought it was unusual, but she arranged it, anyway.

I prayed for guidance on the way to the school. It turned out to be an interesting meeting. Basically, I simply interviewed the teacher, in front of the assistant principal, concerning what had happened the previous day, and why he had made the assumptions he had. He actually said, in her presence, that he didn't think any kids could be trusted, especially these kids. I asked him if he had told them that, and he admitted that he had. The assistant principal showed no reaction, but she asked me what I, as the mother of a special needs student, thought of that.

"I think that's exactly the *wrong* way to go about dealing with them," I responded, "they already feel enough pressure, having to need special classes, at an age when peers are so important. These kids have a great need for a teacher to trust them, encourage them, and praise them for each little accomplishment. Their self-esteem needs to be nourished, not shattered. If you have some proof that someone has cheated, by all means, you should take appropriate corrective action, but to accuse someone, just because you think they might have cheated, is wrong."

"I agree with you, Mrs. Crompton," she said when I finished my little speech. She then directed her attention towards the teacher.

He sat, pressing his hands together, staring at the floor, and softly asked, "What do you want me to do?"

"What do you think you should do?" I asked. I was not about to let him off the hook by telling him what I thought he should know.

"I guess I should apologize to Kelley in front of the class," he solemnly responded.

"That's a good start," I said without expression.

"And I guess I should apologize to the whole class," he offered, looking at the assistant principal.

"Good idea," I said.

I rose, and they followed suit. Extending my hand to shake his, I said, "Thank you."

As I turned towards the assistant principal, it was difficult not to grin. I shook her hand and thanked her for her time. She thanked me for bringing the matter to her attention, and gave me a look that assured me she would stay on top of the situation.

When Kelley got home from school that day, she said, "You were at my school today, weren't you?"

"Did you see me?" I asked.

"No," she replied, "but my special needs teacher came in and apologized to me and the rest of the class. He said he was going to trust us from now on, unless he has proof he shouldn't. That's when I knew you had been there."

Because Kelley and I spent so much time together, we developed a different kind of mother-daughter relationship than the average one. We had many opportunities to discuss numerous issues, while in the car, on the way to and from medical appointments, as well as the many hours we spent together, when she was recovering from something. We knew each other very well.

I never received another call from that teacher, and Kelley never complained of problems with him, either. I suppose he learned something from that little encounter.

# CHAPTER TEN

Out of the blue one day, Kelley asked me, "How do you become a singer?" That was a novel question to ask me. I have no ability to carry a tune.

My children have often said, "Please Mom, don't!" when I have attempted to sing.

I learned to use this non-talent in a positive way. Whenever one of them was reluctant to comply with my wishes, I would simply threaten to sing at them. I was also a wonderful alarm clock. I could walk by the bedrooms in the morning and say, "If you're not up in two minutes, I'll start singing."

"Okay Mom, I'm up," would be the immediate response.

I needed to clarify Kelley's question. "What do you mean?" I asked.

"I've been thinking about singing a lot. Do you think I could take singing lessons?"

"Sure," I said. I would not have come up with that idea, but I thought it was great.

"How can I find a singing teacher?"

"I don't know, I'll ask around. I have enough friends that know about music. Voice lessons would be so different from everything else you've done, it should be fun."

"Well, I can try it," she said, "and if it doesn't work out, at least I'll know I tried." She could be so philosophical sometimes!

While I was in the process of tracking down the right teacher, we had an appointment with one of her doctors, who said, "I'd really like you to do some exercises for those lungs."

Kelley and I both laughed. "As a matter of fact," I said, "I'm in the process of finding a singing teacher for her."

"Super," he said, "that really would benefit her."

The singing teacher we found couldn't have been any better for this particular assignment. I told her that I thought it would be good for Kelley to do something with no pressure involved, and no competition. This woman was in her early twenties, newly married, and very well grounded. She totally understood. Kelley never ventured on a stage to perform as a singer, but once a week, for an hour or so, she had the undivided attention of someone who cared. This woman played a "big sister" role, being a confidant as well as a singing teacher. It was a most beneficial therapy for Kelley's lungs, as well as her emotions.

Two days after Kelley's foot was completely healed, she and Susan started a morning paper route, having seen David earn money from his route. Watching the little one go off at 6:10 AM, on a cold winter morning, with her bag full of papers, was truly inspirational. After the first successful week, she experienced a flare-up in her wrist, causing a good deal of pain in her hand and arm — the right one, no less! We took a trip into outpatient, where they made a splint, and put her right arm in a sling.

"Oh dear," I thought, "she just started this paper route. I don't want this to stand in the way of her making a success of it."

Peggy offered to help, but Kelley said that wasn't right. Peggy was not yet seven years old. I knew Susan was capable of doing the whole route, but I didn't want to impose that on her, and I didn't want to tell Kelley she had to stop. While I was contemplating what to do, the girls came up with their own solution. They combined the routes, and went together, with Susan carrying the load, while Kelley did the actual delivery to many of the houses. Of course, this meant that they had to be out of the house by 6 AM, but I considered it a small price to pay, in order to keep up her spirits.

We had a trip to the city that week that gave us cause for laughter. Since we had established a comfortable rapport with Kelley's orthopedic surgeon, he was the one we usually saw for these problems. He was out ill, and we got potluck at the clinic. I realized that I was starting to age some when I looked at the young man and thought, "Bet he doesn't know the first thing about her disorder."

Taking her very large chart, he looked at Kelley, looked at the latest report, flipped back to the first page, glanced through the middle, and announced, "I think I'll see if I can find her x-rays." He smiled at us, and left the room.

Kelley and I exchanged glances, "He is going to try to find someone who will explain to him what this is all about," I said, rolling my eyes.

When he returned later, he had an older doctor with him, who told us that he had assisted in one of Kelley's operations.

"Has she had a fever?" he asked.

"No."

"How do you know, did you take her temperature?" he almost demanded.

"No, I didn't," I stated, "but I'm her mother."

"Well, I want you to take her temperature three times a day."

I did not answer. He ordered a complete blood count. On the way to the lab, Kelley asked me if I was going to take her temperature three times a day.

"Kelley," I said, laughing, "he just doesn't realize that I've been your mother for fourteen years, and I know, long before any thermometer, if you have a fever. The only reason I ever take your temperature, is to report to the doctor the degree at which it is registering. I haven't missed a fever in you yet. And now this blood work! If I had known that our regular doctor wasn't going to be here, we could have skipped this trip."

"Well, you never know, Mom. God has His reasons. He wanted us here today for some reason," she said. Leave it to her to make me realize that I was sounding pretty negative!

The doctors told Kelley to continue with the splint and return the following week, to see her regular doctor. Bless them. At least they didn't pretend to know anything about her disorder.

Susan was with us on our next visit. She also needed a splint. She had sprained her wrist in gym class. I left the city that day with two girls who had their right arms in splints and slings! They looked as if they had been in a fight, and they both lost. I knew I would miss those two right arms around the house, but I was pleased that they felt they could still handle their paper route.

Kelley checked out the book "Karen" by Marie Killilea from the library.

"I read that book, when you were very young, and it gave me a lot of hope," I said.

"Yeah," Kelley responded, in her typical matter-of-fact fashion, "and it makes you realize how lucky you are, when you read about someone who has had it harder."

It was very good for her to read it, as she decided then to start taking responsibility for her own PT. She was able to put her socks on, by herself, finally, and get her thumb and finger to touch each other. It had taken many hours of therapy for her to reach that point.

The girls and I went shopping at the special shoe store for sneakers for the summer. Susan had a problem that required her to use arch supports in her shoes, and Kelley's wide feet could only be fitted in a store that carried odd sizes. The young woman who waited on us was delightful. She was very relaxed, and she started joking with the children. When the floor was all littered with paper (by her) from Susan trying on sneakers, she said to Susan, "Look at the mess you're making."

We all laughed.

Looking at Kelley's feet, she said dryly, "You've got feet just like mine."

I responded, "Have you got a surgery scar, too?"

"No, has she?"

"Yes," Kelley said, "when my foot got too wide for shoes, the doctor had to take some of the bone off."

"Oh, I don't think I want a scar, either," she responded.

She brought out sneakers for Kelley, chatted with us while she laced one, and then handed it to Kelley saying, "Here kid. You put it on."

Kelley looked at me, and then at her as I said, "She hasn't accomplished that task yet. She can do socks now, but she has a disorder that has affected all her joints, and it is very difficult for her to reach her feet."

The girl's expression did not change. She simply took the sneaker, and while putting it on Kelley's foot, she said, "That's a stupid disease."

We roared! What a refreshing response! Much better than, "You poor kid!" This young woman hit the nail on the head. What a stupid disease! We repeated that remark with laughter off and on, all the way home.

One of the problems that disabled people have with the rest of society is that many people look upon the differences as defining the person, rather than realizing they are simply people who have problems. Everyone has problems with which to deal. Sometimes the physical problems are visible. The best thing anyone can do, for someone with a disability, is to simply accept who they are, and not try to make them conform to someone else's standards and rules.

All humans have growing pains. Our other children didn't have ML III, but they had their share of growing pains, too. They also needed to have us accept them just as they were. Sometimes we didn't like their behavior, but most of the time, we thought they were all pretty great.

Peggy didn't have a live-in playmate like the others did, so she often had friends in, or went to their home. I became more aware, than I wanted to be, of behaviors that were allowed in other homes.

Periodically, when Peggy visited the home of a new playmate, and discovered them getting away with something we didn't allow, she would try it on us, anyway. Just in case. It usually ended up with me saying, "You are not the child that lives across the street, and I am not the mother that lives across the street. The way they do things there is probably different from the way we do here. Our rules have not changed!"

She was a cute little thing who looked so much like me that it was not hard for me to know what her different expressions meant. When this scenario took place, she usually tilted her head to the right, pursed her lips, and frowned at me. I knew she was trying to figure out how I knew what was going on in someone else's house, and, at the same time, she was hoping I would change my mind, if she showed me she was displeased with me.

Disciplining your own children because it is good for them can really be difficult. I always thought my own kids were so cute, the temptation to spoil them was great.

Kelley had a pixie look, with a little nose and dimpled chin. If anyone did anything wrong, Kelley looked guilty, even if she wasn't anywhere near the problem. It is possible she was blamed sometimes for things with which she was not involved.

Susan, on the other hand, could look straight at you with her beautiful big blue eyes, and convince you she wasn't guilty, even if the evidence was in her hands!

David, with his sincere brown eyes, and quick broad smile, was always quick to apologize, when he was chastised for any infraction. He wanted to get the unpleasantness done and over with, so we could all be back on an even keel.

Raising children to be responsible adults is a tremendous challenge. There are many times when letting them get away with things would be so much easier, but spoiled, undisciplined kids never end up being happy adults. Sometimes, one has to be a not-too-popular mother.

Before school was out, Kelley's knee acted up again. I called the orthopedist and told him we missed him.

"What's up?" he asked.

"Kelley's knee," was all I had to say.

"Bring her in. I'll be here. We may have to aspirate."

We looked at the x-ray together. He shook his head, and said, "Those bones look like the Rocky Mountains."

He looked discouraged. Orthopedic surgeons like to be able to fix people. I think of them as carpenters of the body. Their purpose is to get things to work right. This was a frustrating case.

"It's all right," I said, "just see if you can make her a little more comfortable."

As he had done in the past, he aspirated, put a splint on her leg to immobilize it, and gave her a pain medication.

Kelley was out of school 61 days during that year. We decided to plan on nothing more than day trips, for our summer vacation. Susan and David were still doing paper routes. Kelley decided it was one thing to try to continue with an arm in a splint, but on crutches, she had to admit, it was silly to try. We had numerous appointments, in the city, during the summer, and we were making plans for the fall. The older girls were going to high school. The time was right for me to go back to school, at least part-time. I left Real Estate, because with the mortgage rates so high, it was difficult to put anyone into a house, and the company, with which I was associated, closed their doors.

What she lacked in physical ability, Kelley made up for in patience and acceptance. One evening Bob and I were standing in the doorway to the den

90

chatting, when I noticed what Kelley was doing. I motioned to him to watch her. She was completely unaware of us, being deeply engrossed in the television and a needle and thread. The needle was already threaded, and she was trying to tie a knot in the end of the thread, so she could commence sewing. She spent at least five minutes, and eight or more tries, before the combination of fingers and teeth put the knot in the thread. There was no apparent frustration or thought of giving up the project. She was making a purse to match the jumper dress Susan had made for her. She didn't come running to anyone for help. She had become accustomed to working on something until she accomplished it.

I thought about the saying, "Winners never quit, and quitters never win," and I knew that, no matter what Kelley was to face in life, she was going to emerge a winner!

A report sent from the junior high to the high school in September 1978 read in part, "Kelley is a plucky young lady with a positive outlook on life. She is a well-nurtured individual, and in turn is caring of others. She is gregarious and popular and works extremely well in groups. She is reliable at completing assignments and volunteers in class activities."

Freshman year of high school went pretty well. Kelley had been serious about taking on the responsibility for her physical therapy. We had periodic visits to the city, as the orthopedist was concerned about a serious kyphosis of her spine, and was following it closely. Occasionally her knee bothered her. Our family had the usual amount of colds, and Kelley's cough always sounded terrible, but for the entire school year, she missed only 13 days. We didn't have much else to deal with, that year, other than our usual visits to the eye doctors (with three kids in glasses, we were among their best customers), and dentists. We were thankful that Kelley had strong teeth, but the impacted wisdom teeth were of concern.

Since I was going to school, too, the children and I all had homework to do. My children teased me because I was very conscientious about my homework. They found it hard to believe that I really always had done my homework in high school. When Bob told them that they should take an example from me, I asked him not to add to the pressure I was putting on myself.

Our home life was about as normal as any other with three teens and a seven year old. Kelley and Susan took the same school bus, but they didn't do much else together. They usually got along okay, but they had different interests. Susan's interests often took her into other people's homes, especially where there were young children. She loved little kids, and would do what ever she had to, in order to be with them. That included impressing a neighbor by cleaning her house, while leaving her own room at home a mess. She didn't spend much time in her own room, so that didn't matter to her.

Kelley was much more content to be at home. She liked to read and do different kinds of craft projects. She found comfort in knowing that others were around, but she didn't need to be interacting all the time. David liked to tease his sisters, of course! I tried to explain to them that such was the duty of a thirteen-year-old boy. He was active in sports, though, and he had his paper route, so he kept busy. Peggy had many friends in the neighborhood. She was always wanting someone to "eat over," not that she ever ate anything but a grilled cheese herself. Neither Peggy nor Kelley were big eaters, but Susan and David were programmed to be tall, so they had a need for more nourishment.

That summer, I went back to work nights, in a nursing home, to earn enough money for my college courses, with the understanding that I needed two weeks off for family vacation. It was one of the best vacations we ever had. We spent two weeks of perfect weather, having fun! No was got sick or hurt, and everyone enjoyed that camping trip tremendously!

In the fall, I was offered a job at the nursing home as a part-time Activity Director. I accepted because I was able to schedule my time around my classes. It proved to be a wonderful experience. The full time Activity Director was a super lady. I truly enjoyed working with her and the patients. The neat thing about being an Activity Director is that you are the one who provides the fun. The patients are always happy to see you.

Kelley needed her impacted wisdom teeth removed under anesthesia, in the hospital. We went to the medical center in the city in case there were any problems, being somewhat concerned about her breathing.

Before Kelley was taken to surgery, a nurse approached her with a needle and said, "This isn't going to hurt, so don't tighten your muscle."

She immediately gave Kelley her pre-op shot in her thigh, without giving her a chance to prepare. That was not the best way to approach this patient. Kelley promptly passed out.

The nurse was shocked. She looked at me wide-eyed, and asked, "What happened?"

"She fainted," I stated, thinking she should have realized that.

"Why?"

"It's the way her body reacts to shock. Doesn't usually happen if she's lying down, but she didn't get a chance to prepare."

When she was young, our local physician gave Kelley an injection one day, and left the room. I started to help her off the table, from the sitting position she had been in, and she seemed to simply let herself go into my arms. I was not prepared for this, so I wasn't able to properly hold on to her.

The next thing I knew, she was on the floor. On the way down, her leg hit a rolling stool, which in turn banged into a metal cabinet with a resounding clang. The doctor and nurse came running into the room as I knelt down by her.

"What happened?" the doctor asked.

"I guess she passed out," I said as she started to regain consciousness.

"From now on, be sure she is lying down to receive a shot," the doctor cautioned, as he checked her. No damage was done.

Another time, sitting on a chair that had a wooden arm, Kelley got a very large splinter in her thigh. She was wearing shorts. We had not been aware that particular chair was capable of giving splinters. Leave it to Kelley to discover that fact. She was pretty much at ease about it, until Bob removed the splinter. Then she passed out.

This particular day, Kelley came to and asked if she had fainted. When I told her she had, she said, "I'm sorry."

Two doctors came to see me while she was in recovery. First the oral surgeon said that the surgery went fine, and she should be okay. I smiled. Then the anesthetist said, "We weren't sure we were going to be able to go ahead with the surgery. We had some difficulty intubating her. There appears to be a tracheal stenosis. If she ever needs surgery again, you may want to have that checked out ahead of time."

I had no idea what that really meant.

Kelley was of the opinion that having four impacted wisdom teeth removed was a piece of cake! Everything is relative.

# CHAPTER ELEVEN

Kelley's sophomore year in high school was uneventful, except for the fact that she achieved a record for absences — only nine for the entire school year! Because of her personal experience, she chose the Health Occupation course. She was comfortable dealing with medical people. As part of the course, the instructor took them to a nursing home to visit with patients. Actual work would come in future years. Kelley enjoyed doing that, although she did not enjoy that particular teacher. Her grades for that year were the best she had ever achieved, which could have been because she was there most of the time.

This was also the year that Kelley took Driver's Education. Once she had her permit, she needed a lot of practice. To say I found that nerve wracking would be an understatement! I don't know how I did it. I did say many prayers. I didn't want to miss anything, and be responsible for her having an accident in which she would be hurt. Nor did I want her to be a nervous driver, so I pretended to be as relaxed as I thought my mother had been. I found myself wondering if my mother had really been all that calm, after all. Of course, I was the youngest of five, so maybe she was. I was hoping that I would feel more at ease with subsequent children, when they practiced.

Kelley's uncle, Father Jim, having learned that she was preparing to test for her license, sent a check for her to use to buy a used car. He agreed with us that it was important to help her to become as independent as possible. We were able to find the car, before she went for her license, so she was able to practice in the car in which she would actually take her test. That helped.

Summer presented a new challenge. Both Susan and Kelley obtained jobs as counselors-in-training at a camp for handicapped children. It was a much more demanding job than they had anticipated, and Kelley came home exhausted, at the end of each day. However, she stayed with it for the entire summer.

David worked as a grounds keeper at a large park, which was across the street from our house. It included a beach on a lake, tennis courts, and a ball field. The job had been offered to him by men who were on his paper route, as well as on the town park commission. David had impressed them while working as a paperboy. Many aspects of the job were perfect for an active young man who enjoyed the outdoors. The major drawback was the fact that he had three bosses, with three distinct personalities and three distinctly different ideas, as to what needed to be done, and how it needed to be done.

Our son did become a bit confused, sometimes, by their conflicting directions. We told him that it was great training for the future. If he could keep his job and his sanity with three bosses, he should be able to handle whatever supervisors he would encounter throughout his working career. He did keep the job (and his sanity) for many years, earning funds to help with his college education.

Most of my working hours were in the evening or on weekends, but when it was necessary for me to go in during the day, I took Peggy with me. It was a good experience for her, and the residents at the nursing home loved to see her.

We did not take a family vacation that summer, because we were saving for a very special one — a trip to Disney World — in the fall. Planning for the trip was fun for all. We figured out the whole cost, made a large map to hang in the kitchen, and sectioned it off into hundred dollar increments. Every time a hundred dollars was added to the fund, we filled in the space, making us that much closer. The whole family needed to be in agreement with the fact that we wouldn't go to movies as often, or send out for pizza, so we could reach our goal. We also had a "conscience bank" to which individuals had to contribute specified amounts of cash for infringements of family policies, such as being late to supper, not finishing chores, or using words like shut-up. That was the closest anyone could ever get to foul language in our home. We hoped that we taught the children something about delayed gratification, economics and geography with that project.

Before the big trip, Kelley started working part time as a nurse's aide in a nursing home, and she passed the test for her driver's license. We went to what we expected to be just another checkup with her orthopedist, only to have him tell us that the kyphosis (curve in her spine) had reached a point where he didn't dare let it go any longer. He told Kelley that if she didn't wear a brace or have surgery, she could end up being paralyzed, and in a wheelchair.

He illustrated the seriousness of the situation by showing Kelley her x-rays. It was a difficult situation to be in, but she knew that a brace was preferable to surgery, so off we went to the brace makers for her to be measured. On the way home, my mind was in overdrive. I was sure that the reality of all the ramifications had not yet set in for Kelley. I thought that it was tough enough to be very short and physically restricted in your junior year in high school. A Milwaukee Brace, that went from the back of the neck to the base of the spine, and encircled the body, would not only be very noticeable, but would pose a problem in the fashion department. Then I thought about the way the heat always bothered her, and that the doctor had said that she would need to wear the brace for about a year.

"We will buy an air conditioner," I said, as though that was somehow going to make it all seem all right.

"Will it show much?" was the first question she asked.

"Most likely we will have to buy you some new clothes to fit over it. I don't think it will show too much, but I'm sure it will take you some time to become used to it."

I was right about that. Delivery day was a rough one. Kelley had not pictured something quite as large and cumbersome. It did indeed take some time to become used to it. For the first month, she refused to sleep in it. Then the doctor told her that if she didn't start wearing it all night soon, he would have to book her for surgery. She slept in it that night.

She could no longer handle a nurse's aide job, but she managed to get transferred to the laundry room at the nursing home. We had to buy stretch pants and long tops for her. With clothes on, she looked as if she had a strange shape, but the brace itself showed only at the neck.

We planned to keep the children out of school, for the few days before Thanksgiving, so we could extend the school break for our trip. A visit to the space center would be their education for that week. It was the first time the children were in an airliner, so that in itself was quite exciting.

The only upset we had, during the entire time, was when one of the attendants, of a ride at Disney, saw the top of Kelley's brace, and didn't want to let her on that ride. I tried to tell him that she would be safer than any of us would be, with that kind of protection, but he wouldn't have it. The others went on that ride, and Kelley and I went for a walk, while I figured out what to do. We girls all had long sleeve blouses with us, because it was just a little cool when we started out in the morning. I took her blouse, from where she had wrapped it around her middle, and hung it off her by tying the sleeves together around her neck. The brace was no longer visible. She just looked like a chubby kid, and she wasn't stopped from going on any rides after that.

It was a memorable trip, a very expensive part of which was the six of us eating out all the time. On the plane trip heading homeward, I asked the kids what they wanted me to make for supper that night. They unanimously agreed, "Anything but fast food." And we had thought they could never get their fill!

Kelley went back to the nursing home to discover that her job had been given away to the nephew of the owner. Such is life! I thought it was a good idea for her to take a break from working, anyway. While she was wearing the brace, her breathing problems were more noticeable, and she was finding school harder, because she was tiring more easily.

Kelley developed a lump on her tailbone. I assumed it had something to do with the pressure from the brace, so I called her orthopedist. He said he could see us that afternoon. He was seeing patients who had scheduled appointments, but the secretary took us right in to one of the examination rooms when we arrived. The doctor was with us shortly, followed by two students.

"This is one of my star patients," he told them.

After looking at the problem area, he said, "It's a cyst, but not a good enough excuse to get rid of the brace. It is something I probably could treat, but it isn't my specialty, so I'll have another doctor look at you. He knows more about these things than I do. Come with me."

We followed him to an office, where he picked up a phone, called a colleague, and said, "I have a very special young lady here who has a problem you can handle better than I can. I'd like to send her right over for priority care."

The waiting room, in the other doctor's office, was full, but the receptionist approached us, as we walked in, and asked, "Are you the Cromptons?"

We confirmed this, and were taken right in to the doctor. We felt like royalty! The problem was solved in a relatively short time with a powerful antibiotic.

Kelley's health occupation class actually started doing some work in the nursing home, that year. Some of the requirements were difficult for her. She couldn't feel a pulse, and needed to use a stethoscope, so we bought one for her. In time, however, it became apparent that the many physical aspects of a health aide job were too demanding for Kelley. We started to think about alternatives. She had no desire to change into another program at school, even though she didn't like one of the instructors. The woman had been a psychiatric nurse before she started teaching. It appeared that she had some difficulty making the transition. She frequently asked the students how they felt about personal issues. Kelley complained to me that the woman was trying to get in her head. She asked Kelley how often she and Susan fought, and when Kelley said they didn't, the woman found Susan and asked her. She told them it was not normal for them not to fight. I told the girls to ignore her. Easier said than done!

I heard the door slam. When I went to investigate, I saw Kelley's books tossed on the kitchen table. Susan then came in from school, and explained that Kelley was very upset, because of this teacher. Then, I heard the vacuum cleaner running in Kelley's room. I stood outside her room for a few minutes, and heard her yelling things like, "She can't do that to me."

I decided to leave her alone for a while, so she could blow off some steam. At least she was using her anger constructively and getting her room cleaned. I knocked on the door when the vacuum stopped humming.

"Come in," she said hoarsely. I could see she had been crying.

"She's getting to you, huh?" I asked.

"It's not fair!" she exclaimed, "She's supposed to be teaching us, not psychoanalyzing us!"

"What do you mean?" I asked.

"She wants us to write a diary, for her to see, and she wants to discuss our feelings with us. I don't want to tell her how I feel! I don't even like her!"

I sat down and calmly said, "Honey, you don't have to. You don't ever have to tell anyone anything you don't want them to know," I paused to let that sink in, and then said, "No one can get into your head. It is none of her business, and she shouldn't be practicing amateur shrink on students. I don't think you can change her, though, because she thinks she is helping. So just make up something simple to get her off your back. How could she know for sure? I think it's best to share your inner thoughts with someone you can trust."

We discussed the problem for a while longer. That situation did improve somewhat, and Kelley finished the year with only 15 days absent, and no inpatient hospitalizations. She also put herself on a diet that spring, because her orthopedist suggested a little less weight would be beneficial for her spine.

By summer, Kelley had made so much progress from wearing the brace that the doctor said she could discontinue wearing it during the day, but continue for 12 hours every night. Liberation! She could wear her favorite clothes again, and be much more comfortable. As soon as school was out, she set out to find herself a job. It was a long, and often discouraging search. I did wonder if the fact that she was only 4'7½" tall was causing potential employers to think her incapable. The day finally arrived when she burst into the house, bubbling with joy about the job she had found.

"I guess your height wasn't a problem, after all," I said.

She responded laughing, "You should see the woman who hired me. She's not much bigger than I am!"

Kelley worked as a homemaker for an elderly lady, not far from our home, for four hours a day. Although the lady's daughter was sometimes there, she was not well, and they really needed someone they could rely on to be there daily. They became very fond of Kelley. They told the agency that they loved her positive attitude, and wanted her to continue on the job in September. The school Kelley attended allowed seniors to take co-op jobs, and they were willing to let her do the homemaker job, because it was closely related to the health occupation course. The only catch was that she was supposed to work one week, and be in classes the next. I suggested that I could fill in for her weeks she was in school, if that was agreeable with everyone. It was my last year of part time classes (four years to get an associate degree), and I had left the nursing home, when there was a change in administration, so I had the time.

It worked out well all around. I covered for Kelley when she had a cold or a hospitalization, and she worked when she didn't have to be in school. It was a pleasant job. The people in that family were so nice, it felt more like visiting friends daily, rather than going to work.

As time went by, Kelley was becoming tired more easily, as well as more upset with that teacher. I decided to become involved when Kelley told me that her thoughts about going to college were being negated by the woman. She really put her down, saying that Kelley should forget the idea, because she was not college material. I saw red! It was time for me to visit. The teacher was very defensive, and claimed that she was just trying to motivate Kelley. I informed her that it was her job to teach Kelley what she needed to know in order to graduate from High School, and our job to help her decided if she wanted to go to college. I argued that I thought Kelley had enough negative incidents in her life without having a teacher add to it. I resisted telling her what I thought about her attempts to psychoanalyze her students. I thought if I pushed too far, it would backfire.

Kelley succeeded in losing weight, but her breathing was sounding very labored, and she started taking naps every afternoon, in addition to sleeping ten hours a night. By October, she was able to discontinue wearing the brace completely. That was great news! Then a new problem surfaced.

Kelley started to regurgitate part of her meals, sometimes right after eating, and sometimes hours later. It happened with no warning. She also experienced some intestinal pain. I thought we would be able to get the problem taken care of locally, so we saw a doctor, and Kelley had an upper GI series done. It was decided that she had a duodenal ulcer, and medication was ordered. That didn't help. Kelley started walking around with a little paper cup, because she never knew when something would come up without warning. She was not eating much at all, but she gained weight. That really upset her. She knew it was not good for her spine, and she had worked very hard at losing it. She became more fatigued, and had not had a period for months. It was most discouraging.

I finally called our friend, the genetic specialist in the city. He had her admitted for a work up, and what a work up it was! Kelley was seen by hoards of doctors from just about every specialty imaginable. We were under the impression that some of the visits were just because it was a teaching hospital, and the students wanted to see a patient with ML III for themselves.

There was a noticeable improvement in her hospital room, over the last time she had been on that floor. There was more privacy. Many of the rooms that had once been private, had since been converted to accommodate two patients, but there were never any privacy curtains between the beds. It always made Kelley feel uncomfortable. We were happy to see that curtains had been added, and mentioned it to her geneticist. He laughed, and told us that he had never noticed the absence of curtains until his son became a patient. Although there were plans to build a new hospital, he took it upon himself to see to it that curtains were installed, anyway!

It was determined that Kelley did not have an ulcer, after all. She was able to discontinue the medications, which she never did think were helping. She had her first pulmonary function test, which revealed her to have a moderately severe restrictive lung disease. The pulmonary specialist suggested that Kelley's problems with fatigue resulted from a low oxygen level, due to the breathing difficulties. He ordered oxygen for her to use at home, as a supplement, especially when she exercised. She had a stationery bicycle that she used when her knee joints would allow it. She was given a hormone to get her monthly cycle back on track, and while she stopped gaining weight when she stopped the ulcer medication, she did not lose any, either. No one could figure out why she was still regurgitating. I asked if there could be some connection to having worn the brace for so long, that perhaps a nerve somewhere was being pinched. That idea was quickly dismissed. Someone there suggested that it was emotional in origin. I promptly dismissed that idea! They sent Kelley home when they ran out of tests. She was still regurgitating.

The day after she arrived home, I called the chiropractor and told him my theory. He saw her that day. He gave her some manipulations, and told her to return in two days. After the second manipulation, the regurgitation ceased, once and for all. I was a little annoyed with myself that I had not taken her there first. However, I had to realize that the fatigue and lack of monthly periods would not have been addressed as soon, if she had not had that visit to the hospital.

We had two large oxygen tanks in the house, so we would never run out of it. Kelley had a small portable tank that we filled from the large one, so she could have some mobility when using it. It did help. She found it easier to exercise, and she did not require as much sleep. She also said that she found herself to be thinking more clearly.

Weight was still a problem, in that, in order for her to keep from gaining any more, she had to severely restrict her intake. She asked her orthopedist for some exercise suggestions. He offered to write orders for a new physical therapy routine, and a light bulb went off in my head. I called our favorite physical therapist, who was now at home caring for young children, and asked her if she would be willing to work with Kelley. She was delighted, and she taught Kelley well. We really enjoyed seeing her again.

A week before Christmas, Kelley came down with another cold and was sick for weeks. She was glad she lost two pounds during that time, but was very discouraged about her inability to be as active as she had been previously. Her fears about her ability to ever hold down a full time job led to tears, but it was obvious that if she needed a two-hour nap after working for four hours, a full time job would be out of the question.

We still had many questions about ML III, but answers were not available. The condition was so rare that few people in the medical field were working on it.

Kelley was back in school for a few days after Christmas vacation, when another cold appeared. She feared she wouldn't be able to graduate, if that kept happening, so I set up a meeting with the guidance counselor at the school. He had not been aware of all she had recently gone through, and he said he understood her strong desire to graduate that year, yet he was reluctant to provide a home tutor. I could not fathom what his reasoning was, but it looked as if I was up against a brick wall.

I argued with him in my head all the way home, and then called a friend and asked her to let me sound off. Once I got that out of my system, I prayed for guidance, as I often did. Then I realized there was a way to get around it.

I wrote a letter to the counselor, thanking him for his time. I recapped all of what Kelley had just gone through. Then asked him to please reconsider providing a home tutor for her academics, so she would be away from constant exposure to germs, and be able to complete the year with her co-op job. When I sent the letter to him, I sent a copy to the director of special needs in the town. The request was approved.

Kelley was able to finish off the year of working, but before that happened, Susan had a seizure, and had to be taken to the hospital. She had a job in a florist nursery. I still hold the opinion that the chemicals, to which she was exposed at that job, were the cause of the seizures. The doctors put Susan through a series of tests, including an EEG, and they could find no reason for the seizures. She was in the hospital on our anniversary, and she directed us to get the bag out of the bottom of her closet. She had already bought us a gift!

We joked about her wanting her share of hospital time, but we were very concerned about her. She was sent home on medication, but she had one more seizure after that. The first time, it had happened at school, the second time, she was at home. We could not awaken her. Nothing worked! Bob and David carried her to the car, and we took her to the emergency room at the hospital. The staff took her clothes off, and started an IV, without so much as a flinch from her. In about ten minutes, she started to respond. Her doctor was not available, so we saw someone we did not know. After our encounter with her, we decided she was not anyone we ever did want to know. She arrived after the fact, and told us Susan had just been pretending, because she was looking for attention. She claimed if we had stood Susan up, she would not have fallen. I told her there was no way anyone could have faked this, and she insinuated I was an hysterical mother. Bob told me not to pay any attention to her. I was pleased he was with me that time!

Susan's doctor was able to get her stabilized on the medication. She took it for about six months. She did quit the job, at my insistence. She never had problems again, after discontinuing the medication, except for one time, when she was exposed to some fumes, from a chemical that was being used to exterminate insects, in an apartment building, in which she was living. Shortly after high school graduation, Susan decided to get married. We were not surprised. She wanted nothing more in life than to become a mother.

I went with Kelley to the state rehabilitation commission to see if there were any services available to her, since she was disabled. They had her fill out an application, and she was assigned to a counselor. Kelley tried to work with her. I tried to work with her. We both became frustrated.

After a Vocational Evaluation, which required days of testing, suggestions were made that were laughable. Actually, it was pretty sad, considering state taxes were paying for these services. They wanted Kelley to work as anything from a proofreader (after saying she should consider a job working with people) to a bus driver, despite the fact that she had crippling of her joints and severe breathing problems.

When Kelley told the counselor that she wanted to go to college, she received a negative response. Since they appeared to be unwilling to help her work toward becoming a counselor, we looked into alternative courses. We found one at a junior college that would qualify her to be a travel agent. It appeared to us that it would be something attainable, and perhaps they would approve, since only six courses were required for the certificate. It seemed as if it would be a job that would not be physically demanding, and one she could, most likely, do part time. This particular counselor didn't agree, but didn't have any other realistic ideas. When I pinned her down for a reason, she said, "I don't like that school," and she tossed aside the literature we had given to her.

On the way home, I said to Kelley, "I think she's related to that last teacher you had who was so negative. I don't know what is wrong with some people, but never mind. We'll sign you up for one course and pay for it. When she sees that you are capable of college work, she won't be able to find any more excuses." We made our plans without her.

Before the fall semester began, Kelley had some x-rays done by yet another specialist. They showed a collapse of her tracheal walls, which were flaccid. They were supposed to be rigid. It was suspected this problem was connected with ML III, but the doctor said he could not be sure. They scheduled her for a Bronchoscopy and an EEG.

Kelley needed to be able to sleep, after we arrived at the hospital on the morning of the EEG, so she stayed awake until 2 AM. She only slept for 45 minutes for the actual test. Next we went for coffee. We checked in at the admitting office at 11 AM to give them her name. We waited. At 12:20 PM, they sent her for blood work. There was a long line ahead of us, so we visited the cafeteria for lunch. Her blood was taken at 1:15PM. Next, she needed an EKG, and then x-ray. By this time, my girl was really exhausted and hyper-excited. She started talking loudly about nothing. She was very anxious about the test scheduled for the next day, and the loss of sleep was making her zany!

It did not get any better. After x-ray, we went back to admitting. The time was 2:15 PM. They sent us to see the doctor in the ENT department, then the anesthetist, and back to admitting. At 4:15 PM, we were finally escorted to a room. Kelley was anxious to take a nap. She was so tired, I thought about carrying her.

The room was not at all what we expected. It was smoke filled! This was before hospitals instituted no-smoking policies, and the woman in that semi-private room was a chain smoker. I turned to the aide, and explained, "My daughter is being admitted because of severe breathing problems. She has restrictive lung disease!"

She didn't know what to do with us, but she found a nurse's lounge we could wait in, and she left. Kelley rolled her sweater up in a ball, put it on the table, and put her head on it. After a while, a nurse appeared and told us that all they would have was a private room, and that the present occupant was just being discharged. Of course, we had to wait for it to be cleaned. Kelley was in the private room about 5:30 PM. It was a wonderful room, the silver lining of a long and tiring day. Kelley went to sleep in the bed, and I took a nap in the comfortable wing back chair.

The results of the test the following day were that Kelley had tracheal narrowing and tracheomalacia. There were no suggestions as to what to do about it.

Kelley left the hospital with a very sore throat from the test, but we made the best of the situation by stopping on the way home to see the delightful movie "ET."

The geography course Kelley took in the fall was very interesting. It was also very extensive, and she put a lot of time into the homework. She had no trouble with the content, and passed the course. We felt that now, perhaps the counselor at the rehab would believe that she was college material.

Kelley also became involved, at that time, with a church group for young adults, which proved to be a very rewarding experience for her, for many years to come.

Another specialist did another Bronchoscopy in January 1983. This one was a surgeon. He came up with the same diagnosis, but he also proposed a solution.

I was waiting in her room when he came to see me. He spoke quickly, and got right to the point. He said that he would need to remove her trachea and replace it, and that it should be done soon, so she would not end up needing emergency surgery, if she got into breathing difficulty. In response to my question about her prognosis, if she chose not to have it done, he painted a very grim picture. He also admitted that the surgery was so risky, she could die on the table. This was a bit much for me to accept all at once. It sounded so drastic! I had never heard of such a thing as replacing a trachea. I didn't even know that such a thing was possible.

After I thanked him, I stood looking out the window of Kelley's room at the people going about their business on the sidewalk and streets below. I wondered about the best way to tell Kelley. I knew it had to be her decision. She was almost twenty years old, and I did not want to influence her. I knew Bob would find this news very unsettling. As usual, I prayed for guidance. We had wanted answers, but we were not expecting anything so drastic.

Kelley wasn't in recovery very long, so before I had finished thinking the whole thing through, she was back in her room. I chose not to tell her, just yet, what the doctor had said, since she was still somewhat under the influence of anesthesia.

Later, when her geneticist came to see us, Kelley was resting, so I went in the hall to talk to him. I related my conversation with the surgeon, and he said that he agreed that a replacement of her trachea did sound drastic. His advice was that we should wait to see if the problem progressed. That was good to hear. He was always conservative in his treatment, and his level head was very much appreciated by me that day.

I told Kelley of these conversations after she was home from the hospital. I also told her that her father and I would honor whatever decision she made. She chose to wait. Whew!

Right after this, I followed up on something I had read about regarding food intolerance and arthritis. I reasoned that if people with arthritis could derive some relief from swelling by staying away from foods that their bodies could not tolerate, perhaps there would be some benefit for Kelley by trying the same. I did some research and discovered that there were many other symptoms, from which people suffered, because of an inability to process some foods. The reason given was that there was a lack of some enzymes. Now it made even more sense to me, because ML III involved missing enzymes. I asked Kelley if she wanted to try an elimination diet to see if it made any difference. She was game.

After the trial and error process, Kelley said she noticed a difference when she stayed away from dairy products and wheat in any form. After a time, she tried wheat again without telling me. Later she did tell me, saying, "I'm never going to do that again. It had a definite effect on my breathing. Just walking up the stairs was like it used to be before I started on this diet!"

We were both surprised. We were looking for joint improvement, which she did receive. The improvement in breathing was a real bonus! She wasn't hungry on the diet, but she lost weight. That was another bonus.

We found a lab that did a complete testing on blood samples for food allergy and intolerance, so she learned which other foods to avoid, also. Kelley said that staying away from the offending foods was a small price to pay to feel better.

We had not found a cure, but the longer she stayed away from the offending foods, the better she felt. She was able to stop using the oxygen. We kept it in the house for a while, though, just in case! She still had a problem trachea, but she was not becoming swollen like she had been, so her oxygen supply was sufficient.

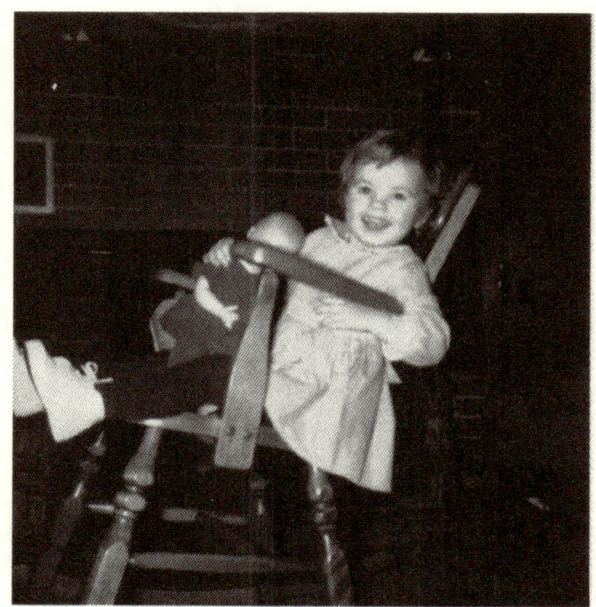

**Kelley Christmas 1965**

**Age 2 ½**

**Kelley in traction 1968—age 4**

**Above: David, Susan and Kelley**

**Christmas Photo 1968**

**Below: Clowning Around!**

Kelley's First Day of School

September 1969

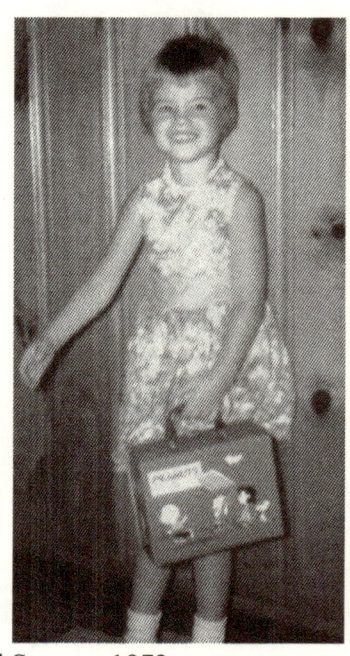

David, Kelley, Peggy and Susan—1972

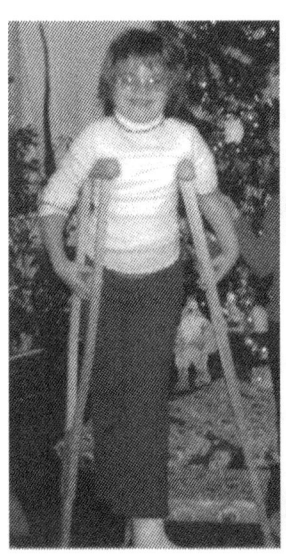

1977 After foot surgery    High School Graduation—1982

June 1987                Kelley's 24th Birthday July 1987

Kelley while hiking in July 1988

The "toilet trained" STAR

1989—Kelley visiting with her uncle, Father Jim

Christmas time 1995
Kelley and Peggy in back of
David and Linda with Paul, Bryan and Emily

October 1998
Aunt Hilary, Kelley, Aunt Mary Lou and Kelley's Mom

Kelley and her Dad on
Vacation 2001

Kelley

Crompton

The
Journey
Continues

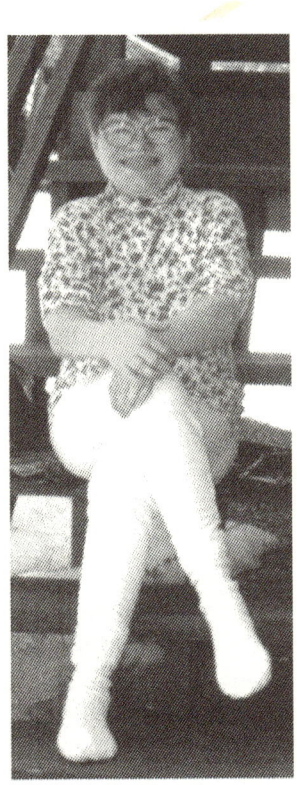

# CHAPTER TWELVE

The rehab counselor continued to give Kelley grief. I wanted to stay out of it, but the day Kelley cried after speaking to her on the phone, I became involved. Kelley spoke up to her, and she chastised Kelley, saying she was going to have to "write her up." I thought if anyone needed to be written up, it was the counselor! In a meeting with her regarding Kelley's desire to get a college education, even part time, she said, "She'll be thirty by the time she finishes."

"She'll be thirty, anyway," I countered, "Wouldn't it be better to be thirty with a degree, rather than thirty without a degree?" I pointed out that Kelley had passed a college course already.

I went on to say that my husband and I were becoming fed up with an agency that was funded by our state taxes refusing to help a disabled person.

An agreement was reached that would allow Kelley to work toward an associate degree in mental health, with their help. I wondered how many people had been put down by this particular counselor, who was so superior to everyone she met. After successfully adding a few more courses to her credit, Kelley took a semester off to have another repair job on the foot that had previously bothered her. The toes had crossed over again, causing severe pain. The orthopedic surgeon said he took a lot of junk out of her joints, and he put pins in to help straighten the toes. Now that she was fully grown, the repair was expected to have a more lasting effect.

The anesthetist opted to try a spinal, in an attempt to avoid more breathing problems. Administering the spinal proved to be difficult, however, because of Kelley's abnormal spine. She still had some breathing difficulties, and said that she would not have a spinal again. She explained that it's one thing to have trouble breathing if you are sleeping and don't know it, and an entirely different thing if you are awake. She also said that listening to the hammer on her foot was pretty scary, but listening to the saw was too much!

During this hospitalization, when the volunteer came around with the activity cart, Kelley chose to try her hand at needlepoint with a kit they provided. She did a wonderful job on her first endeavor.

The cast was split, this time, so it could be easily removed, if necessary. She wore it for about six weeks. It proved to be a successful operation, with no real complications.

Kelley had another pulmonary function test done that surprised everyone. It was much better than the last one had been. It was still not up to normal standards, by any means, but much better than before.

She talked to the counselor about signing up for a few more courses, and was given an okay. When she arrived at the college, the voucher was not there. Returning home upset, she called the counselor, who informed her that it was necessary for them to have a meeting first. Kelley explained that registrations would be over in a few days, so she needed to see her right away. The response was that the counselor didn't have an opening for another week. When Kelley asked why she had not been told about this stipulation, when they had previously spoken, she was told that she should have known. Once again, Kelley hung up the phone and cried. I was glad that I was home when that happened.

Picking up my checkbook, I said, "Come on, let's go down to the college. You sign up and I'll pay. I'll deal with those people later."

There was no way I was going to deal with that woman again. I called her supervisor and asked for Kelley to be transferred to another worker. He claimed that that was an unusual request. I asserted that the attitude of the counselor, who was supposed to be helping Kelley, was hurting more than helping. I said that I hoped it was an unusual one at the rehab. I said that I thought, before taking it any further, I would give them another chance with different worker. I was willing to chock it up as a personality conflict, and let it go. He started to defend his worker, so I quickly reminded him that my husband and I were both taxpayers in that state. Therefore, we were paying his salary, and I thought it would be a good idea for him to accommodate us. He did. The next worker was better. Not a gem, but better.

Kelley did so well with her next two courses, that she went on to take two more in the summer, and four in the fall. She continued to take courses, and do an internship at a private school with special needs adolescents, fitting in her doctor appointments around her school schedule. On the physical front, her knee was still causing problems, and except for an occasional cold, her breathing problems were manageable.

Feeling much more self-assured, Kelley went about having her case transferred to a rehab in another city, where she planned to continue her education after she received her associate's degree. They were impressed with her grades, and felt that she was worth the investment. This was a very big step for her. She lived away from home that year, in an apartment just off campus, with a few other girls. She was only an hour from home, so most of her weekends were spent with us. We were delighted to watch her achieve that much independence.

Sharing an apartment with two other girls, one of whom was not at all reliable, was not the same as having her own room, though. Kelley was just a little disappointed with that part of the experiment. Since her sister, Susan, had separated from her husband, and was having trouble making ends meet, with three little girls to care for, Kelley moved in with her next. She went on with her education from there.

In the spring of 1987, Bob and I celebrated our twenty-fifth wedding anniversary. Whoever said that opposites attract, must have had us in mind. Coming from an Irish heritage, I have dark hair and eyes. I am given to verbally expressing my feelings, and readily showing affection. Of course I was attracted to a fair-haired, blue-eyed reserved man of English heritage. Bob is a man of few words, but when he speaks, his words count, and he has a most charming English wit!

We became good friends during the three years we knew each other before our marriage. We shared the same core values, such as honesty, fidelity, and keeping promises. Neither of us makes a promise quickly, simply because we take them very seriously.

We had to learn to accept some of our differences however, and work through to compromises on others. Bob's mother was the last of the big savers, and mine was the last of the big spenders. My mother was also the "queen" of the house, while his took the role of servant. My mother talked little, and my dad had a story for every occasion. With Bob's parents, she was the talker, and he was the quiet one.

By the time this anniversary arrived, we had already been through a great deal together, sharing our laughter and our pain. We knew each other's strengths and weaknesses, no longer needing discussions regarding who would do what. His strengths are my weaknesses, and vice versa. Best of all, we can make each other laugh!

To make a marriage strong, both partners must be willing to grow, and to turn to God for help. In that way, a marriage becomes stronger as life's trials present themselves.

We rejoiced with each pregnancy and birth. Parenting presents many opportunities for mistakes, and we made our share, but we sincerely put a lot of love and effort into doing the best we could. We both felt it was important for us to have a modest home, where a parent was present most of the time. This was more important than a home that two full time paychecks would provide, but would, also, necessitate the absence of both parents, at the same time. We didn't buy many things for the children. Things have a way of being broken, worn out or lost. We did give them experiences, and took them to as many places as our budget would allow.

My husband and I went on a cruise to celebrate our anniversary. It was a wonderful week, and while we were away, our children (including David's future wife, Linda) were up to something sneaky. On our return, they presented us with a large, framed photo portrait of them all, including the grandchildren. It was a complete surprise, and they were very pleased with themselves for keeping the secret.

Kelley went back into the hospital in October 1987, for arthroscopic surgery on her problem knee, four years after her last surgery. Once again, the doctor talked about taking junk out of her joint. It was worth it for her to have the surgery, because she did get some relief from this procedure. She had postponed signing up for courses because of the operation, but then she was offered a job. The idea of earning some money again was enough of a temptation for her to decide to take a year off from school.

Kelley became a full time Nanny for four children, ages one to seven, going into their home five days a week. The rest of the time, she was in Susan's home with three children, ages one to five. She was happy with this arrangement, but her breathing tubes were not.

Susan called me one day, sounding very upset, "Can you talk some sense into your daughter?" she requested.

"What's wrong?" I asked.

"Do you remember how Kelley's lips used to get blue when she went swimming?"

"Yes."

"Well, they're that way now, and she hasn't been swimming. She has a terrible cold, and she says she just needs a nap. I'm afraid if I let her take a nap, she might never get up again!"

"We'll be right there," I responded, realizing why Susan sounded so upset.

I gave Bob the details on the way to the car. Bob was always ready to go. We had become accustomed to doing so. His mother had been very ill for years, and had died the previous month. We were relieved that she did not need to suffer any more pain. We were also very concerned about his Dad, who had not only lost his partner of sixty-two years, but was not well, himself.

My mom was in her sixth year in a nursing home, suffering from Alzheimer's disease. She was no longer the person we had known, but we visited often, just in case she had a moment or two when she recognized us, or knew we were there. We spent many weekends, on what we called, our whirlwind tour. Our parents were located a good ninety minutes drive from us. We visited at two nursing homes and at Dad's house. Bob tried to do what he could to keep up the yard. Dad did have a homemaker visit, daily, to help him with meals and keep the house clean. Nevertheless, he was lonely now that his wife had died, and we went to visit often. We had our share of emergency calls during those years. It had become a part of life. We were relieved that our children were grown by the time all of this had started to happen.

By then, in 1988, David had finished college, was working, and still living at home, with plans to be married to Linda in June. Peggy was a junior in high school, and most helpful to me. I had opened a small bookshop, which specialized in self-help books. Peggy became my right hand. She usually came into the shop after school, and took care of things during the supper hour, so I could go home to have supper with Bob. At that time, the shop was only a few blocks from our home, so she was able to walk there. My shop was open until 7 PM, so I went back after supper. Sometimes she stayed with me until closing. I was operating on a shoestring, and Peggy really became my assistant manager. It was good experience for her, and I had someone that I knew I could trust, in charge, when I needed to be elsewhere. I believe it was very good for our relationship, with each other. I was able to see a side of her that I would never have seen, otherwise. She was a bright girl, and very reliable. When she found the job boring, if there were no customers in the shop and I had not left her enough busy work, she did little drawings, or wrote up funny remarks on my cardex files. I always had a good laugh when I ran into Peggy's little creations. It was fun for us to share some of the experiences we had with the customers. Working with the public can be very rewarding, humorous, and exasperating, too.

It was wise for Susan to have called us when she did, to tell us of Kelley's condition. It seemed to be that when Kelley's oxygen supply was hampered, she wasn't able to think clearly. Indeed, she was in much worse shape than she herself had realized. She just knew that she was tired, and wanted to sleep, but she was laboring to breathe. We immediately took her to the nearest hospital. They took one look at her, in the emergency room, and didn't even bother to ask her name. The nurse told me to take her to room five, and pointed the way. She came from behind the desk to meet us there, turning on the oxygen supply and grabbing the mask. By the time Kelley was on the bed, with the oxygen going, a doctor was in attendance. He asked me a few questions, and ordered an injection, which helped in a matter of minutes. Then they started doing breathing treatments. Once the x-rays were done, she was admitted to the hospital intensive care unit. Her cold turned into bronchitis, then pneumonia. The care in that hospital was wonderful, and we did not have to worry about her when we were not there.

Kelley recovered and went back to work. We had a few misgivings about her living with and working with little children, knowing how easily little children acquire colds and respiratory infections. However, we did not want to interfere with her independence, so we just talked about it ourselves, without saying anything to her. She seemed to enjoy being able to earn some money and take care of herself!

When Kelley's right hip started causing her a considerable amount of pain, her orthopedic surgeon sent her to a new orthopedic surgeon. This one specialized in hips. He wanted to do a special type of x-ray, using a dye, to get a good look at her hip joints. She put it off until July, so nothing would interfere with David's wedding.

We were all delighted that David had met Linda, and she was going to be a member of our family. Kelley and Peggy were her bridesmaids, and Susan's oldest girl, Shaunee, the flower girl. Linda's sister, Sue, was the matron-of-honor.

Everything for the wedding went as planned, and I realized that the empty nest syndrome was going to hit me, once David was really gone. Peggy was the only one living at home, and we had all those empty bedrooms. I had complained when they were not straightened up, and now they were neat all the time — and unoccupied. Bob and I started talking about selling the big house, and finding something smaller. Peggy would be off to college, before we knew it.

Two days after the wonderful wedding, Kelley was back in the hospital again, with another case of pneumonia. The time had come to mention to her that we were concerned about her constant exposure to germs, from all those children. She was in the hospital for three weeks that time, and the doctor said he would not let her leave in the hot, humid weather, unless she could go home to air-conditioning. We did not want to force her to move back home, so we bought an air-conditioner for her to take to Susan's. She was still hanging on to her decision to live there, but she did admit that the job was probably not too helpful to her breathing problems.

The test for her hips revealed severe deterioration of the right hip, and some deterioration of the left. This surgeon advised replacing the right hip with a new one. We told him about her breathing problems, and he determined that a new evaluation of her trachea should be done, before he took her into surgery.

Before that was done, she had another infection, for which medication was ordered. That was when we discovered her sensitivity to sulfa drugs. Another trip to the emergency room was necessary. Her trachea just about closed up, and she needed medication and oxygen again.

Knowing that she would need help, after her hip operation, Kelley decided to move back into our home. It was a little easier on us to have her there, although we felt badly that she had to give up her independence.

That August, the long awaited phone call came that my Mom had died. Beautiful Margaret Kelley, loved by everyone who knew her, had finally been released from the prison of a body that restricted her ability to live as the person who had always been there for others. A body where just about everything else had stopped functioning well, except her heart.

For myself, the mourning had already taken place. It had started seven years earlier, when the doctor gave us the diagnosis of Alzheimer's Disease. My nursing home experience had taught me enough to know what to expect. My sisters and I cried our tears together during that time. The tears at this time were those of relief.

Margaret loved her children, and was proud of any accomplishments any of us made. I do think that her proudest moment was when her newly ordained son said his First Mass, one snowy, February Sunday in 1961. There is a special bond between a priest and his mother. She will always be the woman in his life. She may lose him to the world, but when he goes home, it is always to her home he returns. A mother might stay close to a son who marries and raises a family, but the bond is different.

There had been many priests concelebrating my Dad's Funeral Mass, fourteen years earlier. Now, because of the closeness priests have with each other, and the closeness they usually experience with their mothers, there were even more priests at Mom's Funeral Mass. It was a glorious day at the church she had always loved, a fitting way to say good-bye to a very special lady!

In October, Kelley and I laughed when a clerk handed her a plastic hospital card at yet another hospital. She was collecting hospital cards as though it was a hobby! Presumably, the specialist she would see, at this facility, would be able to shed some more light on the situation, after he did a Bronchoscopy.

His report to the hip surgeon indicated that Kelley's trachea was deformed and softened, leaving very little air space for breathing. In addition, during breathing, the back and front walls intermittently contacted one another, essentially blocking off the airway. He also noted some deformity of the bronchial tubes to both lungs.

We had a clearer picture now, but still no idea if anything, short of radical surgery, could be done about it. At least the anesthesia department would know what they would encounter, when she went in to have the hip surgery.

The operation was scheduled for November, and the hip surgeon made an appointment for us to see a specific anesthetist, ahead of time, so all bases would be covered.

Kelley became sick, in the car, on the way into the hospital. We hadn't realized that she was coming down with a bug, at the time. We were stuck for a while in highway traffic due to construction. I suggested turning around, to go back home, but she said that since we were almost half way there, we might as well continue. If we didn't see that doctor, on that day, the surgery might get postponed. We found some plastic bags, in the car, that she used, when she needed to vomit. I felt badly for her. I thought if I was in that situation, I would want to go back home, but if she wanted to continue, I would take her. Once we were out of the stop-and-start traffic, her vomiting stopped. Then we reached the city, with traffic lights and more traffic congestion, and her stomach became upset, again. She was okay walking from the car to the building, but we had to take the elevator up to the fifth floor. We stopped on three to let someone off, and the motion of the car reaching a stop set her esophagus in motion again. There was very little left to come up, so she had a case of dry heaves at that point. Being the polite person she has always been, she apologized to the others in the elevator!

When we arrived at the anesthesia department, the secretary told us to have a seat. Kelley went to the ladies room to freshen up as best she could. A man in surgical scrubs came out to meet us, and I immediately asked him if he could get Kelley some Compazine. He looked perplexed, and I realized that I should have explained the situation first. The doctor sent his secretary to get the medication for Kelley, and took us into his office, where he had all the reports. The patient dry heaved a few times again, so I answered the questions for her.

The doctor looked very compassionately at Kelley. He seemed to be a very kind man, and genuinely concerned for her. The Compazine arrived in short order, and it was successful in getting Kelley's gastric reflexes to relax. Her ride home was much more tolerable. It turned out to be some kind of bug that lasted for a day. We were relieved about that, because once she made up her mind to the date of the surgery, she was ready.

I gave Bob a run down of our visit with the anesthetist, and we were both confident that Kelley would be having the surgery under the best circumstances possible.

Having nothing by mouth after midnight isn't too bad, if you have surgery at 8 AM. The later in the day the surgery is, the more difficult it becomes. Since something as extensive as hip replacement surgery takes a long time, and the surgeon didn't want to be tired at the start, Kelley was assured of an early OR time. She liked this idea, because she found it very difficult to go a long time without food. She was admitted the day before, for the usual tests and x-rays, as well as visits from students for a history and physical. They always asked what surgery had been done previously, and when and where, as well as any other hospitalizations and what allergies there may be to medicines. In the past, we looked at each other, trying to

121

figure it out, feeling like a couple of dunces. This time we were prepared! I had typed up a report with all the pertinent information, and made copies so we could hand one to anyone who came asking questions. They were impressed. I also had a list for the dietary department, and asked to see the dietitian the day Kelley was admitted. Everyone who saw my reports said they wished more patients thought to do as I had done. It really did make the whole process much easier.

The timing of the students' visits often coincided with the arrival of the dinner tray, which they thought was incidental, and of secondary importance to their function. Kelley was usually accommodating, but this November night, her tray was late in arriving, because she was a new admission, and had a special diet. She had just started to eat, when two students arrived on the scene. One started to move the table, which contained her dinner tray, away from her. No one was more surprised than I was, when she pulled it back, telling them that, since this was to be her last meal for a while, and she was hungry, she was going to eat it. They could examine her later.

The students stood there and looked at each other, appearing a bit dumbfounded. One shrugged, and the other said, "Okay, we'll be back in about twenty minutes."

They went off to bother someone else. Hopefully, it was someone who had finished eating. I wanted to laugh out loud!

Kelley is a very nice person, and it is easy to get along with, and to live with her. There were times that I was concerned about her being a pushover. Now it appeared that the time living away from home had been beneficial. She had learned to assert herself more.

I did not anticipate a phone call, the next day, telling me she was in recovery, until after noontime, so I was surprised to hear the doctor's secretary, on the phone, at 11 AM. I was more surprised when she told me the surgery had not yet started. Some of the blood work from the previous day had shown results that were suspect, so they drew more blood and were waiting for the results. She promised to call back as soon as she knew any more.

So much for the benefits of early surgery! I called Bob at work, so he would not be expecting to hear the surgery was done. A few hours later, the surgeon called me to say that it took so long to get the results from the blood work, they had to postpone the surgery. The blood was okay, but they never knew for sure how long this type of surgery would last, and he did not think it was wise to chance the team becoming tired. This is not the type of project that can be left, and finished up the next day.

I was glad he was being cautious, but I felt badly for Kelley, getting all prepared for something that didn't happen, and knowing she would have to go through that, again. The surgeon said I could take her home, because he did not know when they would be able to reschedule.

Peggy and I had already made an arrangement for her to take over the shop, right after school, so I called Kelley to tell her I would get there, as soon as I could. She said she had not eaten, and had a bad headache, besides feeling sick to her stomach. I told her to have a nurse get her something. When I arrived a few hours later, there was a tray with mostly foods she could not tolerate, and Kelley was vomiting.

One of the nurses had called down for a tray, but no one noticed that Kelley was on a special diet, so they sent her a regular tray. She tried a little of what she could have, but it did not settle. It came back up with gastric juices, and she vomited until she had dry heaves. Getting an order for Compazine was easier said than done. The discharge order had already been written! I told a nurse that I was not going to take a person, who was already sick to her stomach, as well as being prone to car sickness, out in rush hour traffic!

She managed to find someone to write an order for the medication. I waited until I was sure it was going to work, before we left. By then, most of the rush hour traffic was gone, and I had been able to get some Jell-O from the cafeteria for her to eat. An added benefit of Compazine was that it made her sleepy. The patient slept all the way home.

We reasoned that God had some reason for the surgery being postponed, though we could not figure what that reason was.

Late one night, a short time later, we received a call from Bob's sister, telling us that their Dad had been taken into the hospital, and was in intensive care. We were soon on our way.

Bob's brother and wife, and sister and husband were there, and we were all able to personally say good-bye to a man that we all loved. We knew he had been failing, but it still seemed unexpected. It was a blessing for him that he did not have to spend a long time in the hospital, but there were tears shed that night for a man who would be missed. We reasoned that he had simply given up since his wife had died just nine months earlier.

We were lucky to have had my father until he was seventy five, and all three other parents well into their eighties, but in nine short months, our children lost all of their remaining grandparents. It occurred to us that, although we did not feel old enough, we had now become the older generation. It was hard to believe! It was also hard for the co-workers of Bob and David to believe that they needed time off for a funeral again. It started to sound like a phony excuse.

I looked back, with gratitude, upon the relationship I had been able to have with my husband's entire family, and the great job his parents had done raising their children. I have known many people who have had problems with a spouse's family, and I felt fortunate to have been granted the joy of simply extending my family, with John and Florence Crompton, as an added set of parents.

Florence had had a difficult time, dealing with the many complications she had suffered from diabetes, and she had fought back valiantly, time after time. I remember visiting her at the hospital, after she had had a leg amputated. We thought she would be devastated, because she always said she thought that would be the worst thing that could happen to her.

Instead, she said, "I don't want you to think of me as not having a leg. I'll get a new one, and learn to use it!" She did just that!

Throughout this time, John, who was more comfortable making things in his workshop than anywhere else, learned to be a cook and a nurse.

During the years that I knew them, I was able to listen to many of Florence's stories. I came to appreciate all they accomplished, as a couple, after both having had difficult times, in their youth.

The Christmas before they died, the whole family was able to gather. All the children and grandchildren were there. I am sure we will all treasure, in our memories, the happiness of that day.

Of course, my children laughed at me when, a few days after Grandpa John's funeral I said, "Oh, my gosh, Bob! You and I are orphans now!"

It seemed as if we could see a reason for Kelley's surgery being postponed, after all. This would have been much more difficult to handle, if she had been in the hospital, recovering from surgery during that time.

# CHAPTER THIRTEEN

In the beginning of December, the surgery finally took place. That was an extremely long day. I did call the doctor's secretary before noon; to be sure Kelley had actually gone in to the OR. I called her again just before 5 PM, assuming she would leave soon. I felt that she would be my best hope of receiving any information. She called me back a few minutes later, to say that Kelley was okay, and they were just finishing up, so I would hear from the doctor within the hour.

Bob and Peggy were both at work, with me, by this time, so we did our waiting together. I had no idea why the surgery had taken that long. We were expecting it to last about five hours, not more than eight hours!

"Kelley's okay," the surgeon started, "We had to do more than anticipated. The prosthesis wouldn't have fit into her thighbone the way it was, so we had to break the bone and rotate it. Then we put in a plate and a couple of pins. If we hadn't done that, she would have had an unnatural gait. We will be keeping her in recovery over night, and you can see her there in a couple of hours. I'll tell them to expect you."

Bob and I left Peggy in charge of the shop, and stopped to eat on the way in to the hospital. I was suddenly very hungry!

A nurse met us, at the entrance to the recovery room, to give us an update. She explained that Kelley was still on the respirator because one of her lungs had collapsed, but she was doing all right.

What a sight our girl was! Besides the respirator, which is a very noisy machine, there were tubes going in and out of her all over the place, and a host of different monitors keeping track of everything. She was very swollen from the fluids they had pumped into her. It was amazing to see how different she looked, amazing that one's skin could stretch enough to accommodate all that fluid!

The nurse attending to Kelley gave us a run down of the function of some of the machines. Then the anesthetist, whom Kelley and I had met before the surgery, gave us a complete report of how she tolerated the whole procedure.

Kelley had received nine units of blood. Bone surgery, especially when they cut into a bone as they had done with her femur, causes a loss of a large amount of blood. High doses of antibiotics were being pumped into her to prevent the chance of infection. The doctor said that the collapsed lung was most likely due to a combination of her particular breathing problems, and the fact that she had been positioned on her side for so long.

I appreciated knowing all of this, and thought I had processed it. Then, while looking around the room, I noticed the x-rays of her lungs on the screen. I guess I took a deep breath and held it, as the seriousness hit me. The doctor noticed, and quickly offered me a chair. I felt rather silly, when I realized my reaction showed! He did not say anything. He simply offered the chair. I started wondering how many hours he had put in that day. Apparently he had been there through the entire surgery, and he was still there. Usually we only met the anesthetist quickly before surgery, and never saw them again until the next time. It gave me a lot of confidence to see how he was following up with her.

We stayed long enough for Kelley to realize that we were there. She was in and out of sleep. It always takes time, to wake up fully, after having anesthesia. We left feeling reassured, knowing she had the undivided attention of one nurse, for the entire night. We were told to call, in the morning, for a report.

We talked on the way home about how hard it was to see her going through so much. Mostly, we just held hands.

The morning report was that Kelley's lung had started working again, but they would transfer her to the surgical intensive care unit, because she was still on the respirator. I was told to call that unit around noon.

"Sic U," the nurse said, answering the phone. I quickly realized that was an abbreviation for Surgical Intensive Care Unit, but I wanted to tell her that I wasn't the one who was sick. I imagine she had heard that response before.

Kelley had a wonderful primary nurse in SICU. She was very receptive to a mom who was helpful. I managed to find a few people to help me, at the shop, during the hours Peggy was in school, so I could spend most of my time at the hospital. I learned what the different beeps of the various machines meant, so I would know when to call the nurse. Kelley's breathing was a major concern, and the anesthetist checked on her frequently. Bob and I were both there, when he came in with some other doctors, and said he thought it was time to try Kelley off the respirator. I volunteered that we would wait in another area. If they ran into any trouble, we would have been in the way. They probably would have asked us to leave, anyway.

The anesthetist came to find us, a short time later, to tell us that Kelley was breathing on her own. He smiled and reassured us that they would keep a very close watch on her. She could be put back on the respirator if necessary.

Kelley was very lethargic, for many days, and was not taking anything by mouth, except ice chips. She was given strong pain medication. I was pleasantly surprised when she told me that she wanted coffee. Margaret, the nurse, and I laughed, and she said, "If coffee is what she wants, coffee is what she will get."

I gave her just a tiny medicine cup worth at a time, which she took in sips. After she had three or four, over a period of a half hour or so, she started to brighten.

"That's it," I said, "from now on, I think they should give her coffee in her IV, right after surgery!"

When Kelley was able to eat, I discussed with the nurse what foods she could have. She said they could order it from the kitchen, but she didn't know how soon it would arrive. I told her I would be glad to get it at the cafeteria. That was when she showed me how to go to the cafeteria and get back in, through the back door, so I wouldn't have to buzz, from the front door, and wait for someone to let me in. From then on, I used the back door. No one complained.

The surgeon checked on his patient often, and said he was sure her hip would be in very good shape, but he was going to have to put her in a cast, before letting her get out of bed. Even with the plate in her leg, it would need extra care, until it started to knit. This hospitalization would be longer than we had anticipated.

When I did need to leave Kelley, I felt confident about her care. I called at night before going to bed, and again when I got up in the morning. Everyone I spoke to was cordial and accommodating. They also went into her room to tell her I called.

After a few times, of some very anxious moments with her breathing problems, when her oxygen level would plummet, the staff came up with the right combination of medicine to give her, in order to open her airway again. Then she could breathe more easily. Her trachea kept swelling. It did so slowly. She could feel this happening before it registered on the machine. The nurse asked Kelley to let her know before it got severe, and she gave her the medicine. That worked like a charm! The treatment was needed every three or four hours. Kelley never showed any signs of panic. She was confident of getting the help she needed by simply saying, "I'm having trouble breathing again."

Bob and I were with her, in SICU on Sunday, when we were told she was to be moved down to the orthopedic floor. That was surprising! We didn't know she was doing that well, but did not question the decision, assuming they were prepared for her arrival on orthopedics.

The transfer was a major production. A trip around the world might have been easier. They transported her, and her bed, and an enormous amount of equipment, all piled on top of the bed, or pushed by an attendant. They went through a few sets of double doors, down a hallway, and onto an elevator. This elevator was in the new building, so it was large enough and smooth enough in operation as to not cause any problems. However, they managed to bang the whole bed into a wall a few times. It looked as if they didn't know there was a patient in the bed. Upon leaving this elevator, they proceeded down a short corridor and up a ramp, which led into the old building, where the orthopedic floor was located. Then, there was another elevator ride, on an old and small one. We could not fit her bed, equipment, two attendants and us on that elevator. One of the attendants took the stairs with us to meet her at the destination. There was no other way to do it. It was one of those "you can't get there from here" situations.

We arrived just before the elevator door opened to reveal a very shaken Kelley. She was jounced by the elevator, and further jounced exiting it. It had not come to rest at the same level as the floor, so the bed had to be coaxed a bit. By the time they got her settled in the new location, she was exhausted. Kelley had been taken from a relatively quite, uncomplicated routine atmosphere, and catapulted into a tilt-a-whirl ride at the carnival!

David and Linda paid a visit, but didn't stay long, when they saw how tired she was.

The oxygen level monitor was set up next to her bed, in a private room. It could not be heard in the hall. That disturbed us. The nurse's station was down the hall, and around the corner. I thought it would be necessary for me to stay all night, so someone could alert the staff if Kelley had any difficulty. When the evening shift came on, Bob and I discussed the fact that it appeared there was not enough coverage to handle someone with a severe breathing problem, in addition to an orthopedic concern.

Kelley was resting as we stood in the doorway, when the monitor started to beep. I went to her side to see if the sensor on her finger needed to be repositioned. Kelley opened her eyes and said, "Oh, you're here. I thought you left."

"We were just over by the door, so you could rest," I explained, "I'm going to try this sensor on a different finger."

"I am starting to have some trouble breathing," she said, "I think I'll need some medication soon."

I put on the signal for the nurse and talked to Kelley while we waited. Bob stood in the doorway watching for a nurse. Ten minutes passed. Twenty minutes passed. The oxygen level dropped a little more, and Kelley told me she felt her breathing getting worse. I went to look for a nurse. When I found one in another room, I asked her if she would get Kelley her medication for her breathing.

She was able to leave the patient she was attending, so she went into Kelley's room, with me behind her. She looked at the monitor and said it wasn't too bad. I explained that, although it wasn't yet, it would be if Kelley did not get the medication soon. She said she would get it, and left. A few minutes later, she returned to ask me what medication I was talking about. There was only an order for pain medication.

"You mean she didn't come down with the same orders she had in SICU?" I asked.

She nodded.

"Please get an order soon, before Kelley gets into serious trouble," I requested.

I tried to comfort Kelley while we waited; telling her help was on the way. She was starting to become anxious, and couldn't understand why she was not getting the medicine she needed. I was feeling pretty anxious, too. Bob was pacing by the door, looking for the nurse to return.

Then a doctor showed up — a Sunday evening resident! I described in detail what her condition was, and exactly the medication necessary. He checked the monitor, and rather offhandedly said the level was not that bad yet. I didn't want to say more in front of Kelley, so I went toward the door, and rolled my eyes at Bob. The doctor followed, and I turned around and said firmly, "She *knows* when she's getting into trouble. She can *feel* her trachea swelling. I'd like to keep this from becoming an emergency. She needs that medication. *Please get it!*" I had remained calm and quiet, but I was feeling very annoyed. I felt like telling him that I had run into arrogant residents before, who didn't know as much as they thought they did, but I decided that alienating him wouldn't accomplish anything. Nevertheless, I was not going to give up my mission. I knew how serious her condition was.

"The nurses will keep an eye on her," he said.

I took a deep breath, then explained that we had previously waited twenty minutes for a nurse, and I had to go looking for her, "Besides, they can't even hear that monitor from the corridor," I said, and just about pleaded for the medication.

Once again, the man ignored my request, so I walked down to the nurse's station and *ordered* the nurse to call the evening supervisor for me *immediately!*

Apparently, she understood, because she picked up the phone and paged the supervisor, STAT!

I went back to Kelley's bed. The oxygen level continued to drop, and Bob was trying to tell her to hang on, because help was on the way. He and I exchanged glances of fear and frustration.

When the supervisor appeared at the door, I rushed to meet her. I informed her that they were not equipped to take care of Kelley on that floor, and I insisted she be transferred back to SICU, where they knew what to do for her. I pointed out that having her hip replaced was not going to do her any good, if she stopped breathing!

This woman was very professional. One does not become a supervisor until after many years of experience. She said she would get right on it.

I went to find Bob. He had walked down the hall, and was pacing near the nurse's station. He said that he had to get away, before he said something to her that he would later regret. I was praying for divine intervention, when I saw the resident heading back toward Kelley's room. As I turned to follow him, the supervisor approached us, and said they would be moving Kelley back to SICU. I thanked her, and asked her about getting the medication. As we were talking, the anesthetist we knew arrived at the nurse's station. His back was toward us, and I didn't notice him until I heard a nurse say to him, "You know Kelley Crompton, don't you?"

"Yes," he replied, "is something wrong?"

"She's having trouble — in 314."

He headed down the hall, not knowing we were right behind him. He approached Kelley and the resident, who was then playing with the sensor, and sized up the situation quickly. He told the resident to get her the exact dosage of the exact medication that I had been saying she needed. The resident did not make eye contact with me on his way out of the room.

The anesthetist started to speak very softly and slowly to Kelley, telling her that he knew she was having trouble breathing, but that she should just listen to him, and try to breathe as slowly and deeply as she could. He told her that the medication would be there shortly, and she would be back in SICU, as soon as she was able to travel. He continued to talk to her, even after she received the medication. He stayed right with her until it took effect, and she was relaxed. I don't know when he realized that we were in the room, but when he was sure she was out of danger, he turned around to reassure us. My eyes were watery by then. I wanted to hug him. All I could do was to say, "Thank you," somewhat hoarsely.

He started to walk toward the door, saying that she would be okay now, and he would have her moved back to SICU. As we walked with him, I told him I had just talked to a supervisor about that. Once we were out of Kelley's hearing range, he said, "I didn't know they had moved her down here. Someone must have thought she was doing better than she was. It was close. They were paging anesthesia, because they wanted someone to do an emergency tracheotomy."

A feeling of alarm showed in my face.

He smiled as he said, "Don't worry. Everyone in Anesthesiology, in this hospital, knows Kelley. None of them would have done that!" He went on to explain that he was at the nurse's station, because he was going to see a few people, who were scheduled for surgery, the next day. I told him that I was certainly very relieved, when I saw him.

With her breathing stable, Kelley was able to take some food and fluid before taking the trip back to SICU. When they took her to the elevator, we told her we would meet her up there, and we took our own route back. As we walked along a corridor, we passed a nurse's station where a number of staff members were sitting at various desks, doing paper work. There was a young man in a lab coat swinging a chart around, and almost yelling, "Doesn't anyone here know anything about this patient?"

The others were all ignoring him. Bob and I looked at each other and burst into laughter. I don't think it would have struck us so funny at any other time, but with having just shared a very tense situation, it was a welcome release from the stress.

Margaret was waiting for Kelley at SICU. We went for a bite to eat, after getting her settled in, and for a refreshing walk, on the city streets, in the cold night air. I think that was when my breathing returned to normal. After calling home, to tell Peggy that we would be later than we thought, we went back to SICU, to be with Kelley, until she was ready for sleep. Margaret told us not to worry, as Fred would be taking care of Kelley, when she went home, and he had been with her, at night, all along.

I leaned my weary head back against the wall in the elevator as it descended, "I'll be able to sleep well tonight, knowing Margaret and Fred are taking care of her," I sighed. My mom and dad were Margaret and Fred!

The hip surgeon stopped in the next day. He looked squarely at me, as he approached my position next to Kelley's bed, shook his head and said, "That will never happen, again. She will not leave this unit again, without *my* order!" He was very serious!

"It was quite an afternoon," I said, smiling, "I can't tell you how happy we were, when we saw a doctor we knew!"

"I heard all about it," he responded, before turning his attention to Kelley's drainage tubes, dressings and traction.

I imagined that many of the hospital workers had heard all about it. I remembered, from working in a hospital, how quickly some stories got around. I wondered when they were going to start teaching residents that sometimes patients and their parents know what they are talking about!

"You saved her life yesterday!" I exclaimed gratefully to the anesthetist, when he visited.

"No, Kelley did," he humbly answered, walking over to her, "You did it all. You stayed calm and followed my directions. You can be proud of that."

Before leaving, he told us that there was a doctor, at another hospital, in that same city, who specialized in problems involving the trachea. He

131

suggested Kelley might want to see him, once she recovered from this surgery. We thanked him, and wondered why no one else had ever mentioned this doctor to us. Surely, the others we had seen must have known about him!

The next time Kelley was transferred to the orthopedic floor, she was in much better shape. Most of the post-op swelling had subsided; she was eating fairly well, and was no longer on the strong pain medication. Her right leg was still suspended in traction, but the drainage tubes had been removed. The pressure stockings that she found annoying were still being used on her legs. They were plastic balloon type affairs that were attached, by tubes, to a machine, that intermittently inflated and deflated them, to assist the circulation and prevent blood clots. She wasn't allowed to get out of bed until a cast was in place. I don't know if it was by design or not, but this time Kelley's room was right next to the nurse's station. The staff on duty, at that time, really seemed to understand and appreciate Kelley. She never made demands, and always asked for help with a most polite manner. No matter how sick she has ever been, her personality has never altered at all. The nurses seemed happy to do the extra things for her, like washing her hair and hanging up greeting cards around her room. Sometimes, one would just visit with her for a while. That made this part of her recovery much easier.

December is not the best month to visit the hospital in the city. Traffic gets heavier with people Christmas shopping. Unpredictable weather is an added nuisance. However, in spite of these deterrents, I did manage to make the trip there every day. As Kelley continued to improve, sometimes another family member went to visit her early, and Bob and I went in the evening. I knew a few ways to get into the hospital, after hours, when the main entrance was locked, and the nurses on that floor treated me as if I belonged there. To my way of thinking, I did!

The anesthetist continued to visit Kelley, after she was moved. During one of his visits, we learned that he would not have been the one attending her, if the surgery had been done in November. He had left a detailed report for the doctor who would have attended her, because it was necessary for him to be out of town. Now we knew another reason the surgery had been postponed. We talked about God's timing. We might not have ever learned about the doctor, who was a trachea specialist, if she had not had this particular doctor. It was unusual to become so well acquainted with an anesthetist. I have the highest regard for anyone who dares to engage in such a tricky situation involving other people's lives. This particular soft-spoken, humble man is truly one of the medical profession's finest!

We were anxious for the cast to be put on, so Kelley would be able to get up and around, and home for Christmas. Finally, one day, I entered her room to hear the words, "Wait 'til you see this thing."

None of us had thought about how large it would be. It was so wide and long, that she was restricted to either lying down or standing. No way to sit in it! It went all around her middle, from just under her breast, almost to her tailbone, and on the right side, it continued all the way down her leg. Obviously, she would need a great deal of help, when she got home. It would not be safe to leave her alone in a contraption that would so limit her mobility. Peggy was due for school vacation, but that would not last as long as the cast would. We thought about getting a part time home health aide to cover the time I was at work, and Peggy was in school.

"I'll need my crutches, when you come in tomorrow, so I can start to get up," Kelley told me. She had been doing some exercises in bed, under the direction of a physical therapist, all along. She would be able to stand up, once the cast was dry.

Her bed was very wet, when I arrived with the crutches, the next day. She had asked someone to change it. They said sure, but it hadn't been done. The cast, during the process of drying out, kept getting the bed wet. I looked around for a nurse, to no avail, so I found clean linen and went into Kelley's room and closed the door. I had just about finished the job, when we heard a quick rap at the door.

"Come in," we said in unison.

Her surgeon opened the door, took a few steps into the room, and stopped. Head tilting slightly to one side, he frowned as he asked me, "What are you doing?"

"I changed the bed," was my matter-of-fact answer.

"But, why?"

"Because it was wet. From the cast," I thought he would have known that.

"What I mean," he patiently explained, "is, why didn't a nurse make the bed?"

"Oh, I don't know," I replied, "They're all busy. No reason why I can't do it. She's comfortable now." I gathered the dirty linen and headed down the hall, thinking that *I was her nurse!*

The good news he gave Kelley was that she could go home, after a few days of walking around on the crutches. We discussed our plans with him, about her care at home. It looked as if she would make it for Christmas, after all. That would make life much easier for all of us. I measured her in the cast, and measured the back of my car, with the back seat folded down, planning to get her in through the hatchback for the trip home.

Before going in the following day, I bought a large foam wedge that would help her to be in a position resembling what could be done with a hospital bed. She could not sit up, but could have her head elevated, which was a better position for her breathing. When I arrived at the hospital, I found Kelley with tears in her eyes, and quivering lips.

"I'm not going to make it home for Christmas," she sort of squeaked.

"Who said?" I asked, bewildered.

"The physical therapist."

"The physical therapist?" I was incredulous.

"Yeah. She tried to get me up today, and I was too scared, so she said if I didn't get up today, I wasn't going to be home for Christmas!"

"You know, I used to think physical therapists were patient people, because it takes so long, sometimes, to see progress," I responded, "but some of them aren't very patient at all, are they? Don't you let her intimidate you! I'll get you up later. We'll show the nurses and ask them to chart it."

"But, I really am afraid to get up," she admitted.

"Of course you are!" I declared, "I would be, too! That cast is big and bulky, and you haven't been out of bed in weeks. Anyone would be scared. She just hasn't looked at it from your angle. Wait until after supper. You'll feel stronger then."

Sometimes, you have to take matters into your own hands.

After supper, I picked up the crutches and went around to the left side of the bed.

"Why are you over there?" Kelley asked.

"To help you get out of bed. We can take our time. Don't worry. I won't push you."

"She was going to get me up from this side," Kelley indicated with her right hand.

"That's crazy!" I exclaimed, "You can't even bend that leg. No wonder she scared you. Where on earth was she trained?"

I raised the bed a bit, so she could easily slide off the edge, rather than go down, and pull back up again. The first thing I wanted her to do was simply to stand, with me holding her, then go back. She kept saying she was scared, and I kept telling her it was okay, but I would not let her go. I also compared her size to her brother's, and admitted I would never attempt such a task with him, but I knew I could support her.

When that went well, we did it with my support and one crutch. I continued to reassure her, as we progressed to two crutches, promising I would let go, only when she gave the word. Once she had her bearings, she said I could let go. After she stood for a moment, I told her it was time to rest. We exchanged smiles of satisfaction.

The next time up, she needed little assist. Then she took a few steps. Back to bed again. We kept progressing, watching television in between the attempts. Finally, she stood up and walked to the door, with only minor help. I opened the door, and Kelley walked out into the hall, on her own, using the crutches. One of the nurses was at the desk with her back to us, so Kelley said a real perky, "Hi!"

The nurse jumped, turned and exclaimed, "Oh, Kelley! You're up!"

She went down the hall to round up a few other nurses. They appeared and cheered. I asked them to chart the event.

Now that she knew how to do it, Kelley gave directions to the physical therapist, the next day, as to how she would get out of bed.

The surgeon was pleased with Kelley's progress, and scheduled her to leave the hospital two days before Christmas. She took it upon herself to speak to social services about finding a home health aide, for four hours daily, as soon as possible. We knew we could make it through ten days or so, between family and friends, if there wasn't one available, on such short notice.

The day preceding release day, Kelley called me at work. She was very upset. The physical therapist was now saying Kelley had to have a hospital bed at home, so she called to have one delivered, and she wanted someone to be there to receive it. She also claimed that she needed verification that Kelley had a home health aide, or Kelley would not be able to leave the hospital. What next?

I called the hospital and paged the physical therapist. I did not tell her to take a flying leap, although that is what I wanted to do. I did tell her that I would not accept a hospital bed into my home, that I could adequately take care of Kelley's bedding needs, and I wanted her to call the supplier back and tell them not to deliver the thing. I advised her that we had learned years before, that the sooner Kelley returned to as normal a routine as possible, the better her recovery would go. One doesn't get dressed every morning in street clothes to sit around on a hospital bed.

When it was apparent to the physical therapist that she lost that round, she tried another tact, saying that she was very concerned that I was going to go out to work and leave Kelley home, alone. I enlightened her to the fact that she did not know what she was talking about, but I was going to take Kelley home the next day, and I wanted her to back off. I called Kelley back and told her not to worry.

The next day, I went to the hospital and helped Kelley get ready to leave. A nurse came in and told us that Kelley's doctor was in surgery, but he wanted to meet with us before we left. She asked us to wait.

In response to my questioning, she said that she didn't know what it was all about, but she thought it had something to do with the physical therapist. My grimace prompted her to volunteer that the woman in question had been driving everyone nuts, on that floor. She said that her rotation, onto that floor, was going to end in a week, and they were all counting the days. It was nice to know we weren't the only ones having a problem with her. Different nurses visited with us while we waited. Finally, one came in with the report that the good doctor was out of surgery.

About twenty minutes later, he appeared in Kelley's room with the physical therapist. Almost every other nurse on the floor trickled in after them. It all seemed so strange to me. I was completely in the dark as to the reason for this big meeting. The surgeon did not seem to acknowledge anyone else in the room except Kelley and me. He started by asking Kelley how she was feeling. Then he went on to solemnly ask me a few questions.

Did I think we needed a hospital bed at home?

"No."

Was I planning to leave Kelley at home alone?

"No."

He nodded to each of my answers, as though he really knew what they would be. I looked only at him when I spoke.

Next, he asked, "Would you like to leave now?"

I grinned as I gave him my affirmative answer. I had just caught on to the game! As he told us good-bye and Merry Christmas, I looked around the room to see smiles on all of the faces, except one. I wondered if she received the message from this little exercise. She certainly was presumptuous, to be questioning the decisions the surgeon had already made. In discussing the situation on the way home, Kelley and I laughed. We decided that the extra time we had spent, waiting for the doctor, was worth it.

Our observations, by that time, had led us to the conclusions that, usually, the experienced medical people were the most humble and willing to listen to us. Then there were those, like this physical therapist, and a few of the residents we had met, who were so impressed with their own importance, they thought everyone else possessed limited knowledge and/or intelligence. I can appreciate the many hours of schooling they had. Clearly, I did not know many of the things they did, but they did not seem to understand how well I knew this particular patient. Throughout the years, it has always been the experienced ones who have made remarks to us like,

"You know more about this disorder than I do," or, "Tell me, just what is ML III, and how does it affect you?"

We had also observed that this particular hip surgeon was a perfectionist, and agreed that it was a wonderful trait for a surgeon to have. God kept leading us to the right people for Kelley to get the help she needed.

We were never big on attaching great significance to New Year's Eve or New Year's Day, but after the way 1988 had gone for us, we were ready to celebrate the dawning of 1989!

# CHAPTER FOURTEEN

Social services did find a home health aide for Kelley. She arrived there each day in time for me to leave for work in the morning, and stayed until Peggy was home from school. She was a young woman, and she provided companionship for Kelley.

After being at home for a little while, Kelley was able to do many things for herself, but she still needed help maneuvering from a lying down position to standing, and she still needed the bedpan. She disliked that aspect, so she devised a solution one day, after which she happily announced that she was potty trained! Using her good leg, and leaning on the counter, that was right next to the toilet, she lowered herself down to a half-sitting, half-reclining position. It looked very strange, but it worked, and it did wonders for her morale. Once that was accomplished, she adopted a chair that we had in the kitchen that worked like a step stool and had a high seat. We had also used it, at times, pulled up to the table as a high chair, for a grandchild. Because the seat was so high, Kelley could perch on it, or at least half perch on it. Then she was able to eat meals with us, at the table.

Clothes presented a problem, while Kelley was wearing the cast. Jeans simply wouldn't fit, but we discovered that a few pair of her old tights would stretch enough to go over the right side of her, while the left leg could be covered in a normal way. By wearing large, long shirts over them, she was properly dressed and feeling as normal as possible, under the circumstances.

A loss of weight, adding to a loss of muscle tone, resulted in the cast chafing her somewhat delicate skin. That required constant care with alcohol rubs all around the edges, and a frequent reapplication of moleskin to the edges of the cast to keep it as soft as possible. After a few months, I could fit my hand down inside the cast.

Messages had been mixed up, at the hospital, on the day Kelley was due to have the cast removed. All of the people, who could do the job, were in surgery for most of the day. We arrived there early, as we had been told to do. Yet, we had nothing to do but wait around, while reading our books. It was a very difficult day for the patient, and she was exhausted when we returned home, but not too exhausted to head straight for the shower.

Now, she faced the challenge of strenuous exercises, under the guidance of a visiting physical therapist. Kelley worked diligently at her rehabilitation, surprising the physical therapist by progressing very quickly.

However, she was told that she must still use the crutches, until after the first check up with the surgeon.

She had x-rays taken, when we arrived at the hospital that day, and we looked at them, before we carried them to her appointment with the surgeon.

"How did the x-rays look to you?" he asked when he greeted us. How did he know we had looked at them?

Being very pleased with her progress, he said she could eliminate one of the crutches, continue with the therapy, and visit him in another six weeks. By the time she saw him for that appointment, she was more than ready to dispense with that crutch.

The surgeon looked at me, winked and said, "I'll bet she's been walking without it now and then."

I had to confirm that she had.

"Okay, Kelley, let's see how you do walking without it," he said.

She walked for him, and told him she had reached a point where that crutch was more in the way than it was a help.

"I just didn't want you to start overdoing it," the doctor said, "You don't need it anymore."

He also told us that, normally, he would be taking the plate out of her leg, at some future date. However, with the trouble she had with anesthesia, he did not think it was important enough to take her into surgery again. We agreed.

Kelley walked out of there that day, pain free, and without a trace of a limp. I was carrying the crutch.

Following up on the advice of the anesthetist, we contacted the thoracic surgeon for a consult in the spring. A series of x-rays was ordered, at yet, another large teaching hospital. We needed to learn our way around another facility. The place is so big, with so much pedestrian traffic at one of the crossings of two corridors; I dubbed that spot, "Times Square."

The very specialized x-rays took many hours to complete. They were taken from every angle possible. We were also asked to get the report from the last Bronchoscopy.

It amazed us that it took weeks for that report to reach the new doctor, even though the place, at which it had been performed, was, in part, attached to the same facility.

June of that year found us in a flurry of activity. Peggy graduated from high school. We closed the deal on the house we sold, closed the deal on the house we bought, and moved just over the state line. We had spent all twelve of Peggy's school years in the big house, and we all left with many treasured memories. I hoped that the next family would enjoy it as much as we did. I knew I was going to miss the wonderful attic!

The walk-up attic was the place in which we could put anything that we wanted out of sight. I found it to be a great place to hide gifts that I bought ahead of time. In fact, I hid them so well, I sometimes forgot about them.

One day we were having a family gathering, when David went up to the attic to look for something he had left behind. A short time later, he approached me.

"Say, Mom," he said, "could I talk to you a minute?" He motioned me into the hallway, in case what he was going to say was something that the others should not hear.

"I found something up there that I was wondering about," he tactfully explained.

"You found something?" I asked, wondering what he meant.

"It's a very large Snoopy Dog, like the old one Kelley has."

"Oh, my gosh!" I exclaimed, laughing at myself, "I forgot all about it. And I was so excited when I found it, too!"

"Good thing you didn't have any more than four kids, Mom," David teased.

"Well, I guess it will be more of a surprise to give it to her now, months later than her birthday," I reasoned.

David retrieved Snoopy from the large trash bag, in the attic, and we all had a good laugh, at my expense. Kelley was pleased to receive it, and said she would part with the dilapidated one that held all the secrets and tears of her growing years.

The attic also made the switching of clothes, for the change of seasons, very easy. On the other hand, after twelve years of accumulating treasures, cleaning the attic, in order to move, was a major chore!

Peggy was able to help me at the bookshop through the summer, so Bob and I took some time off, for a few holidays, while she was still available. She was off to college in the fall.

That little event, of the youngest going off to college, was not such a little event, after all. Only ten days after she left, Bob asked me what I wanted to do on a Sunday. I asked him if it was silly for us to drive to Peggy's college, to visit her. He indulged me.

"I can't believe she has been gone two and a half weeks, already," I said, as we drove toward the college.

"That's because it has been only one and a half weeks, Denise," he informed me.

I missed her more than I had expected I would. I was pleased that she was not too far from home.

After studying the latest reports and the new x-rays, the thoracic surgeon wanted to do a Bronchoscopy himself. That was arranged for October.

The following month, Kelley and I sat in his office asking him for many details about his proposals, so Kelley could make a decision. He did not propose anything as drastic as trying to replace her entire trachea. He said that he had previously done splinting procedures, on patients with chronic lung disease, which affected only the lower two-thirds of the trachea. Because Kelley's entire trachea was involved, the surgery would be more complicated, in that he would need to be able to get to both parts of the trachea — in the neck, and in the chest.

He explained that the trachea has rings similar to those of a hose on a vacuum cleaner, but the cartilage (hard part), which holds it firm, does not go all the way around. It is approximately like a letter C, the remainder of the circle being of a more pliable tissue.

In Kelley's trachea, the soft part had been stretched out because the cartilage had spread. Therefore, when the back wall hit the front wall, during breathing, the airflow was blocked.

The surgeon planned to pull the spreading cartilage back into shape and "quilt in" some of her pericardium (lining around her heart) to the muscle to hold it. The pericardium would be replaced with a synthetic. This would call for a large incision from back to front on the right side, and another incision across the throat.

The other option, he presented to her, was one he had used for people whose tracheas had been damaged in a fire. That would call for an insertion of a specially made silicone tube in her trachea, with a small side-arm coming out through the neck, to hold it in position. The side arm would be kept closed so she could breathe and talk normally. It would have to be changed periodically, however.

Since the first option could mean a complete solution, if it worked, Kelley decided to select that one. Bob and I had assured her that we would support any decision that she made.

The surgeon was planning to be away for part of the spring, so he gave her an option of January or May to have the surgery. She had originally planned to go to school in January, but she was feeling poorly enough to say she wanted it done then.

Kelley checked into the hospital two days before surgery, since there were many tests to be done, including pulmonary function tests.

One of the first people we met was the chief thoracic resident. I liked him instantly. He proved to be the best resident we had ever encountered. He liked our updated list of Kelley's medical history. When I answered one of his questions using medical terminology, he appeared to think that was fine. For some strange reason, some medical people did not like that. In this man, we found an ally, who was a great help to us during Kelley's stay.

We expected Kelley to go into the OR Friday morning, but the doctor had an emergency that had presented him with complications, so her surgery did not begin until 4 PM. It was supposed to take four to six hours.

One of the benefits of waiting at home, is that you can find more things to do to pass the time, than if you have to hang around a hospital waiting room. The doctor's secretary called to let us know when the surgery started, so when Bob got home from work, we ate supper and watched the evening news. By 8 PM, we started watching the clock, so we began a jigsaw puzzle. We put that thing together in record time! We watched the late news, which seemed to be a rerun of the earlier one. Nothing new had happened, while Kelley was in the operating room. The late show came on next. We had not seen that since before we had children. I couldn't stand the suspense any longer, so I called the hospital. I spoke with a very pleasant woman. She told me that my daughter was still in surgery, and she was sure that the doctor would call me, just as soon as he was finished.

It was after midnight when the phone finally rang. The doctor started by saying that Kelley was okay. Then he went on to tell me that what he found was a deformed trachea, the likes of which he had never seen before. When he tried to pull the cartilage together, it simply would not move. This situation was surprising to him. He tried to repair it, but he was not sure how much he actually accomplished. He said that there was more work to do, but because she had been under anesthesia for so long, they would give her a few days to rest. Then they would take her back in to surgery. He warned us that she would be on a respirator when we saw her, and unable to talk. Naturally, we should expect her to be very heavily medicated, for the next few days.

I thanked him, then looked at the clock, and asked him how he was doing. He said that he had to admit to being tired. I could only imagine! This man was the chief of Thoracic Surgery in a very large, renowned, teaching hospital. We had learned that patients came from all over the world for his care. We felt assured that everything possible had been done. We could ask for no more.

It was too late at night to make any calls to the people we usually keep posted. This turned out to be such an involved situation, that I simply put updates on our answering machine after a while, and let people check in when they could.

TICU is the thoracic intensive care unit. There are x-ray pictures of lungs hanging around all over the place. The staff is experienced in handling people with breathing problems. They had Kelley hooked up to all sorts of equipment. Going into her body were IVs and blood. Coming out of her body were various drains. However, she didn't appear to be quite as swollen, as she was after the hip operation.

Since the surgery had been done on a Friday, I had Bob's companionship and support, while visiting during the weekend. We spent most of the time with Kelley, leaving for walks, or to eat, when the nursing crew had their work to do with her. Most of the time she was zonked! She was unable to speak, because she was hooked up to a respirator, through an opening in her neck. Even in that condition, she managed to mouth the words "thank you" whenever she was aware someone was doing something for her.

A process of weaning her off the respirator took place during those two days, so she would be able to tolerate more surgery. On Monday, Bob was back to work, and I went to the hospital early. The doctors came in, and pronounced Kelley ready to go back to surgery. She was alert enough by then to be eager to be rid of the respirator.

This time, I did my waiting in the visitor's waiting room. It was a large, attractive room with many chairs and couches in various groupings. In some cases, there were whole families sitting together, and then there were people like me, with their books or newspapers. The volunteer in attendance was the designated phone receptionist. The room became quiet every time the phone rang, and she would then ask for a particular family. While the right person went to get their call, people would start to talk again. My call came in about three hours. I didn't know how long it was going to take. I didn't ask. I reasoned it was worse thinking a call should be coming, and wondering why it was not.

The surgeon said that Kelley was doing well. They had inserted a flexible trachea tube (T-Tube) that would keep her airway open. It could be taken care of through a small opening in the front of her neck. While it was only the diameter of a pencil, a small suction tube could be inserted to remove secretions. He planned to have her go back into the hospital in May so he could remove the tube to see if the trachea had any more stability by then, but he honestly doubted that it would.

He went on to tell me that when he saw Kelley's trachea, he wondered how she had stayed alive. If he had known how serious the condition of her trachea was, he would not have given her the option of waiting until May for the surgery. It sounded to me that the man was genuinely sorry that he was unable to repair it completely.

In the days that followed, I started to feel like a permanent fixture in TICU. I was able to be there daily. When I arrived, I had to be sure to report to Kelley that I had fed 'Mr. Fish.' She had cautioned me frequently before surgery not to forget him when she was away. During the week, Bob visited in the evening, allowing me to go home to my chores. On weekends, we went in together.

Peggy took care of the bookshop for me, until she returned to college. After that, I found a few friends to help me. I still needed to attend to my business, though, to pay bills and place orders. Frequently, I received requests for special titles. It would have been too confusing for more than one person to be handling that. Throughout this period, I was telling myself that I was doing just fine with a short supply of sleep. I believed myself, too — right up until I called a distributor I often used. After identifying myself, I said, "I'd like to order a place." I really wanted to place an order!

"And just what kind of place did you have in mind, Ma'am? You know we always like to accommodate."

That was the day that I admitted that I was tired!

For the most part, the TICU staff was great, and we worked together. However, occasionally, some nurse having a bad day, was rude to a patient. The day I walked in to see a fairly young woman yelling at Kelley, the stress we had been under came exploding out of me, and I emphatically told her to leave the room.

On the defensive, she self-righteously declared that she was trying to motivate Kelley so she would get well.

"Motivate to do what?" I demanded.

"She wanted me to push her self-medicate button for her. It's time she started doing it for herself," she proclaimed authoritatively.

"Oh, Dear Lord!" I countered, "This is her first time out of bed after two major operations. No one has even gotten her glasses for her yet, and she has trouble seeing without them, in addition to fingers that don't work well!" I took a breath, and finished slowly and forcefully, "Would it have been too much trouble for you, a nurse, who is supposed to be here to care for patients, to give half a thought to where she is coming from, and push the silly button for her?"

Kelley sat silently, as I went to her and pushed the button, saying, "Since no one has bothered to get your glasses for you, I think I'll go look into it. Oh, by the way, I fed Mr. Fish." I left on a pleasant note.

The nurse was smart enough to say no more.

Kelley's glasses were still on the floor where she stayed before the surgery. Because she was in Intensive Care, the staff had packed up all of her belongings, and placed them in a closet. I had to find the person in possession of the key to the closet. I was not feeling too patient with the situation, since I thought the staff should have already taken care of that detail. I prayed for help, so I wouldn't take my frustrations out on the people on that floor. Praying worked. I returned to TICU with the glasses.

Kelley gave me one of her broad smiles, when I put them on her, and asked, "Are you okay?"

"Yeah," I said, smiling, "I'm fine now, honey. How are you doing?"

"I'm tired, but they just got me up, before you got here, so I want to stay up a bit longer."

"How was she after I left?" I asked about the nurse.

"She didn't say anything. She just finished picking up, and left."

"I couldn't believe it, when I walked in here, to see her yelling at you! I hope she doesn't do that to patients too often. That's no way to help people get well, especially people in intensive care. Does she think you're here because you want to be?"

"I'm glad you came in when you did," she softly murmured.

I knew she was not up to fighting for herself. There have been many times when I have wondered just how much very sick people have to endure, with no one to advocate for them. I saw that nurse a few more times that day. There were no words exchanged, but she was pleasant to Kelley when, with the aid of other nurses, she helped her back to bed.

The patient was exhausted. I pushed the medication button. That little gadget was new to us. A doctor had walked into her room one day and boomed, "Hi. I'm the drug doctor. What would you like?"

Bob and I gave each other one of those, "Did I just hear what I thought I heard?" looks, and giggled.

The doctor explained that what he had in mind was setting Kelley up with an IV, that was attached to a unit, which dispensed a programmed amount of medicine, each time that she pushed the button. Once it was pushed, it would not dispense any more, until the programmed time. If it was pushed too soon, there was no danger of overdosing. One of the real benefits of this kind of self-medication, for the patient, is that they don't need as much of a dose each time, because they can receive it every few hours. In addition, they don't need to wait for a nurse to bring them relief, when they are in pain. Studies showed that, over a time, patients actually used less medication using this method than the old way. Once Kelley had her glasses, and the button was positioned so she could easily manipulate it, she really appreciated the new device.

Her body made so many secretions, in reaction to the surgery; she needed to be suctioned frequently. I was told that I would be taught how to do the procedure, so I carefully observed the process, each time a nurse did it. I really clicked with one nurse in particular. I helped her make the bed, and get Kelley in and out of bed, so I was comfortable when she said to me, "Mom, are you ready to learn how to do this now?"

I was all thumbs! It looked easy and uncomplicated, when I watched the nurses do it, but the steps needed to be taken in a specific order. The object was, not just to remove secretions, thus making breathing easier, but to do so without introducing any germs into her airway. Of utmost importance during the procedure, was to keep a sterile field. The packet of equipment was opened in a precise manner. Then the rubber gloves were put on, and the catheter picked up, and connected to the main tube. Next, the plug to the tube in her neck was removed, and then the actual suctioning could start. If the hand that was supposed to remain sterile touched anything that was not sterile during the process, we needed to start again. I found myself thinking that I could benefit by possessing a third hand.

This young and gentle nurse was a very patient teacher. Throughout the day, each time Kelley needed to be suctioned, I practiced under her guidance. The nurses there worked twelve-hour shifts three days a week. My opinion of that kind of schedule was never solicited. If it had been, I would have asked the powers that be to observe them during the last leg of the third day of that routine. Intensive care nurses keep an extremely demanding pace. Much of what takes place is critical to the lives of the patients. Intensive care breeds intensive nurses. They appear to be quite stressed by the end of that third day.

On the other hand, to the benefit of the patients, there are fewer shift changes. The nurses become more familiar with the needs of the patients, since they spend more time with them.

During the three days this nurse was with Kelley, I had ample opportunity to learn how to suction. I was grateful to have her. She was an excellent teacher.

Generally, patients spend a few days in intensive care, during the critical phase of their illness. Kelley spent eleven days there. Except for that one nurse trying to "motivate" her, the care she received was top notch! The problem nurse was not assigned to Kelley again after that day. I didn't run into her until days later, when she answered Kelley's call light. She was very pleasant, and by then, I had put that incident behind us. I do have to admit though, that I had some trouble letting it go. I wasn't able to sleep, the night of the incident, until I wrote her a letter. My reaction was not only to the way she spoke to Kelley, but to anytime anyone has done something similar to a defenseless person. Yelling at someone, who is already in a position of weakness, should not be a method of motivation.

I had learned, years before, that I could diffuse anger by writing to the person with whom I am angry. That night I wrote at length. When I had it all on paper, I was able to let it go, and get some sleep. The object of my feelings never received the letter. Once I wrote it, I realized that my outburst had been reaction enough. Hammering away at a nail that is already in place does not set it any better. As usual, I did the writing for my own benefit, and as usual, it worked well for me.

Kelley's progress included sitting up for a few hours at a time, then walking a few steps at a time. It required a great deal of effort, and was a major production while she was still hooked up to many tubes and lines. Her first real walk was something to behold. An apparatus, looking like a traditional walker, but being larger, and on wheels, with poles from which to hang IVs, was appointed for this endeavor. She looked lost. The weight she had lost, during this ordeal, made her 4'7½" look smaller than ever, when surrounded by this contraption, with so many necessities hanging from it. The pain medication apparatus needed to be wheeled along next to her, also. The nurse and I accompanied her. We walked by the nurse's station, out a door, down a short corridor, back in through a second door, across the back of the nurse's station, and back to her room. Slowly, she inched along the route covering about sixty feet, returning to her chair both elated and exhausted.

On the Sunday morning following Kelley's second trip to the OR, I looked out the window, remembered he day my sister Mary Lou was married, and said to myself, "Bob Crompton will get us there."

That wonderful white stuff that makes winter memorable was accumulating swiftly. We elected to make the trip in stages, stopping to eat at a restaurant at about the halfway mark. Since my shop was closed on Sundays, except for Christmas season, Peggy was able to join us that day. The wind whipped the snow around without mercy, but Kelley was in the hospital, and we wanted to be with her. Why else would we be out on the highway, under such conditions? It would have been nice to be sitting by a cozy fire, looking out the window at the beauty of it. In lieu of that, I was reassured that Bob was driving. I was confident that we would arrive safely.

Kelley had been lying in her bed watching the snow pile up against the window, and wondering if there would be anything worth watching on TV, to pass the afternoon away. There are no phones by the beds in TICU, so we had not let her know we were planning to visit. The look of joy that lit up her face when she saw the three of us at her door, made the long trip worthwhile. She was especially happy to see her sister, and share her stories about the effects the morphine had on her mind. Kelley said that she would never understand why people took drugs to "go on trips" on purpose. Thinking there was a barking dog or a crying baby in her hospital room was almost as bad as the severe pain had been. The dosage had been lowered by this time, and she was much more alert than just a few days earlier, so it was a good time for Peggy's visit. Can anything be more beautiful than siblings laughing together?

Having shed most of the added attachments, and being strong and stable enough, Kelley was transferred out of TICU, a few days later. Her lunch was arriving, just as they were moving her out. She had not been eating much, at that time, but I planned to warm up some pea soup, once she was at her new location, and we were reunited with her belongings. We always brought some food to the hospital with us. I had not yet started to bring in daily supplies, as TICU did not have the kind of kitchen facilities that were found on the regular units.

The chaotic trip and settling-in process took the better part of an hour. I told a nurse that Kelley had missed lunch, and I would take care of that, if we could have her belongings. She also wanted her tape deck and books, now that she was feeling better.

"Sure thing. Just gotta find out who has the keys," the nurse responded and then disappeared, never to appear again.

Nearly an hour later, I asked another nurse, and received pretty much the same response. It was going on 3 PM, and Kelley was feeling rather weak, when I went to the nurse's station and asked, of everyone present, if I was going to need a court order to obtain my daughter's belongings. "If so," I said, "I'll phone to my lawyer right now, because your patient really needs to eat!" I hoped that I sounded sufficiently serious.

The person with the keys was right there. She claimed to have had no previous knowledge of the request, and led me to the closet that held the treasures. By the time Kelley had her lunch, it was more or less an appetizer for her supper.

We had been given the name of Kelley's assigned primary nurse, but we did not meet her that day. Nor the next day. Or the one after that. The only continuity she was getting in care was that of her doctors. When the thoracic surgeon was not around, his assistant was, and the resident, in whom we were so confident, was there, most of the time. The nursing care left something to be desired. They did know how to take care of her tube, but there seemed to be no understanding of ML III, and the resulting limitations of her physical abilities. We were both becoming tired of explaining things to people, who should have had at least some knowledge of her problems, if they had listened to a report, or read the cardex, or her chart. I expected more from a renowned hospital, so I found the office of the director of nurses. Soon both she and a social worker were visiting Kelley and apologizing for the oversights that had been taking place. A young and energetic nurse, not much bigger than Kelley, was promptly assigned as her primary nurse. It turned out to be a wonderful match. Once again, I felt every patient should have an advocate working for them.

The other patient in Kelley's room was a fairly young woman. Her parents visited regularly. After they watched me in action for a while, doing my best to see that my daughter's needs were being met, they started to ask me what to do about different situations with which they needed help, including access to the kitchen, linen and such. The dad said that he thought I should have a job assisting the families of patients. I don't think there is such a position available, so I will just keep helping, on a voluntary basis, when I happen to be there. Just after that, their daughter was transferred to another floor, and Kelley was alone in that room, momentarily.

The next thing we knew, Kelley was being transferred to another room, where there was one woman, and an empty bed. They needed to provide a room for a man on that floor. This was fine with us, until we arrived at the new room. It was full of bouquets of lovely flowers. They were lovely to look at, but not to breathe, if one has an allergy to them. This was not a good environment for Kelley. I asked a nurse to remove the flowers, which she did. The other patient had a fit! I tried to explain to her that we had nothing against her, or her flowers, but Kelley really didn't have an option. She was already in the hospital because of breathing problems, and didn't need to aggravate her respiratory tract any further. I told her that Kelley had not asked to be put in that room. She had been happy where she was, but the staff moved her. Then, I asked the nurse if there was another room to which Kelley could be moved, so that woman could have her flowers. She said she would look into it, and left. We did not unpack Kelley's belongings, in case she was to be moved again.

The other patient was not consoled. She commenced to make phone calls to family and friends, bemoaning the injustice done to her. She did not know how she was going to recover, without her flowers. We tried to ignore her, but, if she was going to have to suffer the loss of her flowers, she seemed intent upon making us suffer by having to listen to her complaints. They *were* just outside the room in the hall. She could see some of them from her bed. She was also well enough to be up and around. I wanted to suggest that she go out in the hall to visit them, but I knew that would only make matters worse. We turned on the television, and communicated with each other using facial expressions, rolling our eyes and raising our eyebrows.

Kelley's bed was around a corner from the room entrance, so we couldn't see if any staff members were in the hall listening to any of the lady's phone calls. However, after a while, they came in and moved her out, saying they wanted Kelley to stay in that room. They found a room for her to share with a patient who was not allergic to flowers. No one filled the empty bed for a few days, so Kelley had a good chance to get some quality rest.

Now that she was taking food and fluids well, Kelley was able to shed the IV tubes. That made ambulating much easier. We took walks up and down the corridors, as she started to gain strength. Spotting a scale in the utility room, she decided to try it. Her usual 98 pounds had dropped to 85 pounds.

"I suppose I will have to show my license in order to get an adult menu in restaurants," she quipped.

The surgery scars she had now accumulated gave her body a road map appearance. She joked that she should have had them put in a zipper. The healing process moved along nicely. I became very comfortable handling suction equipment, and Kelley started needing less help. As she became stronger, she was able to cough up the secretions, which thankfully, were not being produced as much any more. In addition, her sense of humor had returned.

The new patient that came to occupy the other bed in Kelley's room was a lovely lady. We established a nice relationship with her, and no one sent her any flowers.

It wasn't as necessary for me to spend as much time at the hospital, at that point. It was reassuring that Kelley had a pleasant person in her room.

The little stopper that fit into the arm of the tube, protruding from Kelley's throat, could easily become lost, if it was not attached somehow. As soon as the tube was in place, a piece of black suture thread was run through the stopper. Then a loop was made by tying the ends in a knot. A piece of gauze string was then passed through that loop, and a necklace-type affair was made out of the gauze, when it was tied after encircling her neck. I'm betting they lost a few of those little stoppers before they came up with that idea. The stopper is necessary for two reasons. Any air that enters the airway through that opening is completely unfiltered. That could create problems for her bronchial tubes and lungs. In addition, the opening is located below the larynx, so air is exhaled before reaching it. Speaking is not possible without that opening being covered or plugged.

The thread was very strong, and not a problem, but the gauze became messed up or wet, and needed to be changed frequently. It was also irritating to the skin. Bob and I decided that, once we returned Kelley home, we would have to find a better solution.

The nurses taught her how to take the stopper out and squirt sterile saline into the tube, put the stopper back, and cough up the saline. She was instructed to do that twice daily, to keep the tube clean, and more often if she had a cold. She said she was willing to learn to do the suctioning after she got home. She just did not feel strong enough, at that point. That was fine with me, and the doctors felt that was okay, as long as she was not living alone. After spending two weeks on that floor, we knew all the nurses, and we were comfortable. The social worker seemed to enjoy Kelley, and visited often.

On discharge day, among the things we packed, to take home with us, were a portable suction machine and a supply of suction tubes. Kelley was very nervous. She had felt very secure on the thoracic floor. By the time we got to the car, she had filled up with secretions. In the car, in the parking garage, I used the suction machine for the first of many times.

The visiting nurses came to our home, and I was able to get back to the bookshop. I was only fifteen minutes away. Kelley needed to call me to suction her a few times, so I put a sign up on the door of the shop indicating my return time. My daughter's breathing took precedent over the sale of a few books.

When Kelley was strong enough, we went to a jewelry shop, where she picked out an attractive gold necklace. They sized it to fit like a choker, and we called it a Valentine's Day gift. Next, I found some gold thread to replace the black, so when she is dressed with a high collar, all that shows is the gold necklace. It has worked out well. She wears it full time, and we change the thread occasionally.

# CHAPTER FIFTEEN

Just when everything seemed to be settling down, a nasty cold invaded Kelley's system, bringing with it a lot of coughing. She called me at work, when she started having trouble breathing again. I went home and suctioned her. She seemed to be better, so I went back to work, knowing Bob would be home soon. About an hour later, Bob showed up at my work. He said he would handle the shop, so I could go home and suction her again. This time, the suctioning did not help. Although I was not getting any secretions back, her breathing was very labored. Putting in a call to Bob, I told him to close the shop and come home, while I called the doctor.

Her surgeon assured us that he would alert the emergency room staff to expect us. As time passed, Kelley had more and more trouble getting enough air. I am not known for liking a mad dash down the highway, but that night I had no complaints about the speed. In fact, I was hoping we might be pulled over, so we could have a police escort.

There was a chart with a red sticker on it, waiting for Kelley, in the Emergency Room. She was taken into a room with four beds. There seemed to be some confusion about what to do for her immediately. The staff said they had paged the resident we knew. It appeared that the young doctor and the nurse, who were attending to Kelley, were waiting for him to give them direction. I did not want to blatantly tell them what to do, so I said very clearly, to Kelley, "You will start feeling better, when they get the oxygen going."

They were alert enough to pick up on that as being a good idea. Even with the oxygen, Kelley was really working very hard to breathe. When the thoracic resident arrived, he looked at Kelley, and asked me some questions. He told the other doctor to start an IV. After he ordered a medication, he said he was going to get the portable bronchoscope.

The young doctor asked me to step out while she started the IV. I could sense her discomfort with my presence, so I obliged, and went to find Bob. He had been left with the chore of parking the car. I explained what was happening, and he showed me where he would be waiting. Once the IV was started, I went back to Kelley. She was exhausted. Each breath was a chore. I stood by her, trying to talk as calmly as the anesthetist had done at the other hospital, and waited for the medication to take effect.

"I can't do this anymore. I have to give up," she barely whispered.

I could understand that. I suspect I would have felt the same way in those circumstances. Who could blame her? Of course, I couldn't let her give up, so I tried coaxing her, "Kelley, you've come too far to give up now. Please hang in. We're in the right place now to get the help you need."

She looked toward the door, and I turned to see the resident approaching with the bronchoscope. He spoke very casually to Kelley, telling her about the portable bronchoscope being very valuable to the thoracic department.

"I had to promise my first born in order to take it," he joked.

The medication started to take effect. Kelley became more relaxed from a combination of her trust in him, the medication, and the oxygen. He inserted the scope into Kelley's tube. The other doctor, standing opposite him, looked at me standing at the foot of the bed, and then at him. She seemed to be surprised that he did not ask me to leave.

"I see the problem. We can fix it," he announced in a short time, "Mom, do you want to look?" he asked, addressing himself to me, and further shocking the other doctor.

"Please!" I enthusiastically replied, approaching him. I glanced at the doctor across the bed. She looked horrified at the prospect of a layperson sharing this information.

"See," the resident said, as I looked into the lens of the scope, "right there at the end of the tube. Some of the trachea is still exposed, and it's swollen. It is probably a result of the cold and coughing. Because of the swelling, it is protruding and blocking part of the opening."

"Yes, I see it," I said, "but what can you do about it?" I was wondering if this was going to happen every time she got a cold.

"For right now, we will control it with medication and the oxygen. Tomorrow, we will take her into surgery, remove this tube and replace it with a longer one."

As he was explaining this, I finished looking in the scope, and he offered it to the other doctor.

"I will be calling her surgeon shortly. He wanted to know of my findings. I'm sure he will agree. We will do it at whatever time we can get an OR room," he advised, as he removed the scope from her tube and closed the opening.

"Did you get all of that, Kelley?" I asked.

"I think so. Am I staying here overnight?" she asked, looking for reassurance.

"Most definitely," the doctor responded. Addressing the nurse, he said, "I want her on the thoracic floor."

Before the nurse left, I made a request on Kelley's behalf, "If she's not going to be having any nourishment after midnight, can we get her some now? She hasn't had much to eat."

"Sure, I can get her a milkshake from the kitchen."

"Oh dear," I responded, "I'm afraid that won't do. She's allergic to milk, but I know what you do have in this hospital. There's a supplementary drink she practically lived on when she was here." I gave her the name, and she said she would ask for it.

I left to find Bob, so he could join us, while we waited for Kelley to be transferred to the thoracic floor. The next few hours were interesting. We all felt more secure, and started to notice our surroundings. I've visited many emergency rooms, in a variety of hospitals, through the years. Never have I witnessed the screaming or gushing blood and general excitement as portrayed in some movies or television dramas. There was a situation comedy on television, a few years ago that took place in an emergency room, which was more representative of what I have seen.

People can be very funny, even when dealing with serious circumstances. The interaction that occurs, between those of very different backgrounds, can lead to some humorous misunderstandings. The nurse who was trying to get a urine sample from an elderly woman, who was from another country, was getting nowhere until she yelled, "Can you pee?" No problem! Apparently, that is the same in any language.

There was an orderly walking around doing nothing but complaining of how overworked he was, and a woman who broke her leg in an accident, and was happy she didn't break any fingernails. She had just spent too much money getting them done.

Bob and I often looked at each other and grinned when we observed such absurdities. Taking notice of the behavior of others can take the focus off one's own problems. Laughter is a wonderful tension reliever. The stress was not completely gone, however. We still needed to wait for Kelley to be transferred to a room, and she was facing another operation the next day. The hour was late, but adrenaline kept us going.

When the attendant arrived to tell Kelley she would be taken to room 212 shortly, I said, "Wait a minute, that's not on the thoracic floor is it?"

"I don't know," was the response.

"I don't think it is," I said, being sure that I knew the room numbers on the thoracic unit, "and the doctor specified that she be sent there."

"All I know is what I was told," she responded with a shrug.

I looked at Bob and frowned. Then I set out to find the nurse. She picked up the phone. Whoever she spoke to said there were no beds on that floor. I asked her to page the resident. She did.

He materialized sometime later by Kelley's bed, and said that he was sorry about the wait, but they were making room on the thoracic floor for Kelley. It was then close to midnight.

I asked the nurse about the drink for Kelley. She assured me that she was working on it. There was none in the kitchen, and she was methodically calling the different floors in the hospital in an attempt to locate some. I suggested she try thoracic. If there wasn't any in the kitchen, there might be some in the supply room.

"You were right!" she happily announced, when she brought the drink to Kelley a short time later, "Learn something new everyday!"

No one else noticed that it was after midnight when Kelley downed the drink. She was much more comfortable by then, and she drifted in and out of slumber land as we waited. A patient was being moved, off the thoracic floor at that hour, to make room for Kelley. I felt badly for the patient being moved, but relieved Kelley would be getting the care she needed.

The elevator door opened to the thoracic floor at just about 2 AM. An attendant was behind Kelley's wheelchair, and Bob and I were on either side. Three nurses that we knew were standing there waiting for us, looking like Angels of Mercy. They immediately started to reassure us.

One said, "Kelley, we got your old room ready for you."

Another told Bob and me, "We'll be taking good care of her. We love her, too."

My eyes filled up with tears. A combination of the hour, the anxiety and the relief made me want to bawl, but I decided it would be best to save that for later. I simply said a silent prayer of thanks. Once again, God had led us to the right place, at the right time.

The nurses settled Kelley in her bed, and told us that, now, it was safe for us to go home. We believed them.

I had no idea what time the surgery would take place, so I decided to find out when I arrived at the hospital. First, I had to find someone to mind the shop. At that point, I was wondering if it was worth it to keep the shop operating. The time was at hand when I might actually start to make some money with the endeavor. However, with the events of the previous months, it was starting to feel like an unnecessary burden.

I reached the hospital shortly after noon, just in time to see Kelley as they wheeled her off to the OR. The perky little nurse decided I looked tired, so she escorted me to Kelley's room and ordered me to rest. That was not hard to do. The beds, on that floor, had wonderful upholstered recliners, next to them. Many of the patients slept in the recliners rather than the beds, due to their breathing problems. I made myself comfortable and closed my eyes, until I heard approaching footsteps. They belonged to the social worker, with whom we had become friendly, during Kelley's stay, the previous month.

"What happened?" she asked, as she took a seat on the bed, "I saw her name as being admitted through the emergency room last night!"

With the update from me completed, she looked at me with narrowed eyes, and queried, "How do you and your husband hold up, through all of this?"

Taking a deep breath, I smiled, "For starters, we pray for guidance," I said, "and there's a lot to be said for a long term marriage. It will be twenty-eight years in April! I think if you have a good marriage, it becomes strengthened by something like this, otherwise, it probably falls apart."

"I know what you mean," she said, "I've been married for a long time, too."

"Last night in the ER," I elaborated, "once we knew that Kelley was out of danger, we started to notice some of the humor in the human nature around us. We chuckled together about things no one else would have thought funny, and on the way home, we amused ourselves by recounting them and laughing out loud."

"The nurse in the ER was wonderful," I continued, "Would you do me a favor, please?"

"Name it!"

"I had been sitting here wishing I had the energy to write a note to the director of nursing. My intentions at this moment are great, but I know I will get all caught up in taking care of Kelley again, and I'll forget. I just want her to know how good that nurse was. She made a big difference in our ability to cope last night. It is always easier when you believe that people are on your side."

The other patient, in Kelley's room, invited herself into the conversation, at that point. She made no complaints about the fact that her sleep had been disturbed the night before, with a transfer of patients. Instead, she had a few questions of her own for me. She also informed me that Kelley had vomited a few times before going to surgery. This lovely lady, probably around sixty years old, said that she thought Kelley was just about the bravest person she had ever met, and she wasn't going to complain about her problems any more.

I related that to Kelley later. She never thought of herself as being brave, "You just do what you have to do," she commented, "What good would it do to complain?" That was typical of Kelley!

The new tube settled in and worked well. In a relatively short time, Kelley's mucous membranes adjusted to the changes and stopped producing an abundance of secretions. We only needed to suction two or three times a day. I asked her if she was ready to try to suction herself.

"If I have to keep the tube after I go back in May, I will have to learn," she said, "but, if it's okay with you, I would like to wait until then."

I understood.

There were two appointments set up for March. One was to confirm the May date with the surgeon. The other was with the urologist, who had been called in, when some blood was found in Kelley's urine, following the surgery. He wanted to further investigate by doing a cystoscopy. Kelley didn't think it was of any concern, since it had lasted only a few days, and then stopped, but he was insistent that it was better to be safe than sorry. I sat as a silent observer during this discussion. Kelley had become her own person, making her own decisions. She no longer needed to look at me to see if I had any input. I was pleased with that.

However, I was stunned to hear her say to him, "Well, I'm scheduled to be in the OR at eight on the morning of May 16th, to have my tube removed and possibly replaced. If you'd like to do it at that time, okay."

The expression on the doctor's face led me to believe he was also stunned. Not for long, though. He soon picked up his phone, and asked his secretary to call Kelley's surgeon to see if such an arrangement would be agreeable with him. It was, and all the arrangements were made.

Traveling home, I said to her, "That was quick thinking on your part, to get it all done at once."

"I couldn't see making another trip in there and having anesthesia again, for something that isn't even a problem."

She was right.

Naturally, we were all hoping that Kelley would be able to breathe normally without the tube. I envisioned her feeling that she would be tied to me, if she had to keep it. I knew she was thinking that she, probably, would not be able to manipulate the suction equipment very well, by herself. On the other hand, once she recovered from the initial surgery, she started feeling better than she had for years. She said that the decline had progressed so slowly, she was not aware of how difficult it had become to breathe, until she had the use of the tube.

Kelley checked into the hospital the day before the surgery. I knew my brother Jim, a Navy Chaplain, would be visiting at my brother Fred's, not too far from the hospital, but I did not tell Kelley. They planned to visit her the evening before the surgery, as it would be a long and anxious one.

Late that afternoon, Fred and his wife, Claire, appeared at the door. Kelley was happy to see them. A few minutes after their greetings, her Uncle Jim walked in, and really surprised her! We had a fun visit. My brothers are both good storytellers, as our father had been. Before they left,

Father Jim told Kelley that he would have some time off, around her birthday, so he wanted to fly her out to where he was stationed, for a visit.

She was delighted. So was I, thinking that it might be the perfect incentive for her to learn to suction herself, if need be. She was bright and chipper that night, going into surgery the next day with hopeful anticipation. I stayed late, and went in early, in the morning to spend time with her, before they took her in to surgery. As before, the patient who was her roommate was very impressed with Kelley's attitude.

The actual surgery time was short, but it felt very long in that waiting room. My hope was for Kelley to be freed from the suctioning problem. I was not at all concerned about the actual surgery, because I had so much confidence in the surgeon, with regard to her breathing. My only concern was with the findings.

Finally, the phone call was for me. All the surgeons we have dealt with start the conversation with, "Kelley's okay." Usually, I hold my breath after saying, "Hello," and exhale, once I have heard that. This time I didn't. I held my breath until he told me that he was very sorry, but Kelley's trachea was not strong enough for her to be able to breathe properly, without the tube. He sounded sad. I thanked him for trying. He told me she would be back in her room shortly, as she had not needed much anesthesia.

I had time to make a few phone calls, but first I needed to cry. The volunteer, working that day, asked me if everything was all right.

I said, "No," and briefly told her it was a disappointment. She quickly dismissed me. I guessed she thought it was worthy of tears only if death was imminent. I went to the ladies room for a brief cry. Then I was ready to call Bob at work and speak without my voice quivering. A few more calls were placed to family and friends, and then I went to Kelley's room to wait for her. Shortly after, Bob surprised me by arriving there. He said that he just could not concentrate at work. He needed to be with her, too.

Kelley was awake before we saw her, so she already knew the results. The first thing she did, on returning to her room, was to ask Bob why he was not at work.

"I just told them I was leaving, and I left," he said, smiling.

She laughed. She had just received some very upsetting news, and she laughed about her father leaving work. What a wonder! I talked to her about what the doctor had told me.

"That's okay," she said. That was it.

We discussed the upcoming trip to the other coast.

Kelley was discharged the next day, with plans to have the tube changed in about a year. Before we left, her roommate said that she had to tell us that she had never met a family like ours. We told her that we knew we were very fortunate. She said that knowing Kelley, and seeing her strength, helped her to have the strength to deal with her own problems. Sometimes God uses other people to help us. Sometimes, He uses us to help others.

By comparison, the recovery from this surgery was very rapid. Perhaps, because the question that had been hanging over Kelley's head had been answered, the anxiety was gone, and her body stopped making copious amounts of secretions. She learned that she could suction herself, if need be, though she still preferred for me to do it for her. That's all right with me. I like to feel useful. I just wanted to be sure she could do it, if I was not around. My greatest fear had been that she would feel tied to me. I believed that the most important factor, to her overall well-being, would be for her to be independent of me.

When the report came in that the cystoscopy was fine, Kelley said dryly, "I knew it."

We booked the trip for her visit, with her uncle, on the other coast. She had to speak to the attendant at the airport security station. She knew the metal in her hip would set the signal off, and needed to explain the suction equipment she wanted to keep with her. A female attendant was asked to search her. It was brief, and respectfully done. I watched the plane take off, and kept my eyes on it, until the speck in the sky disappeared. I was thrilled that she was going. If anyone ever deserved a holiday, Kelley did. I was very grateful that my brother had afforded her the opportunity. I knew she would be well taken care of by him. My only request to him was that he would try to remember to go at her pace, his energy being boundless!

When Kelley first had the tube, her body was producing so many secretions; she needed to be suctioned very often. We thought it was going to be that way all the time, so when it subsided, we were pleasantly surprised. She had been given an ample supply of what they called bullets to take home. They are small plastic tubes of sterile water. She was advised to keep some with her at all times. If she ever became congested with mucus that was hard to cough up, a squirt of the water would most likely be enough to take care of it. A maintenance cleaning with the bullets is usually sufficient. Only when a cold or infection cause an accumulation of secretions, too difficult for her to cough up, does the use of the suction equipment become necessary.

Now that her breathing was improved, and there were no operations scheduled, Kelley was able to resume her education. She enrolled at a good college within commuting distance from home.

# CHAPTER SIXTEEN

Kelley was into the spring semester at school, when her other hip needed attention. After looking at the x-rays, her hip surgeon was noticeably concerned. We knew that he was reluctant to take Kelley into surgery again. His frown and silent thoughtfulness caused Kelley to sense his apprehension, so she pulled down the turtleneck on her jersey to expose the arm of her T-Tube.

"What is that?" he asked, his frown turning into an expression of puzzlement.

"I have a tube in my trachea now to keep the airway open," she explained.

"She is no longer a surgical risk," I added confidently.

"That's wonderful!" he exclaimed, as a smile spread across his face.

"I don't want to take any time out of school," the patient hastened to advise him, "I will have it done at the end of the semester."

He seemed to be studying her, as she spoke, "You know what needs to be done, then?" he asked, his eyes narrowed.

"Sure, same thing," she said, sounding as casual as if she was making plans to get a haircut.

The doctor stood back, hands on his hips, and said, "Well, Kelley, if you're willing to put up with the pain that long, it's all right with me." He glanced my way, and we exchanged a look of acceptance. She had made up her mind.

He explained to us that the recent advances, in the prosthesis development, meant that this surgery might be less extensive than the previous one. He was fairly certain that he would not need to do the bone rotation in her left leg, as he had done in the right. That was good news.

Since Kelley was due to have the tube changed in May, and the hip was to be done then, we contacted the thoracic surgeon. We asked if it was something that could be done at the same time, to avoid two separate admissions to two different hospitals. He advised us to have the anesthetist contact him, and said that he would be happy to supply the necessary information.

We then contacted the doctor, whom we now considered Kelley's Anesthetist, at the hospital where the hip surgery would take place, and asked him to do the honors. I told him that I did not want Kelley going into surgery without him. He was most obliging.

Reaching the end of a semester, with the pressure of finals, is a very anxious time for most students. I can only imagine the anxiety produced by facing major surgery upon completion of the school exams. I wondered if the pressure from one helped to take the mind off the other or not. Certainly, she could not really forget the hip. It was painful.

We now had a much better understanding of what she was facing. Educational television had shown a complete hip replacement operation, shortly after Kelley had the first one done. Bob and I watched in total fascination. Kelley walked into the den that night and asked what we were watching. When we told her, she said, "No thanks. They did that to me," and she left.

By that time, the hospital routine had progressed to admission on the day of surgery, which meant we needed to have her there by 6 AM. Bob took a vacation day from work. We stayed with her until just before seven, when they took the day surgery patients away. She was scheduled to be done at 7:30. Heading toward the parking garage, I said to Bob, "I was tempted to stop by the Anesthesia Department to be sure her doctor is in. I would feel much better knowing he was here."

About thirty seconds later, Kelley's anesthetist walked through the door from the garage. God answers prayers.

"We just left her," I told him, "She's all yours now!"

"We'll take good care of her," he reassured.

The surgeon sounded chipper later, when he spoke to me on the phone, to say that Kelley was doing fine. "Sorry to be so late in calling, but it took them awhile to get that tube changed, so I could start," he explained, "I will tell them to expect you in the recovery room."

She looked much better this time than she had the last. The surgery was less complicated, and her lungs were fine. She was swollen, but not as much as she had been after the first hip operation. The blood she was receiving was her own. They had a new apparatus that took blood draining from her, filtered it, and put it back into her. She had needed only one additional unit this time.

"Hi, Mom. I need to be suctioned," she said in a raspy whisper.

I asked if anyone had suctioned her yet. She said they had not, so I approached the nurse at the desk, to ask who was taking care of Kelley, explaining that she needed to be suctioned. She said that she would get her. I went back to Kelley, and around to the side of the bed, so I was facing the nurse's station. When another nurse appeared, I noticed them having a discussion while glancing towards Kelley. It occurred to me that they were used to orthopedics, not T-Tubes. I joined them at the desk, and told them, as tactfully as possible, that I was used to suctioning her at home. I volunteered to do the job, when I was there, if they would provide me with the equipment.

Relief was written across their faces. I know that all nurses learn how to suction during their training. I also know that when one becomes specialized, one may need a little refreshing, to regain previously acquired abilities. Kelley's nurse seemed comfortable enough, with my assurance to ask me to show her what she needed to do, when I was not there.

This done, Kelley was comfortable, and drifted off to sleep. Bob and I were sitting quietly by when the surgeon visited. He was as jovial as I had ever seen him, having just completed another surgery that went well. We received a complete run down of the new hip, and the way it would work. It was a simple hip replacement, if a hip replacement can be considered simple, that is.

The surgeon started laughing as he said, "You should have seen the OR when they were getting ready to change her T-Tube. They were all set up and following the thoracic surgeon's directions to the letter. I think the whole ENT department was there!" His laughter increased, "There must have been ninety people in that OR, and *no one* wanted to be *the one* to pull out the old T-Tube!"

He knew he wasn't going to have to do it, so he thought the rest of them were pretty funny. It is a procedure that takes about twenty minutes at the hospital that specializes in thoracic surgery. It took them two hours here, according to him. It is possible a number of doctors learned something new that day that would help in the future.

All I learned that day was, that the whole business of watching a loved one go through such an ordeal never gets any easier. There are some benefits to being experienced, such as knowing how to find your way around the hospital, and knowing what to expect from the personnel. However, waiting for the surgeon's call, and seeing our girl suffer, was as difficult the fifteenth time as it was the first. It was a relief, however, to know that there were no complications this time.

When I called in the morning, I was told that Kelley would be moved to the orthopedic floor by 10 AM. No intensive care this time! No cast this time! But a T-Tube on the orthopedic floor could present a problem.

Later that day, as I was approaching the nurse's station, I heard a nurse, whose back was towards me, saying to another nurse, "Do you know what we're supposed to be doing about Crompton's T-Tube?"

"Have no fear, mother's here," I interrupted.

Kelley's nurse turned around, and I explained that with the tube change, she would need suctioning for a while, as her body would make more secretions, in reaction. I told her that I had been dealing with it for over a year, and I would be happy to show her how we do it. I let her know what equipment would be needed.

162

Each night, before leaving, I checked to see who would be taking care of Kelley, and if they knew how to suction my patient. The whole crew seemed to appreciate my help.

I did think it would be easier if you could send part of the patient to one hospital, and the other part to another. Specialization does have some drawbacks.

The anesthetist was in to visit a few times. He seemed delighted to have kept her out of intensive care this time. It turned out that he was the one who actually did change the tube, with an audience.

When she was alert, Kelley asked me to measure her incision to see if it was the same length as the other. I guessed she wanted to be well matched on each side. Actually, it was a little shorter.

The problems we encountered during this hospitalization were few. A misunderstanding with a nurse's aide, who couldn't understand why I was there when it wasn't visiting hours, was quickly resolved by the head nurse, who explained that I was not a visitor.

An overzealous physical therapist was putting unnecessary pressure on Kelley one day. Kelley said that she would be ready for that step the next day, and the woman commenced to give her a lecture about the necessity of physical therapy. She was not talking to someone who was a novice to physical therapy! She got my dander up, because her tone was condescending. I told her not to talk to my daughter, or any other patient, for that matter, like that again! Then she tried to talk down to me. I told her that if she did not leave the room, immediately, I would report her for being verbally abusive to a patient. She left. The other patient in the room, a fairly young woman, affirmed my stand.

"Good for you," she said, "She needed that. I think some of them have no idea what it's like to be on this end!"

The next day, the physical therapist sent the nurse in ahead of her, to see if it was okay with Kelley for her to start doing physical therapy with her. She was much more gentle in her approach, for the remainder of Kelley's stay.

Before I left one evening, the other patient asked me the same question I had been asked many times before, "Why do you drive all the way home every night? Why don't you stay over in town?"

Having given the matter serious consideration in the past, I had a pat answer, "I have everything I need at home. I can change my mind about what I want to wear, if the weather suddenly changes. My hair dryer and refrigerator are at home. I like to sleep in my own bed, with my husband, and the cost to stay in town is more than I care to spend."

Beyond all of that, I really don't mind the drive, unless the weather is bad. Then again, I had to care for my little bookshop, which was getting more difficult after one of those superstore book shops came to town. When a customer would find a specific title, and tell me, "I couldn't find *this one* at the superstore," I knew they were finding many others there. I could not compete with their hours. I could not compete financially, because the publishers gave larger discounts to those who could place larger orders. Some of my customers told me that the personal touch was missing in the big store. It appeared to me that all of my customers were shopping there.

Kelley's recovery this time was uncomplicated. She was up and about on crutches, and working on physical therapy quickly and diligently. She did well on crutches, having used them many times before.

Once at home, a physical therapist came to the house to work with her. She also needed blood drawn frequently by a nurse, because she was taking a blood-thinning medication, until she resumed the full scope of normal activity.

By fall semester, Kelley was ready to go back to classes. Medically, it was a fairly easy year. Just check-ups. We knew the routine well. Check in with the hip surgeon's lovely secretary, and then go to x-ray, where they say, "Hi, Kelley. We know you come prepared, and don't have to change," meaning that she does not wear anything with metal. Then we see the doctor with the x-rays.

Kelley set up the date for the T-Tube to be changed as soon as spring semester was finished. It was done on an outpatient basis. We were there by 6 AM, and home by 4 PM.

Celebrating Kelley's 4th of July birthday has always been easy to do. Parades, cookouts, and fireworks are standard fare for Independence Day. Before their birthdays, the children usually start making suggestions for gifts they would like. That gives Bob and me time to make decisions and purchases. In 1992, Bob asked me what we were planning to get for Kelley, a full month before her birthday.

"I don't know. She hasn't mentioned anything yet," I replied, not knowing he had anything on his mind.

A week later, he brought the subject up again, and I still didn't have an answer, but then, we still had time.

When he spoke of it a third time, I asked him if he had something in mind.

"Well," he hesitatingly offered, "I was wondering if you thought she might like a cat."

"You were *wondering* if she *might* like a *cat!*" I exclaimed with uproarious laughter.

"She would?" he asked.

"Bob, she would be *thrilled!*"

Our family was pretty typical in having had our share of cats and dogs through the years. They were family pets. The cats were always outdoor cats. They came in to eat and sleep, but they kept mice out of the cellar and birds out of the garden. The last two we had did not adjust to our move a few years before. We tried, but they were on in years, and set in their ways. They left. We never found them. We went back to the old neighborhood to see if they had found their way back, but no one there had seen them. We could only hope that someone had taken them in. It had never occurred to us to put tags on them. It was a sad time, but we had never talked about replacing them, because outdoor cats did not seem in keeping with our new surroundings.

We had tried a few dogs from the Humane Society when the kids were young, but they didn't work out well. One turned out to be very sick, and the next was too aggressive. A few years later, we did find it impossible to pass up the opportunity to adopt a six-week-old puppy, whose mother was a Golden Retriever and father was (we suspect) an Airedale. Mundy quickly became a family member; treasured by us all for the many years we had him.

The only time the children had pets of their own was when we agreed to let them have cages containing hamsters, gerbils and mice. These were not the most favored pets of the parents in the family. As long as they were all the same sex, if they were to be caged together, we could tolerate them. I never knew how difficult it was to determine the sex of hamsters until the day the kids came running into the kitchen yelling, "Mom, Pepper isn't a girl, after all! Snow White just had babies!"

The only pet in the house at this time was Kelley's Mr. Fish. I never expected Bob to be the one to suggest the addition of a cat. He never seemed to like them very much.

"Are you sure about this?" I questioned. I was going to proceed cautiously, before becoming excited.

"I thought she might like a house cat. We could have the front paws de-clawed, so it wouldn't ruin the furniture."

"Really?" I asked, "You would really be willing to put up with a house cat?"

"I thought she might like it," was his simple reply.

I was so excited that I could hardly contain myself. I love cats. My kids all love cats. I couldn't think of a better birthday gift! I was glad I had not known sooner. Keeping such a delightful surprise a secret would be difficult. I had to share it with Peggy.

We were at the bookshop together, when I asked her, "Can you keep a big secret, a really super secret, from Kelley?"

"Of course I can," she declared.

I knew she could, but I had to build up to it. "This is something very special, though. Something you and I will be happy about, too."

Peggy's quizzical expression told me that I had her hooked. "It was Daddy's idea," I said laughing, "in fact, he asked me if she would like it."

Peggy was starting to grow a bit impatient with the way I was holding out, "So are you going to tell me, or not?" she asked.

"Peggy, you're not going to believe this, but Daddy asked me if Kelley would like to have a cat for her birthday!"

News of a lottery winning never made anyone react more happily than we did that day. Peggy's eyes opened as wide as possible while a grin spread across her face. With her arms on mine, and mine on hers, we actually jumped up and down together like a couple of kids.

"It was really Daddy's idea?" she asked, amazed.

"I couldn't believe it myself," I said, "but now that he has said so, there is no way he is going to get out of it!"

"That is a hard thing to keep a secret," she admitted, "How soon do you plan to get it?"

"As close to her birthday as we can. We'll have to check the hours the Humane Society is open. They always have kittens there."

When *the day* arrived, Peggy took care of the shop in the early evening, while Bob and I went to adopt the cat. Things had really changed since we last visited a humane society. We were required to fill out a lengthily application, and wait while the girl took it somewhere to see if we were approved.

Looking at me, Bob said, "I hope that raising four children will qualify us to be fit parents for a cat!"

While we waited for the big decision, we started to check out the cages. The kittens were all adorable, but one kept calling me back. She seemed to be very spirited. I felt this was the most appropriate choice for Kelley.

We passed! Next, we had to part with our money, and then sign some papers, promising to have her spayed and to keep up her shots. We left with the furry bundle in a cardboard box. Once in the car, I had to take her out of the box to properly introduce myself, and get a very good look at her.

Peggy was anxiously awaiting our arrival, wondering what was taking us so long. It was just about closing time when we arrived at the bookshop. We took the kitten in, so Peggy could play with it. After closing up, we gathered the various other gifts, which we had stored in the shop, out to the car.

"Oh," Peggy squealed as she picked up the new little treasure, "Kelley's going to love it!"

We drove home in anticipation of Kelley's reaction. When we walked in, she was sitting in her room reading. Peggy and Bob were in front of me, and I was carrying the box. We sang the Happy Birthday song. With her head tilted to one side, Kelley looked very perplexed. It was a few days before her birthday. She didn't expect to be receiving a gift, just then. The Humane Society would be closed on the holiday. It would have been impossible to hide a kitten in our house, with her living there. We had to present it right away.

I approached her with the box that I was carrying by the handle on the top. The box had air holes in the side. A small paw appeared through one of them.

Kelley looked at it wide-eyed, and at each of us, "What is this?" she asked, bewildered.

We were all laughing happily, as I said, "Your birthday gift!"

I set the box down, and opened the top for her. She looked in, and looked at us again. She was speechless. With all of us encouraging her, she reached in and lifted out the kitten.

"I can't believe it," she finally declared, "Oh, thank you. Thank you!"

"It was Daddy's idea!" I told her, knowing she would be pleased to hear that.

Then we all talked at once, and Peggy and I ran out to the car to get the other gifts to present to Kelley. We had feeding bowls, a bed, toys, cat food, a litter box, and of course, kitty litter. We spent the rest of the evening playing with the cat and discussing possible names.

The new arrival commanded so much attention; it was as if we had a star in the house. Indeed, she turned out to be a Star! We thought that was an appropriate name, since on the Fourth of July we celebrate the stars and stripes. She had some pretty stripes, so the name Star stuck.

Everyone who owns a cat thinks theirs is the cutest, prettiest or smartest cat on the face of the earth. We tend to think that Star is the funniest. Of course, we do notice her behavior more than we did our previous feline friends, since she spends her time indoors. It appears she is part Bengal in heritage. She is great fun, and sometimes extremely wild, running about, jumping over and off various pieces of furniture, or running from window to window to track a passing animal. She finds strangers to be a threat, and retreats to a hiding place when we have company.

Of all the toys we have provided, Star prefers to play with small crumpled pieces of paper or small balls of yarn. She is most creative with those yarn balls, doing intricate weaving jobs. It is most interesting to watch her unwind the yarn, push it along the floor to a spot she decides on, lay on the floor under the rung of a chair, and with her paws, toss it up and over. She then picks up the ball with her mouth, and takes it along to the next spot, alternately dropping and unwinding as she goes. Then lying on her back again, she tosses it up and over another chair rung. Using two or three balls, she will work at this project until the table and chairs are encircled. If no one has witnessed this project in process, she will find one of us and lead us to see her handiwork. She seems to enjoy our praise. After a while, we re-roll the balls of yarn, and leave them handy for her to do her performance again another day.

Changing the sheets on a bed is something that Star seems to think we do for her benefit. She comes running, when she hears a sheet being shaken. She likes to settle on the bottom sheet, and have the rest of the covers draped over her. We leave a bed made up with a lump in it. She often naps there, and slips out when her nap is finished. Sometimes, we pet her through the covers, and she purrs loudly!

When Star was old enough, we toilet trained her, by following directions in a book. We have two bathrooms. Sometimes she runs back and forth from one to the other, apparently trying to make a decision as to which one to use this time. Taking her on a trip is easy, because of her ability to use a toilet. When we enter a motel room, we simply show her where the bathroom is. No need to take along a litter box!

The only way Star goes out is in the car, or with a harness and leash, to the yard. She has never tried to go outside on her own, probably because she is conditioned to the harness. Kelley finds her to be a wonderful companion. She asserts that Star is the best birthday gift she has ever received.

As Peggy entered into her senior year in college, Kelley moved forward with her education. She did not have many more courses to complete, and hoped to finish, if she could stay out of the hospital. At the same time, I was watching small bookshops in my area hold going-out-of-business sales.

The difficult decision to close my bookshop was based on the fact that I could not compete financially. I was just squeezing by with all of the overhead expenses, so I made plans to keep it going through the Christmas season. My lease was a ninety-day notice type. At the end of October, I gave my notice to the owner of the building, so I would be out of there by the end of January.

Many of my regulars came in to tell me how much they would miss shopping there. I knew I would miss them. I doubted they knew that it had become, in essence, a six-year volunteer job on my part. I never made any money. In fact, I never earned back my original investment, so I really lost money on the venture. Otherwise, I might still be there!

The shop's closing made the front page of the local newspaper — color photo and all! It was a news story, because it was yet, another, small store closing, due to the opening of larger ones in town. I felt satisfied that I had provided a service to people for years, before the big store arrived. It was a labor of love. It took me many more months of work, at home, to wrap up all the accounts. I dealt with over one hundred different publishers. Each one had a different type of billing system. If it was as simple as buying and paying for the books, that would have been easy. Often, they sent the wrong titles, or damaged books. This required packing and shipping them back, which should have, in turn, meant being credited. The discrepancies that occurred, during this process, caused me many headaches. I shall not miss the bookkeeping part of the job. I shall, however, always treasure my memories of the people who came into my life, during the years I devoted to the bookshop.

# CHAPTER SEVENTEEN

It was a joyous feeling that permeated the Crompton household in May 1993. There was a wonderful cause for celebration! Both our youngest daughter and our oldest daughter received their bachelor degrees! Yea!

We chuckled about the remark a state worker had made, many years before, about Kelley's plans for college, sarcastically saying that she would be thirty by the time she finished. Actually, the graduate was still only twenty-nine!

Kelley managed to put off the changing of the T-Tube until that August. It was another day-surgery procedure. All went well.

Next on her agenda, was a job hunt. A bachelor degree in psychology was, at one time, sufficient for one to enter the counseling field, in one capacity or another. After Kelley looked for a while, we started to realize that the jobs she would be most able to handle physically, and had the strongest aptitude for, were the ones requiring a master's degree. She looked into other areas, but the positions for which she did interview, had many other applicants. While we do have laws about not discriminating against the handicapped, it is difficult to know, for sure, that she was not offered a particular job, because she is so small, and her fingers are crippled. She finally decided that the whole scene was so frustrating; she would work as a volunteer. She became a very well qualified volunteer in a junior high. She believed that when the time was right, a job for her would be made known to her. Some of her doctors had expressed the opinion that full time work would not be the best thing for her over-all health. With time, she reluctantly started to agree.

The following May, a crack in the extending arm of Kelley's T-Tube required a quick trip to day surgery to have it changed. We had become very familiar with the routine.

There is a large, pleasant waiting room in the day surgery area, with signs requesting visitors to refrain from consuming food or drink. It is difficult enough for patients to go without anything. Watching someone else eat or drink would feel like torture to some people.

If Kelley is lucky, she is scheduled early. That's not always possible, though. The later it gets, the more difficult it is to find a parking place in one of the two large parking garages. At times, we have spent a half hour or more, hoping someone would vacate their spot.

Check-in usually runs smoothly. There is a sign-out sheet, so the party waiting for the patient can be located, if they leave the area. It is a good system. A nurse takes the patient in for the preliminaries, including a change

170

into the most fashionable clothes one could wear to the operating room. The patient then returns to the waiting room, until called to go into the pre-op room. When that time comes, I accompany Kelley. It makes the time go by faster for her. She receives a visit from the anesthetist, and waits for her turn to go to the OR. The nurses are usually good about updating her. It always feels like a long wait. At one time, there was a television in there, to keep the patients amused. Some of them found it not too amusing the day a program called "The Other Side" was being shown. People were communicating with loved ones who were deceased. That can be a bit unsettling to someone waiting to go into surgery.

After they wheel Kelley away, I have time to go to the cafeteria, which is a most interesting place. Such a variety of people! Health workers, patients and visitors from all over the world are interacting and eating. It fascinates me how many people are there on any given day. I have seen some people going home who look as if they really need to be admitted. Since the insurance companies and the utilization committees in hospitals have decided to cut down on the amount of time people spend there, the discharges sometimes appear, to me, to be drastic. Hopefully, a balance will someday be reached!

After I eat, I take my place back in the waiting room, sometimes striking up a conversation with another family member. You do get to know about the other patients while sitting there. You cannot help overhearing some of the conversations. Everyone seems to be pulling for each other, hoping that all will go well. Usually a surgeon calls from the OR, or comes out, to the waiting room, to talk to a family member. A nurse comes to find me, after I have heard from the doctor. Kelley tells the nurses that Mom will help, so they welcome me. I carry in my bag of goodies, containing the food Kelley can eat. I help my daughter to take some nourishment, and to get dressed. The nurses always thank me. I tell them I would much rather be helping, than sitting out in the waiting room.

On this particular day in May, Kelley was done late, but there were no problems. When we arrived at home, she needed to be suctioned. It usually happens for a day or two. She is pretty sleepy for a few days, too.

It was a short time later when the hip surgeon broke the news to Kelley that she would need a repair job on the first hip that had been replaced. Since she was young and very active, she completely wore out the lining that went between the ball and socket. He needed to put in a new lining and a larger ball.

Surgery was scheduled for November. Since her tube had just been changed in May, there was no need to do that at that time.

It was necessary for Bob to be at work, on the day of surgery, so I took Kelley in very early. After they took her to the patient waiting area, I went up to the waiting room right next to the operating suite to wait. The television was playing. A young man was curled up sleeping, on one of the couches. I settled in to watch the morning news, and eat the breakfast I had brought along. There were no patients in this waiting room, so it was all right to eat.

It is strange how one remembers certain current events. When I hear a reference to a particular murder that took place in that city, I remember one of Kelley's operations. Mention of a particularly tragic highway accident, brings to mind another. Two popular actors were married on a soap opera, at the time she was hospitalized with stomach problems. I can picture her room. I even remember some of the comments made by other people, who were present. If you keep hearing the same news report, over and over, at a time when something very important is happening in your own life, you tend to commit it to memory.

The young man on the couch woke up, stood up, shook himself and looked at his watch. Then he left. I wondered if he was a homeless person, who had found a good place to sleep, undisturbed.

After a while, other people, who had someone in surgery, started to arrive. I watched television, read the newspaper, wrote letters, and just happened to see the hip surgeon walk by, on his way to the operating room. I assumed that Kelley's surgery would be under way before long.

The phone rang. Everyone sitting there just looked at each other. There was no volunteer on duty. No one else moved, so I got up to answer the phone. I repeated the name requested to those gathered. A woman got up to take the phone from me. This little routine repeated a few times, before I decided to position myself by the phone. Apparently there were a number of short operations that morning. Somehow, I became the official phone person. Hours passed. People came and left. Then the hip surgeon appeared. He gave me a report of how the surgery had gone, and said that "they" were almost finished. He assured me that I would hear when Kelley was in recovery, and I would be able to go in at that time. I thanked him, went to make my phone calls, and resumed my wait. I answered the phone a few more times, each time thinking it must be for me.

The volunteer lady appeared, and I lost my phone job. We talked for a few minutes. She went around the room to learn the status of those waiting. Then she went into the surgical suite to see if she could get updates for any of us. Her report to me, upon her return, was that Kelley was still in surgery. I told her that I was surprised, as her surgeon had emerged, an hour before, saying she would be in recovery soon. I wondered what was taking so long. It seemed as if everything was fine when the hip surgeon left her.

Time passed. The orthopedic surgeon, who had done the surgery on her foot, and had referred Kelley to the hip surgeon, came out next. He came right over to me. As I stood, he extended his hands to take mine. Thank goodness he was smiling, or I would have become very concerned.

"She's doing okay," he reassured me, "but it seems they are having some problems. The T-Tube ripped, so they are inserting another one. You will be able to see her soon."

This helped me to understand the delay. I was very grateful to him for, personally, giving me the latest report. I explained to the volunteer that Kelley had received her tube at a hospital across town, but her orthopedic surgery was done here. She asked some more questions about Kelley's condition. I told her that, usually, I went home during the surgery, but this was supposed to be a relatively short one, so I thought that I would just about arrive at home, when it would be time to go back. I laughed and said, "I could have done a few loads of laundry, and cleaned the whole house, in the time this is taking."

More time passed. People came and went from the waiting room. I was the only one left. The volunteer looked at me and said, "You have been the most patient person waiting, and you've been waiting the longest! I'm going to see if I can find out anything else."

Just then, the phone rang. She answered, and handed it to me, saying, "Finally!"

It was a nurse in the OR. She apologized that it was taking so long. She explained that they had trouble getting a tube to fit Kelley's trachea. It was necessary for them to send to the other hospital for one. She said that I didn't need to worry, because Kelley was on the breathing machine, and doing just fine. I had only one question. Was her anesthetist still with her?

"Oh, yes," the nurse responded, "he's not going anywhere, until the new tube is in and working."

I thanked her and placed the phone on the receiver. The volunteer was staring at me, so I smiled and said, "You know how I told you that I wish these two hospitals were combined?"

"Yes," she said, looking confused.

After relating what the nurse had told me, I commented, "I wonder if the tube is being delivered by courier in, perhaps, a cab, or if they are sending it in an ambulance." After we laughed together, I added, "Seriously, though, if someone is driving it over, and they have to find a parking place, we could be here very late!"

"What about the people at home who are waiting?" she asked.

173

"Oh, they really aren't waiting. I called as soon as the surgeon talked to me. They think that I'm in the recovery room with her."

A few more people arrived to take up their places in the waiting room. I had run out of food, so I told the volunteer that I was going to get something to eat. I went out for a brisk walk to revive myself, and then stopped in the cafeteria to buy something, to take back with me. When I realized how late it was, I called Bob to update him, before he left work. He said he would head in to the hospital. That sounded good to me. I went back to the waiting room, and devoured the cheesecake, to which I had treated myself. Comfort food!

The volunteer said that she had to leave, because of a previous commitment. I thanked her for her help. It was nice to have someone pleasant with whom to chat, while I was waiting. She said that she thought that I was just about the most patient person that she had ever seen, in that room. I got a kick out of that!

In my youth, I was not very patient at all. I was probably thirty, by the time I admitted that I needed to work on becoming more patient. I asked God for help. More often than not, I asked the Blessed Mother, Mary for help. I reasoned that she must have been a very patient individual, to accept so graciously all, that God asked of her, so she would be the one I that should try to emulate.

I have heard it said that, when you ask God for help to overcome one of your character defects, he gives you the opportunity to work on it. I guess I had been given enough opportunities. By this time in my life, people saw me as a patient person. The funny thing is, I really was patient. I had come to realize that there are some things I can do nothing about, so getting myself in a fret over them was wasted energy. The only time I become impatient, is when people refuse to listen to me, when I know how to handle a situation better than they do, such as the resident, who didn't want to give Kelley the medication she really needed, a few years before.

The anesthetist had an apologetic smile, when he came out of the operating suite. He said that, this time, I really would be able to see my daughter in just a few minutes. She was being transferred, as we spoke. Then he told me, briefly, about the problems they had had obtaining a tube that would fit.

Kelley looked good, for someone who had spent the entire day in surgery. Of course, she wasn't having much of anything done to her, for most of the time. She was surprised when I told her how late it was. I began to tell her all about what had happened, when I noticed a drawing on the sheet that was under her.

"Someone was drawing pictures of your tube on your bed," I commented.

"Oh, yeah, before the surgery, the anesthetist was explaining to someone how the tube was in there," she said.

There was one nurse attending to Kelley, as well as a student, who was there for a learning experience. This student had many questions about ML III. I produced a pamphlet, which had an explanation of the condition, for her to take. It had become available, only a short time before that. It was a big help to have one on hand for someone who truly wanted to learn about the condition.

Before long, the anesthetist arrived with a sheet of paper for me. He must have had a secretary type it up before she left for the weekend. He suggested that we present a copy to anyone who might attend Kelley in surgery, should she ever need surgery, elsewhere. It was a report of what had taken place regarding her trachea, during surgery, and a suggestion as to the precise T-Tube to have available, in case the present one should become torn, during the procedure. There are some problems one cannot anticipate. I told the doctor that I was thankful that he was the one attending her, and that the other hospital was not very far away!

Bob and I were both able to spend most of the weekend with Kelley. She did very well after this surgery, and was up on crutches in no time. The Tuesday following the surgery, she was able to go home. Her comment about this particular operation was, "No big deal."

As a child, I was able to sleep through any noise imaginable. Perhaps, it was a result of being the youngest of five children. Perhaps, I simply was born with the ability. My family tells me that I slept through the vacuum cleaner being run under my crib. At Girl Scout camp, I slept through a storm. The other campers put down the tent flaps. They told me in the morning about the rain that landed on me. I was probably dreaming that I was swimming underwater. In later years, I was told about the many fire engines and ambulances that raced by the house one night. They had the whole neighborhood up, with the noise they made. Everyone was up but me. I never lost the ability to sleep through noise, or with lights lit. However, from the day I brought my first-born home from the hospital, I have awakened immediately to a baby's cry or a child's need.

One time, when we were all living in the large house, Bob heard me dashing out of the room in the night, "What's wrong?" he asked.

"Kelley fell!" I said. She was at the other end of the house, but my radar was always up for my children.

Yet, when we had teenagers, I was able to go to bed and to sleep, when one of them was out at night. I always felt that if a problem arose, I would be better able to handle it, if I had some sleep first. Pacing the floor and worrying never made anyone come home any sooner, or kept anyone any safer. We did our best to instill in our children reasonable guidelines of caution, and we had to leave the rest up to God. They are, after all, His children. When they went out, we told them that they could call us anytime they were in a situation where they needed a ride home, and we would go to get them. It was understood, of course, that being arrested for drunk driving was not a good reason. We were strict about things like that. It was also understood that, sometimes, one might find oneself in a situation where the driver had been drinking. In that case, we wanted to be called. The phone was next to my bed. We did get up and dressed, a few times, to rescue a teen. We were glad that they knew they could call, without getting into trouble.

There was one time that I did become concerned. I happened to awaken with an upset stomach, and I realized our youngest, who was already twenty, was not in yet. The hour was late. I could not get back to sleep. I got up when I heard her car arrive at home. She was shocked to see me in the kitchen.

"What are you doing up this late?" she asked.

I explained and hugged her. I was so glad to see her home, and all right.

"I'm sorry, Mom," she said, "I had no idea you would be waiting for me. I never thought much about the time, because you are always sleeping."

"Let me tell you, I am glad that I always did go to sleep. My imagination started working overtime, as it became later and later. No wonder some parents are frantic, when their children stay out late. I'm glad I never really knew the time. I think that I would have been a zombie, if I had stayed up every time one of my children stayed out late. I suppose if I had only one child, I might have been able to do it, but with four, no way."

It is a very different situation, when a child in the home is sick. I always wake up, and wide awake, at that. Sometimes I hear Kelley up in the night. I get up to see if she needs me. Sometimes, when she hears me, she says, "I'm all right, Mom."

I say, "Okay, honey. Call me if you need me," and go back to bed.

Sometimes, she does need me to suction her, so I do, and we go back to bed. Such was the situation about a month after she came home from the hospital, after having the hip repair. Apparently, she had a cold, which quickly turned into bronchitis. I suctioned her, and noticed she was having trouble breathing. She does not like to admit it, so it sometimes takes some coaxing to get her to agree to go to the hospital. I felt the back of her neck.

"You have swollen glands," I said, "and your breathing is labored. I think you are not getting enough oxygen to your brain for you to realize it, but you need medical attention."

"I think my trachea might be swollen, and pressing against the tube," she admitted.

"Do you need help getting dressed?"

"No."

"Okay, then I'll go get dressed, too."

By this time, Bob was out of bed, and in a short time, we three were on the way to the local emergency room.

The attending nurse quickly showed Kelley to a bed. Bob went to park the car, so after Kelley was settled, with the oxygen on, I went to find him. The rooms in that emergency room were very large, so even though numerous people were in and out, we three were very comfortable. The doctor on duty was one of the most unusual ones we had ever met. He seemed to be fascinated by Kelley's T-Tube. He asked me to draw an illustration as to how it was placed in her trachea. We have always been surprised by the amount of medical people, who seem to need explanations and drawings. The trachea is a windpipe. It is long enough to reach from the throat to the bronchial tubes. Anatomy 101! They can see the part that protrudes from it, out through the neck. We all understood what it was and how it worked, without diagrams. The first time that we actually saw one, ourselves, was when the anesthetist brought one, which he had removed, to us, in case Kelley wanted to keep the plug, for future use.

I do understand them asking me to spell mucolipidosis. It is an unusual word, even in medical circles. I don't expect them to know about something that rare.

After explaining it all to the doctor, and telling him what worked to take the swelling down, he wanted to try a different method first. I looked at Kelley and shrugged. She was out of danger, so she didn't mind doing it his way. The doctor called the inhalation therapist, who administered the treatment usually ordered for asthmatic conditions. Twenty minutes later, the doctor decided to try it our way. When that worked, he laughed.

"I guess you can teach an old dog some new tricks, after all," he jested.

"You people do know what you're talking about, don't you?"

The type of treatment done requires close monitoring afterward, so once Kelley was feeling better; she still had to wait for hours before leaving. I took Bob home, so at least one of us would be able to get half a night's sleep. Then I returned to spend the rest of the time waiting with Kelley.

177

The doctor came in to visit numerous times. He was a jovial visitor. We were both sleepy, but there would be no sleeping with him around. I'm sure it was his way of monitoring her.

Kelley was sent home with medications to take, and an order to follow up with her local doctor, which she did.

The antibiotic that he prescribed for ten days worked, and she started doing better. Within a week after finishing it, though, she was back in the doctor's office. He gave her another antibiotic to fight the infection.

Two weeks later, the scenario was repeated. This time she was given an antibiotic for two weeks, and another medication to help dilute the mucus. That seemed to help.

Five days after stopping that course of treatment, Kelley lamented, "I hate to admit this, because I don't want to have to go back to the doctor's office. I feel like they are going to think that I'm doing something wrong, but I'm pretty sure I have another infection brewing."

"I think that is the same infection coming back repeatedly," I commented, "none of these medications seem to be doing the trick."

Kelley usually went to the local doctor's office by herself, but I asked to go along this time. Since she frequently saw whoever was covering for her doctor, I thought the continuity of care might be lacking, and no one was really noticing how many times this was happening. She was given another, stronger medication, that should have knocked the infection out of her.

This time, she did get better for a little longer, but it came back again. We lost track of how many times this had happened, when she ended back in the emergency room, again, in August. We saw the same doctor as the last time. He remembered us, and said he would start off with the treatment that we knew worked. We thanked him. By the time we reached the hospital that night, I had become convinced that she had an infection, somewhere within the trachea, that was being fed by the secretions. She could not shake it completely. Another night in the emergency room, and she was doing better. Why do these things so often happen at night?

I called the thoracic surgeon in the city, in the morning. I gave him the run down of what had been happening, since the tube had been changed, in November. His secretary called back, later, to tell us that Kelley had been booked for surgery, in a few days, to change the tube. She was on another antibiotic then, so it looked as if she would be able to tolerate the surgery well.

She did. The surgeon told us that a tube like that was a magnet for infections, and that was a side effect to having one. We had not known that before, because she really had not had that many. We went back to her local doctor with that news. He put her on a low dosage antibiotic, to see if she could avoid contracting another infection, as well as a medication that helps to keep the mucus loose enough to cough up, more easily. Thanks to this combination, Kelley had a pretty good winter.

Kelley had hoped to be able to earn some money again, but was unable to figure out, just where she could find a job from which she may be absent, at any given time, because of another infection, or another operation, or a day when the pain is too severe. She had to accept the fact that the most she is able do is to volunteer, and she has been as faithful to that as her condition allows her to be.

# CHAPTER EIGHTEEN

In the spring and summer of 1995, we had, once again, started making plans to relocate. Bob's company had offered him an early retirement package. We spent some time discussing the pros and cons of the offer. I had entered back into the world of Real Estate, after closing the bookshop, so I searched for properties a bit north of where we were located, and found the housing prices and property taxes to be a better fit for our needs. We decided it would be nice to move away from an area that had become increasingly busy, with traffic, and live at a slower pace. While our house was on the market, we spent many days driving around the area that we planned to call our own. The more we visited, the more we liked it. We happened to choose to sell at a time that was referred to as a "buyer's market." Our house was on the market for a long time, before our buyer appeared.

I didn't want to become involved with new clients, while I was planning to move, so I spent the time going through all of the notes that I had collected, throughout the years of Kelley's journey. There had been ample opportunity to commit many details to paper, while sitting in waiting rooms, or by her bed, when she slept, after an operation. I wrote the first seventeen chapters before we moved. I didn't have a computer at the time, so it typed it. When I bought a computer, and entered the text, I discovered all of the typos that were in the original. Spell-check it great!

We actually closed on the house we sold, as well as the one we bought, and moved in May of 1996, to our mountainside abode in a small town. This is the first time, in many years, for us to live in a really small town. Since this area has lakes and mountains, it is really a tourist attraction. The population here just about doubles in the summer. It is a wonderful place to be, if one enjoys entertaining visitors. While we do need to travel a greater distance to get to the big city, we all feel that this location is wonderful.

Once we were settled in our new home, we quickly found a family doctor to care for the three of us. He was experienced enough to have some knowledge about Kelley's condition, and humble enough to obtain more information. We also had her files from her last doctor sent to him. We knew that Kelley would still need to go to the big city for her major surgeries, but felt that the local hospital, which was only twelve minutes from home, would be just fine for everything else. It wasn't too long before Kelley needed some medications, ordered by her new doctor, for those pesky infections.

Kelley's orthopedic surgeon informed her that her next surgery would be to repair her left hip joint. It was scheduled for July 1996. We requested Kelley's special anesthetist, and asked if he could change her T-tube, at the same time, since it would then be almost time for her annual change. It made sense to eliminate at least one operation. In June, I received a call from the anesthetist, asking me if I had a copy of the report he had given me in November of 1994. It detailed the procedure that he had used to replace the tube. I found it in my files, and sent it through to him, with a reminder that they didn't have the correct size for her, in that hospital. We were very reassured to know he would have the right size ahead of time, and he would be there for her surgery. By this time, he had become the head of the anesthesia department in that hospital. On the day of surgery, he had many other doctors in the OR with him, so they would all know how to change her tube, if it became necessary, in the future.

Surgery #21

Once again
    I'm by her bed.
        She is at rest.
As usual
    I'm busy 'til
        Her next request.
For me
    The longest day
        Is now behind.
For her
    This is the start
        Of another long grind.
Drip, drip
    The drugs flow
        Through the IV.
They'll help
    To dull the pain
        Caused by PT.
We thank
    All those whose prayers
        With her reside,
And know
    Our loving God
        Stays by her side.

Kelley's recovery from this surgery went well, and we made plans to attend a conference that was within driving distance from home. Some years before that time, I had learned about the MPS Society, which I joined. While the majority of the membership is composed of families that are dealing with Mucopolysaccharidoses, the Society is a non-profit support group, consisting of families and friends of those affected with MPS, ML and similar disorders.

There are at least seven types of MPS, and four types of ML. The Society has grown, since it was started, by few parents in 1975. We receive quarterly reports, in which letters from parents are printed, and information, on research progress, is shared. Although the majority of members are concerned with one of the MPS conditions, we felt the conference would be beneficial. There have been some very dedicated medical professionals working to try to find answers to the problems faced by those with MPS and related diseases. Many of the victims of MPS die at a young age, and it is most heartbreaking for the parents to watch their children suffer, while all they can do is treat the symptoms, as best they can. We believe that any answers that will be found for MPS will ultimately help those with ML.

Although we met many families at the conference, we were somewhat disappointed that there were no other ML III patients present. It was a good experience, though. We left there counting our blessings, and being thankful for the opportunity to see the work that is going on behind the scenes. The presentations by the doctors were very informative. We learned about children who were receiving bone marrow transplants, which appear to be helpful to those who are diagnosed, and treated early in life.

There were only a few adult patients attending the conference. The parents, of the younger children, had many questions for the adults, so a panel was arranged, and Kelley was asked to serve on it. She is shy about speaking in front of a group, but once she started, she spoke up clearly. The parents appeared to really enjoy what she had to say about her years of growing up, and going to school. She focused on the theme that, with support from home, children could withstand the teasing of being different. Like her Dad, Kelley is a person of few words. When a parent asked what she thought was the most important thing for parents to do, her response was, "Just accept your children, and let them know you love them."

Kelley's tube was changed, again, in March of 1997. She felt pretty well, for a while after that, but before too long, the infections started bothering her, again. Her local doctor ordered oral antibiotics for her. They did not seem to do the trick. She experienced swelling of her trachea, severe enough to make breathing more limited than usual. She was taking medication for the swelling, but it provided her with only minimal relief. The doctor then ordered a course of stronger antibiotics, to be given by IV.

Our kitchen was taken over by medical supplies, including some medications that needed to be kept refrigerated. The visiting nurses came, to our home, to set it up. They trained me to handle the IV pump, and to change the IV solutions from one to the other, as they ran consecutively. There was a time that a patient would have been admitted to the hospital, for this type of treatment. However, insurance companies have refused to pay hospital rates, for treatments that can be handled at home, and the doctors have decided that lay folks are not too stupid, after all. Most of us can be taught how to handle it.

Kelley also had to do an inhalation treatment, three times a day, using another antibiotic. During the first week, she coughed up a lot of sputum, every time she did a treatment. Her veins were not too fond of the whole ordeal, and it was necessary to call the nurses, a few times, to have them reset the IV line. Kelley always experienced problems, due to her veins shutting down, when she had surgery.

One morning, after Kelley was out of bed, I noticed that she was having a reaction to one of the medications. On further examination, I discovered her body was covered with welts. Luckily, the visiting nurse arrived, shortly thereafter. When she saw what Kelley looked like, she called the doctor to change the order. Her condition had improved greatly, by then, and she was able to cut down to one medication, for the remainder of the time.

Kelley made it through the summer, before she started showing symptoms of the infection, again. Her primary physician decided that it was time to refer her to a pulmonary specialist. That was, probably, one of the best things that could have happened.

The new doctor was a wonderful young woman, who had a great deal of experience with lung infections, including treating patients with cystic fibrosis. We found her to have a pleasant disposition, and felt she could really see Kelley as a whole person, not just someone with faulty anatomy. We spent over an hour in her office, discussing all of the various treatments available, and deciding, together, what would probably be the best course for Kelley, at that time. I asked her if she had any literature on the type of infection most prevalent in Kelley's bronchial tubes, and she followed up with many articles for me to read. Not only did she give me articles, but she also highlighted the parts that referred to Kelley's particular problems. When we learned that she, also, had moved to our town, a short time before, I told her that I thought we had been looking for her for a long time.

Because Kelley was to receive two new antibiotics, by IV, at the same time, she was admitted to the hospital. The plan was for her to receive a course of the treatments, before having the T-Tube in her trachea changed, and then to be sent home with the antibiotics, for another week. We also saw a local ENT specialist, who said that he could change her T-Tube. I gave him the names and numbers of her doctors, in the city, so that he could confer with them, and gain a good understanding of Kelley's condition.

Shortly before this, Bob had had an operation on his foot, as a day patient, at the local hospital, and we considered it to be as good of an experience, as any hospital experience could be.

Kelley was admitted, a few weeks after we saw the pulmonary doctor, and started on her course of antibiotics. She was in a room by herself, and all the staff members were required to wear masks, when they were near her, so that they wouldn't carry any of her germs to any of the other patients. We were impressed with the care she received at that hospital. In fact, we had no complaints about anyone, the whole time she was there. They appeared to be well enough staffed, that people were able to do their jobs, without cutting corners.

After she was on the intravenous medications for a few days, the doctor talked to Kelley, about having a central line implanted. This is done surgically, with a little receptacle, called a port, being placed under the skin, below the collarbone, and a catheter going from it into one of the larger veins. She said that it would be best, for Kelley, to have this done, so she would not have to worry about the small veins in her arms shutting down, as they often did. After the last round of antibiotics Kelley had taken, she was black and blue, from being stuck so many times.

We were told that the central lines can stay in for over a year, and can be accessed, whenever necessary. Otherwise, they just stay there, and don't interfere with anything. Cancer patients, who are receiving chemotherapy, commonly use them. The doctor said that she expected Kelley to continually have reoccurrences of infections, because her bronchial tubes have been damaged, by each assault of past infections. Thus, they have become more susceptible to other infections. She likened Kelley's respiratory problems to those of patients with Cystic Fibrosis. She seemed to have a better understanding, of the situation, than any one else we had met. She gave me more articles to read.

A few days later, Kelley went into surgery and had the port implanted. Then she spent a few days being sick, from the anesthesia. They let the new device settle in for a few days, before they took the needle out of her arm and switched it to the port. Actually, she was given a double port, in case they needed to access two, at the same time. In the hospital, they were running one antibiotic continuously, and interrupting that, twice a day, to run the other. Meanwhile, they kept monitoring her blood, to make sure that she wasn't keeping too much medication in her body. One of the antibiotics that she was receiving has been known to cause kidney failure. The doctor, from the hospital pharmacy, visited Kelley, two or three times a day. One day, he told her she could handle a lot of the antibiotic because she was "young and healthy." That remark provided us with good laugh.

"Why is she in the hospital, if she is healthy?" I asked facetiously.

He explained that he meant that her kidneys were healthy. They didn't let her kidneys go home without her, however.

After about ten days, the time had come to have the T-Tube taken out of her trachea, and replaced, with a new one. She was due to go to surgery at 8 AM. She called me at 8:30, to tell me that she had not gone, yet. The doctors had to attend to an emergency, so they moved her time up to 10:30. We were disappointed. She always suffers from a sick stomach, when she has to go a long time without food.

The doctor called me around noon, and said, "Kelley is fine." Then he added, "But we didn't change the tube. When we had a good look at it, we discovered that the manufacturer had sent us a defective one!" He said that he felt really badly about that, and the best that they could do would be to have a new tube shipped to them, and fit her in, the following Tuesday, for surgery — that was Friday!

She did become sick from the long time without food, and the pre-op meds. At least she did not have anesthesia, that time. I spoke with the pulmonary doctor, next. She said that she could send Kelley home, and we could handle the antibiotics there, with the visiting nurses coming in to help, then go in, as an outpatient, for day surgery, on the next Tuesday. It sounded like a good idea to me. When I arrived at the hospital, I told Kelley what her doctor had said, and she agreed with the plan.

Kelley was vomiting when the doctor entered her room.

"You can be sick at home, as well as you can here," the doctor remarked, "I'll give you some prescriptions, to take with you."

Kelley held a basin in her lap, as I drove her home.

Now, the reason that she was having the tube change, was due to the theory that, since it is made of silicone, some of the infection could have become imbedded between the tube and the trachea, and it would provide an added insurance, against infection, to start out with a new tube. I suspected that the last infection was from the hospital, in the big city, when she had the tube changed there, the past May. Technically, she would be able to go until the next May, before having it changed, but we were trying to avoid the big teaching hospital, where infections are more prevalent.

We were no sooner in the door, from the hospital, when the visiting nurse arrived. He spent over an hour doing an "intake". Kelley was too sick to handle it, so I answered all of his questions. I was rather tired, by then, from working to put some real estate deals together, on houses, and visiting Kelley, as often as possible. I felt as though I was trying to work two full time jobs. Then, just as I thought the nurse was finished with me, he said he was going to give me instructions on how to take care of all of the equipment, myself. I tried to pay attention, but I was into overload mode, by then.

There were many details involved in changing the drugs and the IV equipment, including a computerized pump. The instructions did not register, too well, in my weary brain. When the nurse came back, later that evening, he asked me if I could do the transfer of meds by myself. I laughed, and explained to the young man that I was not prepared to do so, yet. I had, at least, had time to get some sleep and adjust to the situation, before he came back, the next morning. Then the procedure did not seem like such a big deal, and I learned quickly.

About a week later, I told him that I thought that visiting nurses needed to be more aware of the stress placed on a family, when a member is hospitalized, and not bombard them, first, with questions, and then, with lessons, on the day the patient returns home from the hospital. He did listen, and he told me, a few days later, that he shared my comments at an in-service. I hoped that it would help someone else, in a similar situation.

The following Tuesday, I took my patient to the hospital for surgery, and waited for the doctor, in the surgical waiting room. It is always a strain to wait. It never becomes any easier. About an hour or so later, the doctor came to see me. He said that Kelley was in recovery, and the nurse would be out for me shortly, so I could help. Then he told me that they did not change the tube, after all. The tube was OK this time — in fact, they had ordered two, "just in case," and we had taken along an extra that we had at home. This time, the doctors decided not to proceed.

"We were very surprised at Kelley's anatomy," he explained, "We were afraid that we would hurt her vocal chords, or, worse, lose her airway, if we went ahead with the surgery. Of course, we would have done it, if it had been an emergency, but it would be better for her to go back to the experts, who know her anatomy, and have the right equipment, for a case like hers."

I thanked him for not going ahead with it, since he was unsure of the outcome. I think that took some humility, on his part. The pulmonary doctor concurred, when we spoke to her, later. She said that surgeons usually have to overcome a lot of pride to say they don't want to try something.

So, I was the one who was there when Kelley woke up, and I was the one to tell her that she had gone under anesthesia, and she hadn't had the surgery, after all. I said, "You can cry if you want to."

She simply said, "It won't change anything."

Later on, when we talked about it, she was not in the least upset or angry. She has such acceptance! It seems to me that many people would have been pretty annoyed, if that had happened to them, not really at the doctor, but just at the situation, in general. When she was awake enough, we returned home, for her to continue on the IV medication.

The following Sunday, Kelley started to become dizzy. I was first aware that something was amiss, when she said, "Mom, do you think you could help me get to the bathroom?"

As I started to help her, it quickly became apparent she could not navigate, by herself. With every step, it was an effort for her to stay on course, and she said that she was having trouble seeing straight. I needed to stay with her in the bathroom, and take her back to the couch.

"I don't know what's wrong," she said, "but I'm feeling really queasy in my stomach and very dizzy!"

By Sunday evening, I drew the conclusion that she was having a reaction to the strong medication. The nurse had told us, previously, that; technically speaking, Kelley was really on chemotherapy. She had already experienced a loss of hair.

I decided that I wasn't going to administer the next dose of that drug. I phoned the nurse on call, who said that she couldn't give me permission to stop the medication. I told her that I wasn't asking for permission, I was reporting the situation to her, and I expected her to report it to the doctor. She called back later to say that since Kelley had been on the antibiotics for almost three weeks, the doctor said we could stop them both.

Kelley would have jumped for joy, if she had not been so dizzy! She had such a severe case of vertigo that it even caused her to vomit. For days, she could not navigate, from one place in the house to another, without assistance. We did obtain some medication from the doctor that, at least, made her stomach less queasy, but she was still having a difficult time walking around, a week later! Her condition gave new meaning to the expression "bouncing off walls." It started to wear off very slowly. The particular medication, she had been taking, has been known to affect hearing. I reasoned that it had damaged Kelley's inner ear, and her sense of balance was affected.

The positive side of the situation was that we were pleased that the port worked so well, we didn't need to make any emergency calls to have an IV reset.

Kelley's next doctor's visit was to see the local ENT physician. She had a hearing test done there, and it was determined that she had suffered a slight hearing loss. That doctor then made a referral, for her, to a doctor at a teaching hospital. The plan was for him to do a specialized test, by the name of Electronystagmography (ENG), which helps to diagnose dizziness and balance problems. She was not allowed to take any medications, for two days, before going for the test.

Since it was a long drive to reach the medical center, Kelley was apprehensive, as she really needed medication for stability. After we traveled over many hills, and took many turns, Kelley happily announced to me, "Guess what! I haven't felt carsick at all!"

This was surprising, as she normally would have felt carsick, under those conditions. She did need help, to go from the car to the doctor's office, though.

We were very impressed with the new medical center. Kelley joked about collecting hospital cards, the way some people collect credit cards. If anyone ever steals her purse, they will be very disappointed. The only thing they would be able to charge would be a hospital bill!

I sat in the back of the room, to observe the ENG test. It occurred to me that Kelley had previously undergone tests that were named "EKG," "EEG," and "EMG." I wondered how many more letters of the alphabet there were for electro type tests, and how many more she might experience, some day. During most of the test, the room was dark, and lights danced across and around a large screen. I knew it was all making some sense to the tester, who was also working on a computer. From my vantage point, it meant nothing. I was very pleased to learn that the doctor, conducting the test, was able to give us an immediate report, when it was completed. We would not need to wait for something to be analyzed.

My suspicions were confirmed. Kelley's inner ear had been damaged. The doctor advised her that there was nothing that could be done to correct the damage, but he said that she could get some balance back, by retraining her brain. The therapy he advised was to walk, walk, and walk some more. He suggested that she walk close to walls, until her brain received the message, as to where to place her feet, so she could walk in a straight line.

My courageous daughter returned home determined to overcome her latest impairment, once she knew that the outcome would be in her hands. She walked up and down the stairs and hallways over and over again. With the same resolve that she had used, when doing physical therapy, while recovering from hip operations, she applied her new knowledge, to recover from her balance problems. For the most part, the dizziness and nausea disappeared.

In time, Kelley did learn to walk reasonably well, but with great concentration. If someone interrupts her concentration, when she is in motion, she looses her bearings, and walks off in an unintended direction. She usually laughs, and says, "Oops. I didn't mean to do that."

Walking a straight line, on command, is a problem for her. We hope that she is never stopped, by a police officer, when driving, and asked to get out of the car and walk a straight line. With her breathing problems, it would also be just about impossible for her to exhale into one of those Breathalyzer machines!

# CHAPTER NINETEEN

When Kelley received the port, we did not realize that a nurse would visit her monthly, to access and flush the port, in order for it to remain in working condition. It is a procedure that can be done only by nurses, who have had special training to use the specific type of needle that is necessary for the port. We soon became accustomed to seeing the same nurse every month. Usually he visited alone, but on occasion, he had someone, who was in training, with him. In time, his visits started to feel more like visits from a member of the extended family, rather than a medical professional, except that family members usually don't poke Kelley with needles.

Her health appeared to be in check, after the latest round of medications. She had her T-Tube changed in the big city, without any complications. She also had regular orthopedic check ups. During one of those visits, as we sat in the exam room, waiting for the doctor, we heard a knock at the door.

"Come in," we chorused.

The door opened to reveal a visitor. It was the orthopedic surgeon who had done Kelley's earliest operations, and had referred her to the hip surgeon. He had seen Kelley, off and on, through the years, when she was in surgery, but she had not seen him for a long time.

"I told the secretary to call me, the next time you were here, so I could see you," he said smiling.

Kelley and I both said, "Hi," as he leaned forward, to where she was sitting, on the exam table, and shook her hand.

I spontaneously jumped up from the chair in which I was sitting, across from the door, and headed toward him. I extended my right hand, but I was so happy to see him, that I also threw out my left arm so I could hug him. For a brief moment, I felt awkward, wondering if that was appropriate. He appeared to be a very reserved man, when we first knew him, but I felt like I was seeing an old friend, now. His arms went out also, and we hugged. It was wonderful to see him. We had a nice chat, including Kelley's health, computers, and the Internet. He suggested to Kelley that she set up a Web page, so people could get in touch with her, because she had so much to offer. That didn't appeal to her too much, as she doesn't like to type, and she really doesn't like to talk about herself.

After he left, we looked at each other and remarked about how good he looked. "Gee," I said, "You were only 10, when we first met him. That was 24 years ago."

"And now, he is the head of the orthopedic department!" Kelley said.

We talked about how fortunate we had been, to find some really good people to help us, along the way.

The hip surgeon came in and said, "I guess you had a surprise visitor, huh?"

He examined Kelley, said that the x-rays looked great, and he was really pleased with her range of motion. She received a reprieve for an entire year.

During that year, a new movie was released, in which a member of the MPS Society had a starring role. I saw "Simon Birch" three times, and wrote a letter to Ian Michael Smith's parents, to tell them how much I enjoyed his acting job, in a most delightful movie!

In December of 1998, Kelley, Bob and I attended a three-day, MPS conference on Long Island, New York. The participants were from 21 states as well, as Puerto Rico and England.

The first morning, we listened to a panel of adults share their experiences with various MPS problems. They spoke of the challenges they had met, as well as their hard work, surgery, and many accomplishments. It was an inspiration to hear them, and to hear their beliefs about the fact that God has a reason for them to be here. They all said that they turned to God, for the strength they needed, to deal with their problems.

We passed up the workshop that followed, and took a trip into the city instead. We viewed the Big Apple from atop the Empire State Building. Then we visited Rockefeller Center and Radio City Music Hall. That was especially fun at Christmas time. However, the noises, in the busy city, did make us appreciate our quiet home!

On Saturday morning, a doctor presented an overview of MPS. She had observed the course of the disorder in patients, for many years. She was followed by a doctor who gave a detailed account of Gene Mutations in Hunter Syndrome Families (MPS II), complete with diagrams, regarding the way the disorder is passed on. Next, we were treated to photos of animals that were affected with some of the MPS and ML conditions. Some of them had been successfully treated with various treatment plans. Another doctor talked about gene replacement therapy for MPS patients.

In each case, the enzymes that would normally break down certain substances, in the body, are missing. The more the doctor explained, the more we realized how very complicated the situation is, and why it has taken so many years of research to try to find solutions. His colleague discussed the work being done with stem cell transplants. When children, who were diagnosed at a young age, have received the transplants, they have experienced positive results. The disease progressed more slowly, although there had been no real cures, at that point.

191

Denise Crompton

The only disappointment we had, that weekend, was that, once again, there were no other ML III patients attending. Since joining the MPS Society, I had corresponded some other ML III patients and parents on occasion, and had a few phone conversations with others. The Society publishes an annual list of the members, who wish to participate. Very few are listed in Kelley's category. No two people are affected in the same way, but all the victims of these diseases share the struggle with physical limitations, pain and surgeries. We did have that in common with the families that we met at the convention.

The following spring, my sister Mary Lou, her husband, Bob, and their son, Jimmy, moved into our town. They had visited us six months before, and discovered why we loved the area so much. They sold their house in short order, and found one just a few miles away from us. Although Jimmy had become an adult, he still lives with his parents, because he has Downs Syndrome, and is not able to live on his own. He was very happy to move this close to his aunt, uncle and cousin. Now when family members visit, they are able to see more of our family, at one time.

By the time she visited her orthopedic surgeon, that year, Kelley was having considerable trouble with her left knee. It had become difficult for her to walk without pain, and the lower bone went off at an angle, rather than straight up and down.

The doctor looked at the x-rays, then looked at her and said, "There is nothing I can do, unless you are willing to have a total knee replacement."

He has never told her that she had to have surgery, but left the decision up to her. It was apparent to Kelley that she was going to have more pain, and less mobility, as time went by. She made an immediate decision. That was followed by more trips to the city, for some specialized x-rays and measurements. The first plans that were arranged for surgery had to be changed, as the doctor realized a part had to be specially made for her, because of her size. Then we needed to coordinate the surgery time with the anesthetist. The last few weeks before the surgery, the following February, were very difficult. Kelley was feeling a great deal of pain, but she had to forgo taking any pain medication. The only kind that she can tolerate tends to act as an anticoagulant. The ironic aspect of this is that, after the surgery, she usually is given an anticoagulant, so she won't develop any blood clots, due to a lack of exercise.

On the day of surgery, we left the house at 4 AM, in order to have Kelley at the hospital by 6 AM. Her surgery was scheduled for 7:30. That "four hour" operation took more like seven hours! Even though her doctor had replaced both of her hips, and had seen her bones before, he still remarked about the condition of them being among the worst he had ever

192

seen. His job is orthopedic surgery — hips and knees! He came to find me in the family waiting room, to take me to the recovery room. I believe that he told the staff there that I should stay with Kelley. Other patients had family members visit them, for only a few minutes and then leave. The nurses have always asked me dozens of questions about ML III. I had a feeling, that day, that the doctor told them, something to the effect, that *nothing* should go wrong, since we did have a serious problem, in that hospital, back in 1988. Upon leaving the recovery room, his voice was loud and clear, as he instructed me to let him know, immediately, if anything went wrong.

I spend the time observing others in the recovery room, when my patient is resting. There was a patient, who appeared to be about thirty years old, that the nurses had been watching. They were not with her at the time she started grimacing and crying. She pulled the sheet up over her head, rather than calling for the nurse. A nurse turned around, saw her, and dashed to her side. She pulled the sheet off the woman's face, and asked her what was wrong. The response was inaudible to me, but the nurse responded, "Why didn't you say so? I'll get you something."

The woman was medicated, and she drifted off to sleep. About an hour later, she awakened, and attempted to get out of the bed. A nurse noticed, and ran toward her saying, "Wait a minute honey. You can't get up without help. You're still attached!"

It appeared that she wanted to go to the bathroom. The nurse obtained a pole, to which she attached the IV solution. She helped the woman into a robe, and with the help of another nurse, walked by us, with the woman grimacing and holding onto her midsection. After the patient returned to the bed, she had some visitors, for a short while. Once they left, she asked the nurse if she had to stay in bed. She was told that there was a place where she could sit on a couch, and still be observed, after which the nurses assisted her to a different recovery area.

Before another hour had elapsed, two of her former visitors entered the recovery room, demanding to know who was in charge. Their attitude and tone of voice let everyone in the room know that they meant business! They said that the patient never should have been put out, in the other section, on the couch. The nurses walked by each other, rolling eyes and exchanging glances that could not be seen by the complaining visitors, but were observed by me.

Shortly after that, the patient was returned to her bed, looking a bit forlorn. The nurse approached her to apologize, and said, "I'm sorry I upset your family. I thought you wanted to be out there."

"I did!" she declared.

The nurses were not going to chance any more complaints. They kept her in bed, until such time as the hospital room, to which she was to be transferred, was ready.

I spent the entire five hours, in recovery, with Kelley, making sure that she was being carefully watched, because of her breathing. The anesthetist checked up on her frequently, in an attempt to decide if he could let her out of the recovery room. When I told him that I would spend the night with her, he said that that was very good, and he decided to discharge her from the recovery room.

After Kelley was settled in her room, I stayed by her to monitor her breathing. I dozed off and on, in a chair, but she did need to be suctioned, a few times. She was too dopey from the anesthesia and pain medication to cough up the secretions, and too far "out of it" to call for a nurse. She has told me that none of the nurses suction her as carefully as I do. It would have been nice to have a bed next to her bed, so I wouldn't have had to prop my head up on a pillow, as I dozed. It strikes me funny, when I see a show on television, where a family member has a bed, next to the patient's bed. I suppose that might be possible, in a private room, but the quarters were so tight, with all the equipment that had been added to the hospital room, there was just about room for me on a comfortable chair, never mind a bed! Since I brought a change of clothes, a toothbrush and other essentials with me, I did a quick wash up, and changed my clothes, in the morning. Then I bought a large cup of coffee, and by 6 AM, I was ready to "special" my patient for the day.

A physical therapist visited Kelley, the day after surgery. He wanted her to get out of bed, to exercise. She suggested that he try again, the next day. She was too tired to get up.

He responded, "Okay, we'll just do some exercises in bed then." Smart man! By saying that, he showed respect for her feelings, and she tried to do all of the difficult and painful exercises he wanted her to do.

The surgeon visited in the afternoon. I like to observe his face, when he checks up on her. He always shows his concern or pleasure, very clearly. On that day, he was beaming. Everything was going well, and he was pleased with the job he had done. He did tell Kelley that she would have a lot of hard work to do, to get the tendons stretched out, so she would be able to almost straighten out her leg, again. She never could get it completely straight, but he said she was about 5% off before the surgery, and was about 15% off after. She had 10% to make up. I knew she would do it in time, and he would smile and tell her what a prize patient she is.

At that time, Peggy lived only a half hour away from that hospital, so she came to the city, the next night, and took me back to her apartment, to shower and sleep. I really needed a bed, and was happy that I didn't have to drive myself home, before I experienced some quality sleep. I did not have to drive all the way home until Saturday night.

Bob and I went in, together, on Sunday, to spend the day with Kelley, and found her doing so well, that we were amazed. This time her breathing was not much of a problem, and she was up on crutches, walking around. The physical therapist was impressed that she was able to walk up and down stairs. That is a requirement for being discharged, if one lives in a house where there are stairs. Because she had used crutches, so many times in the past, it was almost second nature. Kelley is a wonder to behold! Most people whine, or become grouchy, or impatient when they are in pain, but she never complains, and always thanks the nurses, or me, when we do anything for her. The nurses seemed to appreciate both of us. We saw a nurse, in recovery that had remembered us from twenty-two years before. She had been working on the unit where Kelley was a patient, after one of her foot reconstruction surgeries. Another one came to see us, one afternoon. She was working on the other end of the floor, but saw Kelley's name and remembered her, from one of the hip operations.

She did have one setback, in the hospital, when one of the medications made her sick. We quickly had that order changed.

Kelley felt that she needed a sputum culture done, because the chronic infection was acting up. When the results came in, the surgeon called Kelley's local pulmonary doctor, to find out what medication to order. By the time she was discharged on Monday with six prescriptions, it was 4 PM. We didn't arrive at home until about 7:30. Kelley was happy to be back to her own bed, that night. Our sleep was interrupted, a few times, because the patient needed help to get to the bathroom.

The next day, the visiting nurse came for a 90 minute "intake." My, they can think of more questions to ask! In some cases, it seems as if they are asking the same question, in four different ways. These questions were being asked by the same service that she had been with for over two years, and they already had a file on her. However, they were required to discharge her, when she went into the hospital, only to do an "intake" six days later! It is an exhausting experience for someone, just home from the hospital, after major surgery.

Besides coming home on an anticoagulant, having a nurse draw blood twice weekly, and having a removable cast on her leg, to be removed for really painful physical therapy, she was to take extra antibiotics, and do inhalation therapy, with other antibiotics, three times a day. Each of these treatments lasted about 45 minutes.

By Tuesday evening, Kelley was having trouble breathing. We spoke too soon, when we said that she had no breathing troubles, this time! It was caused both by the tremendous amount of swelling from the surgery, and the three units of blood that were pumped into her, afterward. The swelling causes pressure on the little T-Tube through which she breathes. It is only silicone, and flexible, so pressure against it does restrict her breathing. Normally, we would have helped her to the car and driven her to the hospital, but there was snow and ice on the ground, and she had a cast on her left leg. She was exhausted and starting to feel scared. I knew she needed oxygen quickly, so for the first time in my life, I called 911.

The emergency team was great. Two local EMTs arrived, before the ambulance, which carried three more. Later, Kelley remarked that she wished she had been feeling better, when five nice men came to visit her! When the rescue team began asking their questions, about her medical history and allergies, I produced the list that I call "Kelley's medical resume." They were very pleased and said that they wished that everyone they helped had such information, so readily available. After each major medical change, I revise the list to keep it up to date, however I had not yet included the knee surgery, so I wrote that one in. The list includes her vital statistics, food and drug allergies, a list of all her doctors with their addresses and phone numbers, and the hospitalizations and operations with the dates of each.

Once it was determined that Kelley should be transported to the hospital, I asked the man in charge if I could travel in the ambulance, and let my husband follow in the car. He said I could, if I promised not to play with all the fancy lights and sirens! Actually, we did not need sirens, because Kelley was receiving oxygen and she was pretty stable. By then it was 11 PM. There is very little traffic around here, at that time.

When we arrived at the local hospital, the ER doctor listened to me (thank God!) when I told him the treatment that would be effective, to bring the swelling down. He ordered it. It took a while to take effect, so he said they would admit her. She was settled, into a room, by about 4AM. She was in pretty good shape then, so we decided to go home, to get some sleep. Bob had planned to awaken at 4:30 AM, to go to work. We reached our bedroom in time to hear his alarm go off. We laughed! He did not go to work, that day. I had a few hours of sleep, before going back in to the hospital. The patient was able to come home, that evening, as the fluid had started draining, and she had become much more comfortable. We decided not to notify the visiting nurses of her overnight in the hospital, as we were afraid that we would have to go through the whole intake, again!

The reason Bob's alarm went off so early was that, after we had moved so far from his former job, he was once again offered a position there. He agreed to work three days a week, since it was a very long drive. Although he enjoyed going back, he found the traveling to be very tiring, by the end of the third day.

The physical therapist came to the house, while it was still very difficult for Kelley to ambulate. The therapy was very difficult and intensive. Her incision started above the kneecap and ran for about 7 inches down the front of her leg. Naturally, the knee was still very swollen, and bending it is not what one would choose to do. It looked to me as if the therapist was always trying to push her, beyond a reasonable demand, but, only rarely, did Kelley tell her that was all she would do, for that day. Once she was able to maneuver around pretty well, I took her to the local hospital for her PT, a few times weekly. The therapists appeared to be impressed with the amount of effort Kelley put into the task at hand.

At the end of April, it was time for the T-Tube to be changed again. Kelley had been having some difficulty for many weeks. Her breathing didn't sound quite right, and I was glad that the appointment had already been made. The doctors found the problem. Some material was adhering to the inside of the trachea and pressing on the tube. They scrapped it off, before inserting the new tube. She was able to breath much more easily after that.

Our next successful trip, to the city, was to visit the orthopedic surgeon. He gave the patient permission to dispense with the crutch that she was still using. She had accomplished enough with the PT, that he felt she could complete the process, on her own. Of more importance, to her, was the fact that she was given permission to drive again!

At her next appointment with her pulmonary doctor, for a simple check up, Kelley said that she thought she might want to have the port removed, since she had been able to keep the infections in check, with the medications by mouth. She was tired of being poked every month, and reasoned that she could have another one implanted, if necessary. The doctor said that since it was a surgical procedure, she would need to contact the surgeon, and have his office get in touch with Kelley, to set it up. It was a very long time, before we heard from the surgeon's office, and we were ready to go on a trip, by then. Kelley decided she would get in touch with them, when we returned.

We had a wonderful vacation, with visits to family members and friends. Kelley didn't have any major health problems. Once her knee was repaired, the only problem, with her walking, was that the inner ear damage caused her to walk a bit off course, sometimes, but she said that she was happy that, at least, she no longer suffered from motion sickness!

# CHAPTER TWENTY

In the beginning of 2001, Kelley visited her primary doctor, an osteopath, to see if he could help ease the pain that she was experiencing in her neck. He ordered x-rays, to be sure there was no reason for the pain, other than tight muscles. Since the bones in her neck appeared to be normal, the doctor performed a few adjustments. Kelley did receive some relief from the adjustments, but sometimes she still felt pain in her neck, jaw and head.

While Mother Nature dumped snow on us, over and over again through February and March, the pain in Kelley's neck increased. We finally decided that the pain might be related to an infection settling in that area, and called her pulmonary doctor. She ordered a sputum test. The results showed that Kelley had two different infections, so two antibiotics were ordered, which she was able to take orally. The pulmonary doctor said that Kelley would never really be completely rid of the infections. The medications could help to knock them down, but they would keep coming back. Kelley found that to be discouraging, and started to wonder if the day would come when the medications would not work at all. That news caused her to rethink the idea of having the port removed. She had a good dosage of the antibiotics in her, before going to the big city, to have the T-Tube changed, and all went well. We said prayers of thanks.

During the spring of 2001, after I had volunteered my email address, on the MPS web site, I started hearing from parents of other ML III patients, via the Internet. When Kelley was young, I would have loved to communicate with someone else, who was dealing with the problems that we were facing. I was happy to find a way to reach out to others. Although the condition affects each person differently, we parents share many common denominators, in handling the various problems our children face. The parents, who have contacted me, have asked questions about the prognosis, for someone living with such rare disorder, as they all have children that are younger than Kelley. I have tried to encourage them, without sugar coating the problems that they may face. Perhaps the most encouraging aspect, for younger children, is the fact that the MPS Society has been very active in attempting to find answers to the problems that MPS children share. Anything that they learn should be helpful to ML children, eventually. Since children are now being diagnosed at a very young age, their parents are able to get a handle on the problems they are facing, right from the start. I am sure that the Internet will help us all find each other, more quickly.

Also in the spring, we had the fun of David's five children visiting for a few days, so he and Linda could have some time off, to celebrate their anniversary. The oldest was 12 years old, and the youngest (twins) were almost 3 years old. We had a great deal of fun with our Grandchildren. The day after they left, I sent an email to David asking him to bring them back, because it was too quiet without them.

The next time the infections hit Kelley, her neck and face became very swollen. Her trachea was also affected, and she found walking up a flight of stairs difficult. The doctor tried a few rounds of medications by mouth, but they didn't work too well, and some of them made Kelley sick to her stomach.

When Kelley's nurse visited in September, he was disturbed to see how swollen her face appeared. The swelling had been gradual, so it had not appeared as severe to us, as it had to him. He called Kelley's pulmonary doctor, and we were in her office, shortly thereafter. Tests and x-rays were ordered. Blood tests revealed that she had anemia. No wonder she had been so tired! A CT scan showed her lymph vessels to be clogged. It appeared that the infections had overloaded Kelley's lymphatic system, and it was no longer doing the work it was designed to do.

Kelley was admitted to the hospital. A blood transfusion was ordered, as well as a new type of IV medication. At that point, three different antibiotics were prescribed, one of which made her sick to her stomach. So often, the answer to the problem seems to cause added problems!

Kelley had been in the hospital for a few days, when we all watched the television, in disbelief, on September 11, 2001. Ordinarily, the hospital staff pays very little attention, to the televisions that the patients keep on, most of the day. That day was very different. Just about everyone stopped in their tracks. It was difficult for people to get on with their work, as the events unfolded. Certainly, everyone was affected, to some degree, by the events of the terrorist attack. We shared a profound sadness, with the rest of the country, as well as with many good people, around the world.

After about a week, Kelley was discharged. She returned home with 10 prescriptions, and instructions to keep up two of the medications, by IV. Her recovery proceeded very slowly. There were a few doctors involved, and numerous consults. That course of treatment ran for about six weeks. It was difficult, in that she was not able to do many things for herself, with the needle attached to her port, even though she was starting to feel better.

It was impossible for her to take a shower, so I washed her hair in the kitchen sink. She was able to take a bath, if the water wasn't too high, but needed help to get in and out of the tub. While that treatment was taking place, Kelley's nurse noticed a problem with her port. Suddenly, it became accessible through only one access line, so he advised us to have a doctor look at it. We called the office of the doctor, who had implanted the port, and were told that he would meet Kelley in the Emergency Room, of the local hospital. As it turned out, we did not see the original doctor, but instead, saw a colleague of his, who didn't seem to know what was causing the problem. He did say that he didn't think that it was anything to worry about, as long as one side of the port could still be accessed. He instructed Kelley to follow up with a visit to the office of the surgeon, who had actually placed the port in her. Weeks passed, before she was able to see him. By that time, some of the swelling had diminished. That surgeon was able to access both sides, of the port, in his office, although he did appear to use force, when flushing the line. It appeared, to him, that the access problem was due to the swelling, but he didn't seem to be too concerned, about the swelling. Kelley told him that she would like to have it removed, after she finished the current round of IV medications. He advised against doing so, saying that it would not be a good idea to remove a port that worked that well, because if she needed another, it might not work as well. He also told her that she was lucky to have a port that had lasted that long. Kelley was relieved when the IV was discontinued, and she was able to take a shower, as well as keep an appointment with her orthopedic surgeon, in the city. She asked me not to say anything to him about her latest infection, since he always appeared to be worried, when she mentioned infections. The visit went well, and she was told she could take a year off, before having to see him, again.

The next visit, to the city, was to have the T-Tube changed. We had decided that having the tube changed twice a year, rather than once a year, might be more beneficial in preventing the infections from collecting between the tube and the trachea. Kelley was taken early, for that surgery, and we were in and out, of the city, in record time. The anesthesiologists used a new type of anesthesia, and she woke up much more easily, with only a little after effect from it. In fact, we were able to stop to eat, on the way home.

About a month later, the pulmonary doctor ordered a new chest x-ray for Kelley, only to call her to say she was to go back on the IV! Once the new medication was delivered, to take up a shelf in the refrigerator, and the new pump was on hand, our nurse was back. They keep changing the types of IV pumps, just to keep us all learning something. The nurse told me that I had enough experience, by that time, to make the rounds with him, when he has people on IV meds.

The next thing, that we learned, was that Kelley's doctor had booked an appointment for her, for November 30th, to have an ultrasound and thoracentesis performed, to take the extra fluid out of her lung. That news was a bit anxiety producing, not just because a thoracentesis didn't sound like a fun procedure, but because of the other plans we had made for November 30ᵗʰ. Before we knew that the infection was going to hit so hard, we had purchased tickets to a concert at a new arena, in a nearby city. We had planned a big evening, including taking Kelley's cousin, Jimmy, along, and meeting Peggy there, in time to have dinner, before the show. We had no idea how long the IV infusion would last.

We did all of the positive thinking that we possibly could, while the medication was working on the infection. We did not want to have to take the medication with us to the concert, but I did not want Kelley to miss the concert, either. Since the September disaster had occurred, frisking at public events had become commonplace. It was difficult to know if someone would give Kelley a problem with her portable IV pump and medication.

On November 30ᵗʰ, we went to the hospital on time for the ultrasound. The technician looked thoroughly, but could not see any fluid. She called the doctor who planned to do the procedure. He looked at the ultrasound, and asked Kelley what she did with fluid that had been on her x-ray picture, two weeks previously, because he couldn't do the procedure without the fluid being present.

Kelley simply said, "I knew I was feeling better."

We hurried to the pulmonary doctor's office, only to discover that everyone was at lunch. We waited in the hall. The staff was surprised to see us there, when they returned. We told them of the results of the test, and they took us into the doctor's waiting room, to wait, while they reported the news to the doctor. The nurse came back out to the waiting room and told Kelley that she could discontinue the medication.

Kelley said, "Oh, good! Now I can go to the concert tonight!"

We rushed home. I disconnected the IV, flushed the tubing and used a heparin lock. We called Kelley's nurse to say that we knew it was too late in the day for him to come to the house, but she would be fine waiting, with the heparin lock, until a nurse could come to remove the IV needle. We made some quick phone calls to Peggy, Jimmy, and Jimmy's Dad, to let them know that we would be able to go. We met up with Peggy, at the parking garage, near the arena, by keeping in touch, with our new cell phones. It was a fun concert, and we all had a wonderful time!

The next morning, being Saturday, a weekend nurse came to the house to remove Kelley's needle. She said that she had been in the office, when Kelley's regular nurse received the call. She told us that when he hung up the phone, he exclaimed, "Yes! Kelley is going to the concert!"

Everyone was well through the Christmas season, except for Kelley's ten-year-old cat, Star. Since she was showing all of the symptoms of being diabetic, I bought some urine testing strips, right after the holiday. It was easy to test her, because, as a young cat, she had learned to use the toilet. All I needed to do was to hold the end of the strip under the stream, when she wet. I made the correct diagnosis, and we took her to visit the Vet. Star has always hated to visit there. She hisses and growls at the doctor. He did a blood test, and called us later, to say that Star was much sweeter, on the inside than she was to him. Kelley and I went back to the Vets, to learn how to give the cat insulin shots twice a day.

"Don't worry," Kelley assured the doctor, "My mom won't have any trouble handling it."

I had visions of chasing the cat around the house, twice a day, to try to get her to stay still, for her shot, but that turned out not to be the case, at all. Star has always loved home cooked chicken or turkey. We decided to entice her, with a little piece, when I gave her the shot. In a short time, she associated the shot with a treat. As soon as she would see the needle, or hear me mixing the insulin, when the bottle hit my rings, as I rolled it between my hands, she would come running, and hop up on the chair. She gained back the weight that she had lost, before she was diagnosed, and became a happy cat, again. It was a bit tricky to adjust the amount she needed, so we kept a watch on her urine, and adjusted the insulin accordingly. She has been such a good companion, for Kelley, that we want to keep her around, as long as possible.

The swelling, in Kelley's face and neck, never went away. We attributed it to her having so many infections, and started to become accustomed to her new look. She made it through the holidays, and the beginning of winter without incident. Then, in the beginning of March, the 24-hour IV infusion was resumed, and the medicine was in the special place, in the refrigerator. We took care of the daily medicine change, but Kelley's nurse visited weekly, because the needle to the port needed to be changed. One day, she remarked to him that she seemed to be very tired, and didn't know why.

He responded, "You are sick, my dear. Just because you are up and walking around, doesn't mean you are well."

Kelley never thinks of herself as being sick. She knows she has medical problems, but her bright outlook keeps her on the sunny side, most of the time.

I had decided that I wanted to finish writing this, before we reached our 40th Anniversary, in April 2002. That didn't happen. Happily, our 40th Anniversary did happen, but I didn't have time to do any writing.

Everything in our daily lives changed the day my brother's plane crashed, in Alaska, in March.

Father Jim was a very unique person. He spent 4 years in the Navy, after high school graduation. We had expected him to go to college, when he returned, to train to be a physical education teacher, like our Dad. Instead, he answered a calling, and went into the seminary. After the eight year training, he was ordained, and he served as a parish priest for the next eight years. At that time, he also learned to fly, at an airport near his parish. We were fortunate to see him frequently in those days. However, he had a desire to return to the Navy, so he spent another 23 years as a Chaplain. During those years, his interest in flying only increased, and he learned to pilot many different types of aircraft.

Wherever he was stationed, he volunteered his services to people, in his free time, to do missionary type work. We saw him frequently, when he was stationed near home. At other times, when he was on a ship, or stationed in various locations, different family members would meet him, for visits. We always enjoyed being with him. He had an easy-going nature, and was great company. Jim was full of stories, and had an ability to tell them in an amusing fashion. He had a wonderful, infectious, hearty laugh.

I think we all expected that we would have him back home, once he retired from the Navy, but he had yet another calling! He retired from the Navy in 1991, at the age of 62. But he didn't really retire. Not Father Jim! On March 24, 1991, he arrived in Alaska to serve as a priest, who would take the Church to the people. Now he was able to combine his love of serving with his love of flying. His mission of St. Paul served 23 villages across 600 miles of the Aleutian Peninsula.

He was on his way to celebrate Palm Sunday Masses, in villages along Bristol Bay, when his plane crashed, on March 23, 2002. He was one day shy of celebrating his 11th Anniversary in Alaska. He did come to visit, in the lower 48, twice a year, and we did hear the stories of some of his close calls, in some pretty rough weather, and so the accident was not a *total* shock. Nevertheless, his death was a tremendous loss to many of us.

The first few days after the original phone call were difficult, in that we did not know if he had survived, and we wondered if he was hurt. Once it was confirmed that he had died on impact, in a weather-related crash, we all became very busy. Our extended family all needed to be notified, as well as friends Fr. Jim had made, around the world, and the friends he had retained since childhood. Our brother, Fred, and a friend had visited Jim in Alaska the previous year, and had plans to visit him again. They changed their airplane tickets to attend the two Funeral Masses that were held in Alaska. They also made arrangements for Jim's body to be flown home. When our

Dad died, in 1974, Jim and Mom had picked out a plot, for the three of them, in our hometown.

Thankfully, our Kelley was able to discontinue the latest round of IV meds in time to attend the funeral.

The days that followed turned into weeks, and much of it was hectic, with very little sleep for most of us. The phones were ringing, emails were piling up, with copies of newspaper articles being forwarded, and old friendships were being renewed. It did seem strange to have our brother referred to on some national news shows, when they talked about the 73-year-old flying priest, who lost his life, while on his way to serve. He was a very happy and healthy man. He knew that there were risks to flying, in that area, but he never took foolish chances. If he had, it is doubtful he would have lasted that long.

We really miss our wonderful brother and friend, but feel blessed to have had him, in our lives, as long as we did. We also consider it a blessing that he died doing what he believed God was calling him to do. His was truly a life well lived.

In June, we visited Kelley's primary physician, in regards to the pain she was experiencing, almost constantly, in her head. He had given her a pain medication to take, when it became severe. The condition that we had thought was due to infection, and, therefore, to be temporary, had remained. The doctor said that he was pretty sure the pain was being caused by swelling, and tried her on a new medication. About a week later, on a Friday morning, she said to me, "I think this new medication is going to help."

We were in the kitchen, getting ready for supper, when she told me that I had left the radio on, in the next room. I didn't think I had, but I went to check. The radio was not on.

"Gee, I wonder what I was hearing," she said.

The radio was only the beginning. She started seeing things next! Then we discovered that she had a rash, and she admitted that she had some difficulty breathing. A visit to the local hospital's Emergency Room confirmed our diagnosis of a reaction to the new medication. On the way home from the hospital, she kept hearing music on the radio that wasn't on.

We were disappointed. The doctor seemed disappointed, too because that medication would have worked faster than some others. He started her on a new one a few days later. He said that the results would take longer to take effect.

Two nights later, Kelley was back at hospital, for a prearranged appointment, at the sleep center. Following that, she had a consult with the neurologist, who interpreted the results. She said that Kelley's sleep was disturbed by a combination of some sleep apnea as well as jumpy legs. She suggested another medication, with the hope that if Kelley could receive a better quality of sleep, she would be less tired.

As had become a tradition, for numerous years, we all gathered at David and Linda's house, for a 4th of July cookout, on Kelley's 39th birthday. We did not attend the parade first, because Kelley wasn't feeling well enough. We did enjoy being with our family members, as well as Linda's family members.

Kelley had asked for a small sewing machine, for her birthday. She said she didn't want to do any fancy sewing, but thought she would like to make a new quilt. The last one she had made was hand sewn. She put that machine to work, as soon as she received it, and started making many trips, to the store, for more material.

By late July, Kelley said she needed to be tested, again, for infection. We delivered the sputum to the lab for analysis. It takes a long time for all the testing that needs to be done. We received a call from the doctor's office, about a week later. The nurse said that there was nothing that could be done, at this time, for the pseudomonas infection. It had become resistant to everything that Kelley could safely take. However, they could treat for another infection that might also be causing problems. Once again, she was sick to her stomach from the new medication. She also increased her breathing treatments, to keep the airway as open as possible. She felt so sick, that she found it necessary to leave early, when we went to church. Kelley has always enjoyed attending church, but at times has had to keep her spiritual life nourished with daily bible readings.

We all started to wonder about this new turn of events, just as we were entertaining numerous summer guests. Kelley's head and neck had been looking very swollen, particularly in the morning. She tired easily, and sometimes was out of breath, by the time she walked up a flight of stairs. We wondered what it meant for the future, if nothing could be done about the pseudomonas. After our July visitors left, I called the doctor's office to ask numerous questions. We received a call back shortly after that, with an appointment time to see the doctor. This time, both Bob and I went with Kelley. We all had questions. We spent well over an hour, asking our questions, and trying to understand what it all meant.

We all felt somewhat reassured by the doctor's answers to our questions. She explained that there were still many things that could be done to help Kelley to deal with the infection. She also said that the medical community was constantly looking for more answers to the pseudomonas problem. Kelley is not the only person that suffers from it. Nevertheless, it can be a frightening situation, in that we don't know what to expect next. The doctor said that she has seen patients live many years with pseudomonas. It was our opinion they may not feel particularly well, most of the time.

During August, we entertained some very special visitors. One of the parents of a child with ML III, with whom I had been corresponding, via email, decided her family should take a summer vacation touring in our area, and include a visit to meet us. Jackie and Bret came for lunch, one afternoon, with their two children, Peter, age 11, and Anna, age 7. Anna has been diagnosed with ML III. We had not exchanged photos before our meeting, so none of us had any idea what to expect. As it happened, Anna sat next to Kelley at the table. Bob and I kept looking at Anna, and then exchanging glances with each other. She looked so much like Kelley did, some 30 plus years earlier; we couldn't quite believe our eyes.

After lunch, we offered to take the family for a ride, to see some of the local scenery, since they had not been in this area previously. Kelley decided to stay at home, and I suggested that if anyone was not interested in going for the ride, they could stay with her. Anna made a quick decision to do just that. The two of them hit it off!

After our ride, Bret visited with Bob and Kelley, while Jackie and I took the children to the beach. Peter loves the water and did a lot of swimming, while Anna played in the water, but didn't want it to splash in her face. She and I watched for waves and jumped up to keep them off her face, while her mom went off to swim with Peter. Then we spent some time on the beach, playing in the sand. Jackie and I found we had a lot in common, and I couldn't help but wonder if we were, somehow, related, many generations ago. Anna has the same kind of can-do attitude Kelley has. I know she is going to do just fine dealing with the restrictions that her joints are already imposing on her. I hope that she doesn't have to have trachea problems. As far as we know, there isn't anyone else with ML III, that has. I know that there are MPS patients, who have problems with their breathing, and some of them have needed a tracheostomy.

We had a wonderful visit, with our new friends, and Kelley has been talking about making a return visit to them, since they left. If possible, we may take the 1,300-mile trip, in the spring. I gained a new understanding of the way most people react to Kelley when I met Anna. I was delighted to be in her company.

After they left, I asked Kelley what she thought, when she saw Anna.

"I never expected to ever see anyone else that looked like me," she responded, sounding somewhat astonished.

I gave some thought to that, and realized that most of us, at times, are told how much we look like someone else, be it a family member, or a total stranger. I have often been asked if I am related to this person, or that. I frequently see people that resemble other people I know. None of us had ever before seen anyone who looks like Kelley. This little girl has the same type of hands, arms, legs, impish smile, eyeglasses, and just plain cuteness that Kelley had, at that age. We all fell in love with her!

I hope Anna will have the same kind of perseverance that Kelley has. Kelley's gumption, in struggling to do the physical therapy, necessary to keep her functioning, is remarkable. One of the activities, in which she engages, that I find most interesting, after all the years of working on her fingers, is that she taught herself to crochet. She also joined a church group that makes quilts for babies who suffer from AIDS. In addition, toys and clothes for the toys, vests, sweaters, backpacks, pocketbooks, tablecloths and pillow covers are among the assortment of handicrafts that she has produced. Who would have predicted such?

# CHAPTER TWENTY-ONE

Kelley was taking a variety of medications, by the end of the summer. One was to help her have a more restful sleep. In time, she decided to discontinue that, feeling that it didn't help, and being concerned that it was contributing to the swelling that made her so uncomfortable. The sleep doctor gave her another medication to try.

By the middle of September, when Kelley saw her primary physician, and she described, in detail, the pain she was experiencing in her head, he said that he thought the problem could be with her temporomandibular joints. He referred her to an oral surgeon, who, in turn, ordered a CT scan. He also had his assistant make an impression of her mouth, so an appliance could be made. Kelley was told to return to him in two weeks, with the results of the CT scan. A few days after the scan was done, I obtained the report. We do not have the ability to read the films of the scan, but we can understand the language in the report. It appeared to us that the same kind of deterioration that had happened to her hip joints, had now happened to her temporomandibular joints.

When we returned to the oral surgeon, he looked at the report and said that although Kelley had a TMJ problem, it was not a typical case. His recommendation was for her to receive care at the specialized facility, in the big city. He also told her that if she would wear her new appliance every night, she would feel less pain, in a short time. He said that some of the swelling in her head could be a result of the TMJ, but that he didn't think the swelling in her neck had anything to do with it. He had a very abrupt manner, and although he had originally told us that he knew something about ML III, after that meeting with him, we realized he knew very little about it. Since Kelley had an appointment the next week, in the city, with the orthopedic surgeon, we decided to take the report along for him to see, and to ask for his advice.

The visit with the orthopedic surgeon was interesting. He had not seen her for over a year, and he was very surprised to see the swelling of her face and neck, coupled with her shortness of breath. He looked at the report from the CT scan, and told us he that would make a referral, for Kelley, to see the oral surgeon, at that facility. He checked the x-rays of her hips and knees, and said that everything looked fine there. However, he said that he was concerned about Kelley's swelling and breathing. Her pulse and blood pressure had also started registering higher than what was normal for her. He called the cardiology department to look at her.

We were at a teaching hospital, so she had to see the interns and residents, and answer numerous questions, before she saw the doctor, who was in charge. They ordered blood tests, an EKG, and an echocardiogram. While Kelley's symptoms did suggest congestive heart failure, in some respects, the head cardiologist ruled out that diagnosis. By the time we returned home, Kelley was exhausted. We tried to focus on the good news that the hips and knees were looking good, and a referral to the oral surgeon had been made.

A few days later, Kelley had a follow up appointment with the sleep doctor. We discussed the MRI, of Kelley's brain, that was scheduled for the next evening, in an effort to help solve the mystery of the ongoing swelling problems. The doctor said that she would call, as soon as she had the results from that test. Kelley told the doctor that she didn't like the way that she felt when taking the latest medication from her, so she gave Kelley a different one to try. Later, Kelley decided to wait awhile, before starting on any new drugs.

The following day, we saw Kelley's primary physician. He was pleased to hear that she had an appointment, in the city, with the TMJ specialist, and we all hoped that the treatment for that problem might help to reduce the swelling. Kelley asked him for a different pain medication, as she was to have the T-Tube changed a few weeks later, and could not take any of the medications that inhibit clotting.

Meanwhile, she tried the appliance at night, and found it affected her breathing. She awakened with her trachea swollen, and decided to wait, until she saw the new oral surgeon, to try that again.

The neurologist called to say that the results of Kelley's MRI showed that there were no abnormalities visible, so the reason for the swelling did not originate there. It was good to know that we could rule out that issue, but there was still no answer about the swelling.

The T-Tube change went well. The doctor said that they removed a lot of junk, and added that he found her trachea to be very soft. We hoped that much of what he cleaned out was infectious material, and she would experience some relief after that procedure.

Our hopes were dashed the next morning, when Kelley's breathing became severely impaired. I asked her if she needed to be suctioned, and she said that that was not the problem, so I told her I thought we should visit the emergency room. She said that she couldn't make that decision, to which I responded that I had, already, made the decision.

The staff, at the local ER, has always been good. I told them the treatment Kelley needed, and they gave it to her. It took only one treatment, for the swelling of the trachea to subside. By coincidence, we saw Kelley's pulmonary doctor there. She had been attending to another patient. After a discussion with her, she said that she would find out if we could have some of the medication for that particular type of treatment, that Kelley could keep at home, so she wouldn't have to go to the ER, to have it administered. I told her that I was surprised that we would be able to do it at home. She said that Kelley had had that treatment enough times to be experienced. She did caution us that we should visit the ER, if the treatment didn't provide relief in twenty minutes time.

During the next few weeks, there were days when the swelling in Kelley's head was quite severe, especially upon rising in the morning, even though she had started to sleep in a propped up position. Sometimes, her eyes had crusty material adhering to them, and her lips appeared to have blue tinge. She was tired, and her appetite was poor. She sent a sample of her mucus into the lab, in case another infection was brewing, along with the pseudomonas. Although she was not feeling well, at all, she kept her appointment, with the oral surgeon, in the city. We took the films of the CT scan with us, as well as the report. In addition to looking at those, the surgeon needed to examine Kelley. Her poking, at the very sore spots, took their toll. Kelley experienced extreme pain, and her breathing was so restricted, she had a difficult time simply walking down the corridors. We had to stop frequently, for her to catch her breath. She was glad that she had, at least, accomplished that much. A follow up appointment was made, for two weeks later, to start Kelley on a program, to include physical therapy and other treatments. That doctor said that TMJ can cause some swelling, but she did not think the swelling in Kelley's neck had anything to do with the TMJ. When we arrived at home, there was a message on the machine from Kelley's pulmonary doctor.

The next morning, when Kelley awakened, she said she was having trouble with her trachea, again. We tried the special treatment, which gave her some relief. However, she was extremely nauseous.

I called the doctor's office to learn that the only infection, at that time was the pseudomonas, but the doctor said that she would call in a prescription, to see if it could be knocked down, at all. Bob stayed with Kelley, while I went out to the store, to get the medication. We had reached a point in caring for her, whereby, we wouldn't leave her home alone, in case she needed help.

When I returned from the store, I learned that she had been vomiting, and had not, yet, kept anything down, that morning. She was in severe pain, but couldn't take the pain medication. We decided to take her to the ER, again. She had to keep stopping to catch her breath on the way to the car, and she vomited all the way in to the hospital. I sent Bob back home, because there was food in the oven that I didn't want to burn, and someone needed to take it out.

The ER doctor started her on oxygen, took her vitals, examined her, and ordered blood work. Her blood pressure was up, again. He had them start an IV, through which they were able to give her an anti-nausea medication, pain medication, and the antibiotic she needed. I noticed the look on the doctor's face when he listened to her lungs, so I was not surprised, when he sent her to X-ray.

A short time later, he reported to us that there was a sizeable amount of fluid, in one of Kelley's lungs. She was surprised to hear him say that, because she usually could feel fluid in her lungs, and this time she could not. He said that nothing would be done that night, so he could admit her, or, if she preferred to go home, she could do so, after the antibiotic was run, and then see her pulmonary doctor, in the morning. She was feeling decent by then, and said that she would go home. I called Bob, to have him pick us up. Kelley discarded the oxygen, once she started feeling better. After an hour without it, she had difficulty breathing, again. We told her that we thought she should stay in the hospital. She agreed to do so.

Kelley's regular pulmonary doctor was not available, so one of her colleagues visited Kelley, the next morning. It was the first time that we had met him, as he had joined that practice, a short time before. He explained that the fluid was really in the pleural cavity, and it was pressing against Kelley's lung, thus causing a partial collapse of the lung. He said that he would need to do a thoracentesis, to remove the fluid, but he would not be able to return until after office hours. Kelley's primary doctor made sure that Kelley had everything she needed, to keep her comfortable. We were curious about the fluid, but relieved to know something could be done. We were still under the assumption that it was being caused by infection.

Bob and I were with Kelley, when the doctor returned to do the thoracentesis. We were pleased that he was comfortable enough with us, to let us stay in the room, while he performed the procedure. I was happy that he was behind her, and she could not see the size of the needle he was using. She would not have liked the sight of it. It was a difficult procedure for her to experience, but she didn't complain. He removed some of the fluid into a test tube, and held it up for us to see, explaining to us that it should have been the color of light beer, not the milky white that we saw. We were very surprised to see the amount of fluid he removed. It totaled about 3 pints. He said that he thought it was lymph fluid, but he would wait for the lab results, to be sure. When we asked him how it got there, he said that, at that time, he did not know, but he did know that it did not belong there. He told Kelley that she would start to feel better, once the lung was able to fully expand,

and she could probably go home the next day. We were perplexed, but relieved to have one problem solved, anyway. Since the fluid was in the pleural cavity, and not actually in the lung, we were able to understand why Kelley felt differently than when she had had pneumonia, in the past.

As the evening progressed, Kelley was able to breathe more easily, and her color looked better than it had for some time. We assumed that she would be home, from the hospital, the following day. After a good night's sleep, I sent email messages to both David and Peggy, to let them know Kelley was in the hospital again, but it appeared her condition was improving. Then I went to the hospital with clothes for her to wear home. I was most surprised to see her, and notice that not only were her face and neck more swollen than before, but her arms were swollen, also. I called the nurse, and asked her to observe Kelley, and report the condition to the doctor. She said that the doctor had been in earlier, but Kelley had not been that swollen at that time. As the day went on, Kelley became more swollen, and her arms were looking like those of football player. I called the nurse in again, and, after she saw Kelley's arms, she said she would call the doctor's office, and tell him not to go home, before seeing Kelley.

Meanwhile, David had received my email, so he called the hospital. I let him know that Kelley would not be going home, after all. He said that he would be able to get away from work early, so he would visit. He stopped by his home on the way, so he brought cards that the children had made for Kelley. The three older children did wonderful drawings, and wrote empathetic messages. Linda wrote the comments from the 4-year-old twins. They told Kelley to have fun in the hospital.

Shortly after David arrived, Kelley's primary physician and the pulmonary doctor, who had done the thoracentesis, came to see her. When her primary doctor said to her, "Kelley, I'm very concerned about you." I thought, "Thank God, someone else is concerned!" Actually, I was feeling quite alarmed.

The pulmonary doctor said that the lab confirmed that the fluid he took out was lymph fluid. Then, one of them told us that they had called a vascular surgeon to see Kelley. He arrived shortly after, made a quick assessment, and sent her to have a CT scan of the area where the port was situated. The results confirmed his suspicions, that there was a problem with her superior vena cava. It is the vein, into which, the line from the port was placed. That was when we learned that the pulmonary fluid normally drains into that vein. He drew an illustration, to show us how the vein had narrowed, and where a few blood clots had lodged. The lymph fluid had nowhere else to go. Apparently, for a while, it had found a route into the pleural cavity, but once the lung had been expanded again, it blocked up into her head, neck and arms. The vascular surgeon said that it appeared to have been failing, for over a year.

He discussed Kelley's options with us. He said that the port needed to be removed, but, since she had other complications, such as an impaired airway, our local hospital couldn't handle it. He recommended a transfer to the big city. He explained that the vein could tear, or one of the blood clots could travel to a lung, therefore, the port needed to be removed by someone who was very experienced. We talked about doctors in the big city, and he asked me if I had phone numbers. I took out the little date book, that I carry with me at all times, and suddenly realized that I had more phone numbers of doctors, than of family and friends. We agreed that the hospital, at which her thoracic surgeon practiced, would be the best choice. Since it was a Friday night, the doctor knew he wouldn't be able to contact the city doctor until Monday. He said that they would keep Kelley in the hospital, on medications, to keep the swelling from becoming any more severe, and to keep her blood from forming more clots. He assured us that the doctors in the city, would do their own work up, and decide on the best way to handle the situation.

When I spoke to Peggy on Saturday, she told me to take something to the hospital, for Kelley to wear on Sunday, with the colors of their favorite team. Kelley put her team shirt on over her hospital johnny. A few years before that, Kelley had started wearing the team colors, every time they played. She knew that her clothing choice had nothing to do with their wins and losses, but it was her way of participating. She said that if they lost, she didn't want to feel guilty. It was a good thing that I brought the shirt to her. Their team won, on that particular day.

The staff made Kelley's weekend stay as pleasant as they could. A respiratory therapist, who Kelley had seen, numerous times, during previous hospitalizations, happened to enter her room, just as she was waking up from a nap. Apparently, she wasn't displaying her usual smile, when he first looked at her, so he asked her if she was having a grumpy day.

"She never has a grumpy day!" I quickly responded.

He looked at me, and asked, "Really?"

"Really," I said.

He looked back at her, and exclaimed, "Marry me!"

On Monday, the vascular surgeon told us that he was able to speak with the thoracic surgeon, who, in turn, recommended a vascular surgeon, at the city hospital, who agreed to see Kelley. Our first assumption was that we would take her in there, based on what one of the doctors had said.

Since we didn't know how long she would be in the hospital, or what kind of hours we would keep, it was important to have someone care for

Kelley's cat. She needed insulin shots. We knew that if we were not at home, a visitor would have had to hunt all over the house, to find her hiding places, so we called the Vet's office. As it turned out, our usual Vet's kennel was full, because it was Thanksgiving week. Luckily, we did find another one, on our next call, and we delivered Star to them.

We returned to the hospital, ready to take Kelley into the city. However, the vascular surgeon said that he wanted her to travel by ambulance, because she needed to be monitored with the IV. After we received that news, we learned that she could not leave then, because there was a problem with the admission process. I was asked to see the case manager. When I arrived at her office, she was working with two phones. She told me that when she called the admitting office, at the other hospital, they said that they didn't have any knowledge of Kelley being on their list. I suggested that she call the thoracic surgeon's office. I was sure that his secretary could clear it up. When she did, she learned that Kelley was being admitted under the name of a vascular surgeon, rather than the thoracic surgeon, whose name she had given to them. That was good. One problem was settled, but next she had to wait for a bed to become available. That was a long day. We were all somewhat apprehensive about the kind of surgery Kelley would be facing, and what complications could occur. The nurses kept us updated about the progress that they were trying to make. They repeatedly called the city hospital, on Kelley's behalf, with the hope that the squeaky wheel would get oiled. On Tuesday morning, when Kelley's primary doctor visited, he said to her, "I don't want to see you here tomorrow!"

Another long day followed, and, just as we were about to give up, a nurse told us that a bed had become available, and Kelley only needed to wait for the ambulance to arrive.

The nurses at that hospital were wonderful. They seemed to really appreciate Kelley. When she was on the stretcher, ready to leave, one of the nurses gave instructions to the paramedic, and then told the ambulance driver to drive carefully, so Kelley would arrive safely.

It was late in the evening, so we knew that nothing would be done to her, once she arrived there. We returned home. Before we went to bed, I called the hospital, in the city, to be sure that she had arrived and was comfortable. We arose very early in the morning, to go to the hospital, because we knew that the doctors would be in to see her early. We made it in time, and found her on the vascular surgery unit. Kelley's thoracic surgeon visited her, to tell her that he would be available, if they needed him. We found that comforting. Then the vascular surgeon arrived, and told her that she would be going to the X-ray department, where the radiologist would do a CT scan, with a dye, and try to stretch out the vein, by doing an angioplasty. A special type of balloon is inserted for that procedure. We thought that the vascular surgeon would be in attendance at that time, and the port would be removed, also. A short while later, the radiologist came for her. He told us she would be gone for about 2 hours. To our relief, she did return in just about that time. She was awake, but sedated during the procedure. She explained to us that they performed the angioplasty by going in through her jugular, and that they told her it was successful. She was surprised that the radiologist didn't want to remove the port. We all believed that it was the port that had caused the problem, so we couldn't understand that. We stayed at the hospital until 8 PM, hoping to see a doctor again, but later learned that the vascular surgeon had visited Kelley after 9 PM.

When we arrived the next morning, we were pleased to see that the angioplasty was indeed successful, as the patient was looking much better than she had the previous day. Kelley told us that the vascular surgeon was also surprised that the port had not been removed. He had expected the radiologist to do so. The radiologist had told Kelley that she wouldn't be able to get an IV any other way. We assumed that was because her arms were so swollen. The vascular surgeon did tell Kelley he would take care of it on Friday, but he didn't write it in the chart. Consequently, after we arrived at the hospital on Thursday, a nurse came in to talk to us about Kelley being discharged. We told her that was not the plan, and she said that the discharge order had been written. I asked her who had written the order.

She said a name, which I had not previously heard, so I asked, "Is that a resident?"

The nurse said that it was, and asked if we wanted to talk to her.

"Absolutely," was my response.

Sometime later, a young woman (most of them seem young when one reaches my age) came into the room, with an air, about her, that seemed to suggest, that she planned to straighten us out. I managed to keep it to myself that I had, in the past, run into residents that made snap decisions, on weekends and holidays, without getting the whole story, and I would not let my daughter suffer for it, again.

Kelley was feeling well enough, by then, to fend for herself.

The doctor said to her, "I understand you have questioned the discharge order."

"Yes," Kelley said, "The vascular surgeon told me, last night, that he would take out the port tomorrow."

"Well, you had the angioplasty, and you are doing fine. You can have the port taken out at your local hospital," she claimed.

Kelley then pulled herself up in the bed, to the tallest position she was able to obtain, and announced, "I waited 4 days, in another hospital, to come here, because they can't do it there. I don't intend to leave here, until it is done." It was obvious that she was serious.

"Oh," the resident conceded, "Then, I'll let them know that you want to have it done tomorrow, and you can go home after that."

We all thanked her.

The nurse returned later, to say that the discharge order had been reversed. She appeared to understand the situation very well.

The hospital cafeteria provided a decent turkey dinner, on that Thanksgiving Day, and we gave thanks to God that there were people who knew what to do to help Kelley. She pointed out to us that she had never been in the hospital before, on a major holiday. We recounted the times that she had been sprung just before holidays.

Before we returned to the city on Friday, we rescued the cat from the Vets. We had been in touch with them, and learned that she was protesting the visit, by not eating. That is not good for a diabetic cat. She was so happy to be home, she went straight to her food. We were relieved that they kept her alive for those days, and made out lives a little easier.

We didn't see the surgeon on Friday. In the late morning, they wheeled Kelley away, and she was gone for about 2 hours, again. It seemed longer, as we didn't know if there would be any trouble while they were removing it. As it turned out, Kelley said that the doctor did have some difficulty, but there were no real consequences.

Sometime after Kelley returned to her room, the nurse told me that the doctor was on the phone, at the nurse's station, and he wanted to talk to me. He told me that he had expected the radiologist to remove the port, and that he had come in, on his long weekend off, to do it for Kelley, because he felt badly for her, since it had not been done. He said that he didn't think that he needed to do any follow up with her, and that I could call her local doctor to tell him that she should stay on the anticoagulant medication, for the next 4 to 6 months. He said that our local doctor would be able to handle that. I thanked him for his help, and wished him happy holidays.

Although he told me that Kelley could go home, no one had written the discharge order. We were not able to obtain that signature until 7 PM. At least the heavy traffic had left the city, by that time.

Along with the patient, we brought home some medications, to be delivered by injection, by me, for the next 10 days, and prescriptions for other medications, as well as pages of notes that had been faxed to the local visiting nursing association. I enjoyed reading the part of the note, where the nurse wrote, about the patient, "she is very pleasant, and it has been a pleasure to have taken care of her." It is so nice to know that others appreciate her.

Of course, the visiting nurse came on Saturday, to do a 90-minute intake, again. Since it was a weekend, we didn't see our regular nurse, but we knew that we would see him soon. We were looking forward to having a discussion with him about the problem with the port. We believed that the doctor, who had implanted the port in her, should have done a better follow up job, when Kelley had gone to see him the previous year. Almost every medical person, upon learning that she had the port for 5 years, expressed surprise. It seemed to us, that if he was going to implant the devices, he should have had a better idea of the type of problems they could cause. If he had done a CT scan, a year before, when the problem first started, he might have seen the problem before it had become so severe, thus saving Kelley an extra year of pain, hospitalizations, procedures, and so forth. I made a list of the physicians that she had seen during that time. It was the 17$^{th}$ or 18$^{th}$ doctor who was able to discover the problem, and only after the situation was severe. I wouldn't expect most of those doctors to have made that connection, but that surgeon knew where he had placed that port, and he should have known that the lymph system drained into that vein. She was already swollen in the face and neck when she saw him. I determined to send a letter to him, as soon as I was able to write it. I hope that it will help him to be more aware, in the future. During that year, Kelley had X-rays of all types, and an MRI of her brain. She had CT scans, an echogram, a cardiogram, and blood work, all of which could have been avoided.

After she was home for a while, we were amazed at how much better her appearance was. By the time her regular nurse visited, he was delighted to see the old Kelley again.

She was home, less than a week, when her stomach refused to keep food down, again. It happened to be a day off for her primary physician. I took her in to the local hospital, again, so they could start an IV, and keep her from becoming dehydrated. They were also able to give her the medications she needed. She stayed over night. We were not sure if the stomach problem occurred from a combination of medications and exhaustion or something else. When her doctor saw her the next day, he discontinued one of the meds, and gave her a prescription for an anti-nausea medication.

The day before Christmas, Kelley's nurse visited. He always seemed to enjoy the fact that one of us would be at the door, to greet him, whenever he visited. We usually knew what time to expect him, and we could always hear his car approaching. It became somewhat of a game, after a while, to be able to open the door, before he could ring the bell. Since Kelley no longer had the port, and was not in need of the visiting nurse's services for any other reason, he told us that there was no need for him to return. We all felt a little sad. He really had become a reliable and trusted friend, over the course of five years. We were happy that Kelley didn't need him, and we knew that he might be back, at some time, in the future. Nevertheless, it was a bit difficult to say goodbye.

The treatments for Kelley's temporomandibular joint are due to take place next. Kelley hopes that will help, without surgery being necessary, because the pain that it causes is severe.

Kelley's journey continues, with visits to doctors and trials with medications to see if they can find something to make her more comfortable. She doesn't like to take the medications that make her feel groggy. When she is feeling well enough, she is able to take herself places, in her car. At this point in life, Bob has retired again, and I have cut my work hours down drastically, so we can take her wherever she needs to go, when she is not able to drive.

Whenever I hear people complaining, about what they don't have or can't do, or how badly life has treated them, I want to put Kelley in front of them. It's what you do with what you have that matters. Complaining, about what you don't have, is wasted energy. Kelley uses her energy in the most positive ways that she can find. She has a body she can't trust. Because of that, she has been denied many opportunities that others take for granted, and yet, she never complains. She doesn't display any moodiness. I have seldom seen even a hint of anger or depression. She derives joy in doing what she can for others.

One day, when we were discussing people, who gripe about trivial problems, I asked Kelley how that made her feel. She responded, "Nobody ever said you had to like it, but you don't need to complain, either."

As a voracious reader, fantasy is Kelley's favorite subject. She is also the "town crier" in our home, faithfully keeping up on world and national affairs. Often, she is the first to tell us the latest news. She has developed some pretty strong opinions about some issues, and sometimes talks back to politicians on the television.

Kelley has the ability to enjoy the daily, small gifts of life. She is quick to laugh, even at herself! We all do our fair share of laughing, in our home. We love to play with words. Bob is a master of the art, and we can often tell when he is about to share a gem with us. A small grin, at the corner of his mouth, gives him away.

Anyone who visits with us, for any length of time, usually joins our laughter. No matter how graceful or well coordinated they are; they are bound to drop or spill something.

The first time that this happens to our visitors, they seem to be surprised, or even embarrassed. When they start to apologize, we tell them not to worry. It is just part of the effect that we have on people in our home.

*Denise Crompton*

We do try to be neat and orderly, but we are also droppers and spillers. We don't know how we impose this attribute upon others, but people, who say that they never have such a problem, at other times, do so in our home.

"It's us!" we tell them, laughing. We are very accustomed to picking up objects and cleaning up spills. Living with challenges has taught us to expect the unexpected. Does anyone know the twists and turns one's paths will take? A close friend, and a power of example, in accepting God's will, when he died of cancer, some years ago, often said, "Serenity is not the absence of problems. It is the ability to deal with them."

Our grandchildren enjoyed having their aunt baby-sit for them, when they were younger. She loves them dearly. When Kelley was taking care of Paul, Bryan and Emily one night, some years ago, precocious Paul, at the age of six, gave us all the reassurance, for Kelley's future, that we will ever need.

"When Nana and Grandpa get too old to take care of you," he solemnly told her, "we will."

# ABOUT THE AUTHOR

Denise Crompton has worn many hats in her life, with a variety of positions in a variety of professions. She considers her most important role to be that of wife and mother. Denise has been happily married to Bob Crompton for over forty years. Together they have raised four children. Their daughter, Kelley, has a rare disabling disorder.

Denise has chronicled the many events that have taken place, as all members of the family have made adjustments, due to the demands made by Kelley's condition. She hopes that by sharing their experiences, they will help others to keep knocking on doors, and praying for help, when seeking solutions to life's challenges.

Denise is a member of the National MPS Society. Her email address is: kelleyc@worldpath.net

www.ingramcontent.com/pod-product-compliance
Lightning Source LLC
Chambersburg PA
CBHW030310290526
45785CB00001B/295